Pre-publication REVIEWS, COMMENTARIES, EVALUATIONS . . .

"This book includes excellent descriptions of highly applicable group activities relevant to a wide range of groups of a wide range of types, from training groups to addictions and grief resolution and support; to working with children, adolescents, and college-age members; and couple and family groups. The descriptions of the activities are detailed, with a sound rationale, and appropriate lists of props and copies of forms. An especially useful element in each description is a section on contraindications of the activity to alert group workers to limitations and potential problems.

Students and new professionals will find this notebook very valuable, and seasoned group workers will also benefit from this new collection of activities through which to provide increased breadth and depth and additional stimulation into their groups. This book makes a solid contribution to the practice of group work and to the group members we serve."

—Donald E. Ward, PhD
Professor and Chair,
Counseling Committee,
Department of Psychology
and Counseling, Pittsburg State
University, Pittsburg, Kansas;
Editor, *Journal for Specialists
in Group Work*

"*The Group Therapist's Notebook* includes straightforward and powerful learning activities that can be used in groups that focus on a wide variety of goals. Each contributor does an excellent job with providing theoretical insight into respective counseling issues and following up with procedures that take full advantage of group process.

I found the activities throughout the book to be relevant across age groups, populations, settings, counseling specialties (e.g., school, mental health, psychology, social work, etc.), and counseling issues. This book provides a unique and valuable contribution to both the practitioner and the trainer. It also offers the reader a comprehensive compilation of state-of-the-art resources for each counseling issue.

If I were to have compiled a notebook of my best activities and resources that have withstood the test of time for conducting group counseling, this would be it."

—Russell A. Sabella, PhD
Professor, Florida Gulf
Coast University

The Group Therapist's Notebook
Homework, Handouts, and Activities for Use in Psychotherapy

HAWORTH Practical Practice in Mental Health
Lorna L. Hecker, PhD
Senior Editor

101 Interventions in Family Therapy edited by Thorana S. Nelson and Terry S. Trepper

101 More Interventions in Family Therapy edited by Thorana S. Nelson and Terry S. Trepper

The Practical Practice of Marriage and Family Therapy: Things My Training Supervisor Never Told Me by Mark Odell and Charles E. Campbell

The Therapist's Notebook for Families: Solution-Oriented Exercises for Working with Parents, Children, and Adolescents by Bob Bertolino and Gary Schultheis

Collaborative Practice in Psychology and Therapy edited by David A. Paré and Glenn Larner

The Therapist's Notebook for Children and Adolescents: Homework, Handouts, and Activities for Use in Psychotherapy edited by Catherine Ford Sori and Lorna L. Hecker

The Therapist's Notebook for Lesbian, Gay, and Bisexual Clients: Homework, Handouts, and Activities for Use in Psychotherapy by Joy S. Whitman and Cynthia J. Boyd

A Guide to Self-Help Workbooks for Mental Health Clinicians and Researchers by Luciano L'Abate

Workbooks in Prevention, Psychotherapy, and Rehabilitation: A Resource for Clinicians and Researchers edited by Luciano L'Abate

The Psychotherapist As Parent Coordinator in High-Conflict Divorce: Strategies and Techniques by Susan M. Boyan and Ann Marie Termini

The Couple and Family Therapist's Notebook: Homework, Handouts, and Activities for Use in Marital and Family Therapy by Katherine A. Milewski Hertlein, Dawn Viers, and Associates

The Therapist's Notebook for Integrating Spirituality in Counseling: Homework, Handouts, and Activities for Use in Psychotherapy edited by Karen B. Helmeke and Catherine Ford Sori

The Therapist's Notebook for Integrating Spirituality in Counseling II: More Homework, Handouts, and Activities for Use in Psychotherapy edited by Karen B. Helmeke and Catherine Ford Sori

Interactive Art Therapy: "No Talent Required" Projects by Linda L. Simmons

Therapy's Best: Practical Advice and Gems of Wisdom from Twenty Accomplished Counselors and Therapists by Howard Rosenthal

The Christian Therapist's Notebook: Homework, Handouts, and Activities for Use in Christian Counseling by Philip J. Henry, Lori Marie Figueroa, and David R. Miller

The Therapist's Notebook, Volume 2: More Homework, Handouts, and Activities for Use in Psychotherapy by Lorna L. Hecker, Catherine Ford Sori, and Associates

The Group Therapist's Notebook: Homework, Handouts, and Activities for Use in Psychotherapy edited by Dawn Viers

Introduction to Complementary and Alternative Therapies edited by Anne L. Strozier and Joyce Carpenter

The Group Therapist's Notebook
Homework, Handouts, and Activities for Use in Psychotherapy

Dawn Viers, PhD
Editor

Routledge
Taylor & Francis Group
New York   London

Routledge
Taylor & Francis Group
270 Madison Avenue
New York, NY 10016

Routledge
Taylor & Francis Group
2 Park Square
Milton Park, Abingdon
Oxon OX14 4RN

© 2007 by Taylor & Francis Group, LLC
Routledge is an imprint of Taylor & Francis Group

Printed in the United States of America on acid-free paper
International Standard Book Number-13: 978-0-7890-2581-8 (Softcover)
Cover design by Kerry E. Mack

Library of Congress Cataloging-in-Publication Data

The group therapist's notebook : homework, handouts, and activities for use in psychotherapy / edited by Dawn Viers and associates.
  p. cm.
  ISBN 13: 978-0-7890-2581-8 (soft. : alk. paper)
  1. Group psychotherapy—Handbooks , manuals, etc. I. Viers, Dawn. [DNLM: 1. Psychotherapy, Group—methods. WM430 G8833 2007]
  RC488.G725   2007
  616.89'152—21   2006035687

Visit the Taylor & Francis Web site at
http://www.taylorandfrancis.com

and the Routledge Web site at
http://www.routledge.com

As always, to my family

CONTENTS

SECTION I: GETTING STARTED

SECTION II: INTERVENTIONS FOR ALL GROUPS

SECTION IV: INTERVENTIONS FOR ADOLESCENT AND COLLEGE-AGE GROUPS

SECTION V: INTERVENTIONS FOR COUPLE AND FAMILY GROUPS

ABOUT THE EDITOR

Dawn Viers, PhD, is Prevention Supervisor at New River Valley Community Services (NRVCS) in Blacksburg, Virginia. Prior to this, she was a Prevention Specialist at NRVCS, where she facilitated parenting and divorce education groups. Dr. Viers has facilitated groups on women's issues, children of alcoholics, substance-abusing teenagers, and school-based groups. She edited, with Katherine Hertlein, PhD, *The Couple and Family Therapist's Notebook: Homework, Handouts, and Activities for Use in Marital and Family Therapy* (Haworth, 2005). She has been published in *Contemporary Family Therapy, Journal of Feminist Family Therapy, Journal of Clinical Activities, Assignments, & Handouts in Psychotherapy Practice, American Journal of Family Therapy,* and *The Therapist's Notebook: Homework, Handouts, & Activities for Use in Psychotherapy.* Her research interests include wellness groups for children and grandparents acting as parents.

Contributors

Jennifer T. Aberle, MS, earned her master's degree from Colorado State University's (CSU) Marriage and Family Therapy Program and her doctorate in education at CSU, specializing in theory and practice of experiential learning and teaching, women's studies, and diversity. She teaches both graduate and undergraduate courses in the Human Development and Family Studies Program at CSU. Jennifer wrote the FAIR (Fairness for All Individuals through Respect) curriculum and children's book, along with Dr. Toni S. Zimmerman. This book is currently under review by publishers. In addition, Dr. Aberle has published in the *Journal of Feminist Family Therapy*.

Mary Ann Adams, PhD, LMFT, is an associate professor in the Marriage and Family Therapy Program at the University of Southern Mississippi. Her clinical interests are gender specific programming for juvenile female offenders, fatherhood and single parent families, mother-daughter dyads, and adolescents with attention deficit disorder. Her previous works have appeared in *The Encyclopedia of Human Development* and the *Journal of Child Sexual Abuse*.

Susan A. Adams, PhD, LPC, ACS, is an assistant professor at Texas Woman's University in Denton, Texas. She received her PhD from Texas A&M-Commerce in counselor education. Her publications include the *Mississippi Counselors Association Journal* and *Texas Counselors Association Guidelines*. Her areas of specialty are grief work and shame-based identity. She has presented at state, regional, national, and international conferences. She also maintains a private practice.

Marcia K. Anderson is a professor of athletic training in the Department of Movement Arts, Health Promotion, and Leisure Studies at Bridgewater State College, Bridgewater, Massachusetts. Dr. Anderson is author of several textbooks, including *Foundations of Athletic Training: Prevention, Assessment, and Management*. Dr. Anderson is an athletic training educator and has treated athletes for more than twenty-five years. She began her career as a high school physical education and health instructor. Dr. Anderson is a 2005 inductee into the ATOM Hall of Fame.

Victoria L. Bacon is an associate professor and chair of the Department of Counselor Education at Bridgewater State College, Bridgewater, Massachusetts. As a licensed psychologist, she was trained to work with children, adolescents, and families with a focus on trauma and dual diagnoses. Dr. Bacon's current areas of clinical expertise, research, and writing include work with athletes and the physically active population around addictive behaviors and critical incident stress debriefings with athletes and teams. In addition to training counselors, Dr. Bacon provides consultation and instruction to athletic trainers, physical therapists, and sport nutritionists in the greater Boston area.

George W. Bitar, MMFT, received his master's degree in marriage and family therapy from Abilene Christian University in 2002. He is currently employed at the Southwest Institute for Addictive Diseases at the Texas Tech University Health Sciences Center, where he provides individual, couple, and family therapy services for individuals who are transitioning from prison into mainstream society. He is also a doctoral student in the Marriage and Family Therapy Program at Texas Tech University. George is a licensed marriage and family therapy associate and a licensed professional counselor intern.

Markie L. C. Blumer, MA, MEd, is a doctoral student at Iowa State University in human development and family studies, specializing in marriage and family therapy. She earned her master of arts in marriage and family therapy from the University of Louisiana at Monroe in 2002 and her Master's in Education from Northern Arizona University at Flagstaff in 1998. Her academic interests include sexual minority issues, social justice, therapeutic and supervisory evaluation, and prevention of adolescent high-risk behaviors. She is currently a member of the editorial board for the *Journal of Feminist Family Therapy* and is an associate member of the American Association for Marriage and Family Therapy. She is a two-time recipient of the Alice M. Ford Scholarship and was named the 2005 Outstanding Graduate Student of the Year by the Iowa Association for Marriage and Family Therapy. She is currently serving as a visiting professor in the Department of Psychology at the University of Alaska at Anchorage, where she teaches primarily life span development and abnormal psychology courses. She has worked in various therapy contexts over the past six years, ranging from university clinics, to drug treatment centers, to adult mental health facilities, and programs involving homeless youth. In her leisure time she enjoys traveling, skiing, running, and dancing, as well as spending time with her husband, Tim, and their animal companion, Dax the cat.

Dave Bryant is a licensed professional counselor as well as a board certified music therapist. He is associated with a community (public) mental health, mental retardation, and substance abuse agency in addition to maintaining a private counseling practice. The bulk of Dave's experience with groups, group process, and group dynamics came from his years of experience as a music therapist in an inpatient setting. Dave enjoys being married and being a grandparent.

Nancy G. Calley, PhD, LPC, is an assistant professor in the Department of Counseling and Addiction Studies and the director of counseling programs at University of Detroit Mercy. In addition, she is the clinical director, Spectrum Human Services, Inc. & Affiliated Companies. Her clinical specialties and research interests include the juvenile justice and child welfare populations, solution-focused practices, professional identity issues related to counselors, and professional ethics. She was the 2004-2006 ethics chair for the Michigan Counseling Association. She has previously published in the *Journal of Counseling and Development.*

Christopher M. Faiver is a summa cum laude graduate of Hiram College, where he majored in religion and Spanish, attaining honors in both undergraduate majors. He is a member of Phi Beta Kappa. His master's in student personnel administration in higher education (counseling specialty) was conferred by Case Western Reserve University. Dr. Faiver also received his PhD in educational psychology (counseling specialty) from Case Western Reserve University. Licensed in counseling and psychology in Ohio, he is certified nationally as a counselor by NBCC and as a clinical consultant in hypnosis by the American Society of Clinical Hypnosis. He is listed in the National Register of Health Service Providers in Psychology. He has extensive clinical experience in a variety of settings. He has made numerous presentations and is the author of many journal articles and two books, one of which is in its third edition. Dr. Faiver is professor and coordinator of the community counseling master's program at John Carroll University in Cleveland, Ohio.

Trey Fitch is currently an associate professor at the University of Cincinnati-Clermont College. He has an EdD in counseling and has licensure in Kentucky and Georgia. Trey Fitch's specialty is counseling with children and adolescents. His previous works have appeared in *Professional*

School Counseling, Education, Community College Journal of Research and Practice, Counselor Education and Supervision, and *Journal of Critical Thinking.*

Robert Gee III, EdD, received his master's and doctorate degrees at Texas Tech University in counselor education. He is the associate director of the Southwest Institute for Addictive Diseases and assistant professor in the Department of Neuropsychiatry at the Health Sciences Center at Texas Tech University. He is a licensed professional counselor and approved supervisor.

Elwood R. Hamlin II, PhD, ACSW, is a professor in the School of Social Work at Florida Atlantic University. He is a clinical member of the American Association for Marriage and Family Therapy (AAMFT). His interests include family treatment, family violence, and clinical practice.

Randall L. Hilscher has a master of arts in education degree from the University of Akron (2004), and a doctor of ministry from McCormick Theological Seminary (1989). Mr. Hilscher is a licensed professional counselor in Ohio and a doctoral candidate at the University of Akron in the Counselor Education and Supervision Program, with a specialization in marriage and family counseling/therapy. Mr. Hilscher is employed as a counselor at the Interval Brotherhood Home in Akron, Ohio, a residential substance abuse treatment center. Mr. Hilscher is also currently a lecturer at the University of Akron, teaching issues in sexuality for counselors.

W. Jeff Hinton, PhD, LMFT, is an assistant professor in the Marriage and Family Therapy Program and director of Clinical Services at the University of Southern Mississippi. His clinical interests are in working with troubled and delinquent adolescents and their families and clinical supervision. Dr. Hinton's previous works have been published in *The Comprehensive Encyclopedia of School Psychology, The Encyclopedia of Human Development, The Researcher,* and *The Family Journal.*

Michael Kane, PhD, MSW, MDiv, is a licensed social worker in Florida and an assistant professor in the School of Social Work at Florida Atlantic University. His interests include ageism in aging, dementia, managed care, and clinical practice.

Jennifer L. Krafchick, PhD, earned her master's degree from Colorado State University's (CSU) Marriage and Family Therapy Program and her doctorate degree in education from Colorado State University, specializing in education, counseling, gender, and diversity. She currently serves as the assistant director in the Office of Women's Programs and Students at CSU, providing services for survivors of interpersonal violence, and maintains a private psychotherapy practice in Fort Collins, Colorado. She teaches both graduate and undergraduate courses in the Human Development and Family Studies Program and Women's Studies Program at CSU. Dr. Krafchick has published numerous articles on sex education, parenting, and social justice education for counselors and family therapists.

Glenn W. Lambie, PhD, LPC, NCC, NCSC, CCMHC, is an assistant professor in the Department of Child, Family, and Community Sciences in the College of Education at University of Central Florida in Orlando, Florida. His areas of specialty and interest include professional school counseling; individual, group, and family therapy with children and adolescents; and counselor development.

Jennifer Marshall is currently an associate professor at the University of Cincinnati-Raymond Walters College. She has an EdD in counseling and has licensure in Ohio and Kentucky. She was previously director of counseling at Berea College and ran groups with college students. She specializes in working with college students and adolescents. Her previous works have been published in *Professional School Counseling, Education, Inquiry: Critical Thinking Across* *the Disciplines, Counselor Education and Supervision,* and *Journal of Humanistic and Educational Development.*

Meredith W. Neill, ThM, LMFT, is an adjunct faculty instructor at Valencia Community College and a certified sex therapist in full-time private practice.

Brigid Noonan, PhD, NCC, ACS, LCPC, is an assistant professor in the Department of Counselor Education at Stetson University. She has had experience working with individuals, couples, and families while working for employee assistance programs, in private practice, and consulting for companies. Her areas of interest include the addictive disorders, eating disorders, working with women, chronic illness, advocacy within the counselor education field, working with diverse populations and career development.

Aaron Oberman, PhD, NCC, is an assistant professor of school counseling at The Citadel. He earned a doctorate in counselor education from the University of Tennessee. He has completed internships in community and school counseling, and worked as a career counselor. His specialty areas include career counseling and group and individual counseling in the schools.

Loan T. Phan is an assistant professor at the University of New Mexico. She received her MA in marriage and family therapy and PhD in counselor education and supervision with an emphasis in school counseling and multicultural counseling from the University of Nevada, Reno. Dr. Phan has worked extensively with multicultural and diverse populations including ethnic minority children and families, people with disabilities, students of color in high school and college settings, women of color, and LGBT racial minorities. Dr. Phan has expertise and publications in the areas of multicultural counseling, social justice issues, group supervision, racial and gender identity development, gender issues with women of color, ethnic minority students, family therapy and group work with ethnic minorities. She teaches courses in multicultural counseling, group counseling, assessment in counseling, and career counseling.

Jeffrey A. Rings, MA, is a doctoral student in counseling psychology at the University of Denver. He received his BA in psychology from Pepperdine University and his MA in counseling psychology from Northwestern University. He has cofacilitated many psychotherapy groups over the last seven years, with populations ranging the chronically mentally ill to college students. He also currently serves on the board of directors for the Colorado Psychological Association as the APAGS representative.

Maria T. Riva, PhD, is associate professor and training director of the Counseling Psychology Program at the University of Denver. She has been actively involved in facilitating many types of counseling and psychotherapy groups over the past twenty years. She teaches both group counseling and advanced group counseling courses, and her teaching style is strongly influenced by group and leadership theory. In 2001, she was awarded the University of Denver Distinguished Teaching Award. She has numerous publications on group counseling and psychotherapy. She belongs to the Association for Specialists in Group Work (ASGW, Division of ACA) and Group Psychology and Psychotherapy (Division 49 of APA). She was on the editorial board of the *Journal for Specialists in Group Work (JSGW)* for six years and currently serves as its associate editor. She is a fellow of ASGW and in 1997 co-edited a special issue on group research for *JSGW*. She also co-edited the *Handbook of Group Counseling and Psychotherapy,* published by Sage in 2004.

Jane Roberts, PhD, LCSW, is an assistant professor in the School of Social Work at the University of South Florida (USF) in Sarasota, Florida. Dr. Roberts obtained her PhD in gerontology from Virginia Tech, where her research interests and doctoral work emphasized age-biased attitudes and prejudicial views toward older people. She is currently involved in a project involving the familial and socio-cultural influences on adults of the WWII era. Her clinical and administrative career has included psychotherapy with couples and individuals, hospice and hospital administration, and children's and elders' protective services. She is a licensed clinical social worker and teaches BSW and MSW students at USF.

Floyd F. Robison is an associate professor in the Counseling and Counselor Education Program, School of Education, at Indiana University. He has a PhD (1982, Indiana University) in counseling and educational psychology. His research interests include the study of group counseling processes and leadership, as well as the applications of groups in mental health, social service, and school settings. He has authored twenty-two professional journal articles and delivered more than fifty presentations at regional and national professional meetings. He is a licensed health service provider in psychology, licensed marriage and family therapist, licensed mental health counselor, and national certified counselor. In addition to his academic work, he maintains a private psychology practice, specializing in psychological assessment, group and family therapies, and treatment of children and adolescents with emotional and behavior disorders.

Jessica A. Russo has a master of arts degree in child life therapy from The University of Akron. Ms. Russo is a fourth year PhD student in marriage and family therapy at The University of Akron in Akron, Ohio. She is a social worker for Cuyahoga County Department of Children and Family Services and specializes in working with families, specifically expectant mothers who expose their unborn child to drugs or alcohol. She has presented at APA and AAMFT. In addition to a chapter in this book, she has two book chapters in press.

Shari M. Sias, PhD, LPC, is an assistant professor in the Department of Rehabilitation Studies at East Carolina University in Greenville, North Carolina. Areas of specialty and interest include substance abuse counseling, individual and family counseling, and counselor development.

Shirley R. Simon, LCSW, ACSW, is a faculty member at the School of Social Work, Loyola University Chicago with over thirty years of continuous college/university teaching experience. She coordinates the group work sequence at Loyola and has engaged in a variety of social work practice activities, including private practice in clinical social work with adults and families, group work leadership and consultation, and agency practice with women and adolescents. She has been published in *Social Work with Groups, Child Welfare League of America, Journal of Teaching in Social Work, Journal of Social Work Education,* and *Jewish Community Center Program Aids.*

Laura Simpson, PhD, is a licensed professional counselor, national certified counselor, and approved clinical supervisor. She is employed as the Adult/DD Services Coordinator at Region I Mental Health Center in Clarksdale, Mississippi and serves as an adjunct professor for the Department of Counselor Education at Delta State University. She received her PhD from the University of Mississippi. Her special interests include spirituality, secondary traumatic stress, and supervision.

Pat L. Sims, EdD, LMFT, LPC, is an associate professor and director of the Marriage and Family Therapy Program at the University of Southern Mississippi. Dr. Sims's clinical interests include sexual trauma, at-risk children and youth, juvenile delinquency, and clinical training. Dr. Sims's previous works have been featured in *The Encyclopedia of Human Development, The Researcher: An Interdisciplinary Journal, The Family Journal, Journal of Child Sexual Abuse,* and *Journal of Family and Consumer Sciences.*

Randyl D. Smith, PhD, is a licensed psychologist and assistant professor at the Metropolitan State College of Denver. She has more than ten years experience facilitating groups in such varied settings as inpatient psychiatric facilities, residential treatment centers, community mental health organizations, and public schools. She has trained others in group leadership skills, has written articles on group therapy, and is particularly interested in ethics applied to group work.

Paul Springer, MS, received his master's degree at Auburn University in marriage and family therapy and his bachelor's degree at Brigham Young University in marriage, family, and human development. He is currently a student at Texas Tech University, where he is completing his doctorate degree in marriage and family therapy. Paul works at the Southwest Institute for Addictive Diseases where he continues to do individual, family, couple, and group therapy. He has his associate license in marriage and family therapy.

Donna Starkey, PhD, LPC, is a licensed professional counselor, national certified counselor, and approved clinical supervisor. She is currently an assistant professor of counselor education at Delta State University in Cleveland, Mississippi. She received her PhD at the University of Mississippi. Prior to returning to an academic setting, she was a community counselor in a regional mental health setting. Her areas of interest include clinical skills development, ethics, and supervision.

Laura Tejada, MA, is a student in the PhD program in Marriage and Family Therapy at the University of Akron. She is a registered play therapist and was a K-5 elementary school counselor at Roosevelt Elementary School in McPherson, Kansas, as well as a classroom teacher in Whiteriver, Arizona, and Gallup, New Mexico.

R. Valorie Thomas, PhD, LMFT, LMHC, is an adjunct faculty member in the Counselor Education Department at Rollins College. Formerly, she was an assistant professor at Stetson University. She is the cochairperson of the ethics committee of the Association for Specialists in Group Work, a division of the American Counseling Association (ACA).

Edil Torres-Rivera has a PhD in counseling psychology with a concentration in multicultural counseling from the University of Connecticut, Storrs. He is an associate professor at the University at Buffalo, SUNY. Dr. Torres-Rivera has published articles in the areas of group work with ethnic minorities, technology, chaos theory, supervision, multicultural counseling, prisons, and gang-related behavior. He also has presented at national and international conferences. He also has coordinated the school counseling program at the University of Nevada, Reno, and presently is the director of the school counseling program in Singapore.

Charles K. West, PhD, LMFT, is an assistant professor, Department of Child and Family Studies, University of Southern Mississippi. His clinical interests include issues around continuing competency, eating disorders, supervision, and the impact of divorce on adult children. Dr. West's previous works have been featured in the *Journal of Divorce and Remarriage, Journal of Systemic Therapies,* and *The Clinical Supervisor.*

John Joseph Zarski, PhD, was the former director of marriage and family therapy and a professor at The University of Akron. He was a licensed psychologist and a licensed marriage and family therapist. He had over fifty publications. Unfortunately, during the production of the chapter in this book, "Maintaining Stability: Life Cycle Transitions in Families Coping with Childhood Cancer," Dr. Zarski unexpectedly passed away. His contributions and dedication to the field of marriage and family therapy are innumerable. He will be missed greatly.

Toni S. Zimmerman, PhD, is a professor in the Human Development and Family Studies Department at Colorado State University (CSU) and licensed marriage and family therapist. The graduate program at CSU, directed by Dr. Zimmerman, was awarded the Best Training Program by the American Association for Marriage and Family Therapy in 1999. This award was granted to the department largely based on the dedication in training family therapists who are sensitive to issues of diversity. Toni has published over fifty professional journal articles, eight book chapters, and three edited journal volumes primarily focusing on issues related to fairness and equality.

Foreword

The Group Therapist's Notebook: Homework, Handouts, and Activities for Use in Psychotherapy is an excellent resource that builds a bridge between theoretically based texts on group counseling and collections of group exercises. The publication is a practical aid for group psychotherapists who are in the process of beginning a group practice or already utilizing groups as part of their practice. The section Getting Started is particularly helpful for beginning groups. As an example of the use of professional resources in this workbook, one of the chapters in this section details a disclosure statement, which is based on the Association for Specialists in Group Work (ASGW) Best Practice Guidelines. An actual disclosure statement used in ASGW training workshops is provided.

The workbook model is useful for group specialists in creating their own exercises to fit the needs of their clients. The organization of the exercises into type of contribution, objectives, rationale for use, instructions, suggestions for follow-up, contraindications, and readings and resources for the professional and clients provides a comprehensive grid for completing additional exercises. Some exercise descriptions add suggestions for variations, so a group specialist can adapt an exercise for maximum flexible application. An important addition to this workbook, not often see in other collections of group exercises, is the inclusion of contraindications. These cautions show the concern for ethical and best practices in using the techniques. The resources listed after each exercise, including conferences, workshops, and resources offered by the Association for Specialists in Group Work, are extremely helpful for professionals who need background information on techniques and advanced knowledge with specific populations.

In reviewing the workbook and the client concerns addressed by the exercises, an experienced psychotherapist is immediately aware that Dawn Viers and her associates have included group treatment techniques for the major issues clients bring to group counseling. Another observation is the inclusion of a variety of theoretical approaches. Many authors tend to focus on a narrow array of client problems and operate from one or two theories. Professionals using this workbook will find a variety of valid approaches that effectively address their clients' concerns.

In summary, this publication is the product of group specialists who obviously have experience in the field. This workbook helps new and experienced professionals begin a group practice or effectively include new approaches in their group work. The reader is encouraged to evaluate his or her own group facilitation skills and identify those group skills that could be improved from professional development. Because of the breadth of client concerns addressed by the exercises and the use of multiple theoretical approaches, this workbook contains something of value for any reader who is a group specialist.

M. Carolyn Thomas, PhD
Auburn University Montgomery
2005-2006 ASGW President

Preface

In an era of managed care, reduced health benefits, and increasing client loads and productivity standards, group therapy is seen as a valuable, and often optimal, way of providing treatment for individuals, couples, and families (Buchele & Price, 1995; MacKenzie, 2002; Villeneuve, 2001). Group members can at once commiserate with, cajole, and challenge each other. This process is unique to this modality and factors in the success and popularity of group therapy. Across a variety of studies, group therapy has been found to be as effective, or even more effective, than individual therapy (Fuhriman & Burlingame, 1994; McRoberts, Burlingame, & Hoag, 1998). Being part of a group has also been linked to an increased perception of quality of life among participants (Michalak, Yatham, Wan, & Lam, 2005; Tkachuk, Graff, Martin, & Bernstein, 2003; Yildiz, Veznedaroglu, Eryavuz, & Kayahan, 2004). Further, as group work can be used to treat a greater number of clients with fewer resources, group therapy is often viewed as more efficient than other treatment approaches (Brabender, 2002). Clearly, group work has many benefits.

Professionals who engage in group work come from many different backgrounds and professions. Psychologists, marriage and family therapists, social workers, counselors, prevention workers, nurses, psychiatrists, ministers, and educators have all facilitated groups. Group therapy has been employed to treat such varied issues as mood and thought disorders, abuse and addictions, couple enrichment and relationship concerns, and parenting issues. Groups can vary in duration and can be used in prevention, in treatment, in short-term crisis counseling, as a support source, or as after-care. Further, group work can be conducted in many different settings. These benefits make group therapy an almost universal treatment approach.

This book offers both new and seasoned professionals resources and ideas for organizing and implementing groups for individuals, couples, and families. In contrast to many group therapy books, this book includes practical resources for a variety of presenting problems and population types, as well as ideas for organizing and facilitating groups. Each chapter presents detailed instructions for use, suggestions for tracking the intervention in successive meetings, contraindications for use, and resources for the facilitator and client. Further, each intervention is backed by a theoretical or practical rationale for use. Models and theories include such varied approaches as experiential, behavioral, existential-humanistic, solution-focused, and attachment theory, ensuring that group facilitators will find an approach that fits their practice.

Group work requires facilitators to utilize different skills than they would use in individual or even family therapy. Facilitators must find ways to take clients with their own unique needs and preferences and form a cohesive unit where group members feel comfortable exploring personal, and often painful, topics. To meet this need, the authors in this book offer practical tips for engaging group members, facilitating open dialogues, and ensuring active participation. Further, many of the authors present clinical vignettes. These vignettes demonstrate the intervention in action and allow readers the opportunity to envision how to use these tools.

Audience

Mental health professionals in all areas and settings will benefit from using this book. This includes group facilitators in nonprofit agencies, counseling centers, private practice, school settings, hospitals, and inpatient or outpatient treatment facilities. Facilitators who specialize in treating a specific presenting problem will likely find interventions tailored to their particular population, as well as ideas for taking a group from induction to termination. Mental health professionals who facilitate many different groups will find a myriad of ideas and tools for their practice.

Professors and instructors at colleges, universities, and training centers will want to have this book on hand when they are teaching students group facilitation skills. It can also be a handy resource for supervision and practicum. Students and novice facilitators will benefit from the step-by-step instructions when they first engage in real world practice. More experienced facilitators may gain a new perspective for treating specific problems or ways to jump start their group processes. Increasing the adaptability of this book, the activities, homework assignments, and handouts can be used as presented or can be adapted to fit different group curricula or presenting problems.

Organization

This book is comprised of five main sections. The first section, Getting Started, begins with a chapter designed to help instructors teach group facilitation skills. The next chapter gives tips and ideas for facilitating a group. The final chapter in this section provides recommendations for developing a professional disclosure statement, a critical tool for the group facilitator.

The second section, Interventions for All Groups, offers activities, assignments, and handouts from the introductory phases of a group to the conclusion. The first chapter in this section features a fun and easy icebreaker, while the second chapter presents activities designed to reduced stress and increase coping mechanisms. The third chapter helps group members problem solve through the use of fantasy. The fourth chapter uses group members as de facto family members for a sculpting exercise, while the fifth encourages congruence between thought and actions. The next two chapters can be adapted for individuals, couples, or families. One helps group members connect via the meaning of their names, while the other teaches self-awareness and management skills. Last in this section is a chapter devoted to activities used during the termination phase of a group.

The third section, Interventions for Population-Specific Groups, showcases a variety of interventions for specific populations or presenting problems. The first chapter teaches anger management skills. The next two chapters help group members ease feelings of shame and guilt. The fourth and fifth chapters present activities for groups of substance users and children of alcoholics. The last two chapters spotlight interventions for dealing with grief and loss.

The fourth section, Interventions for Adolescent and College-Age Groups, targets teens and young adults. The first four chapters are targeted at groups in a school setting or mental health facility. First is a chapter that guides teens through the steps necessary for change. The second chapter focuses on the often contradictory states of independence and belonging, while the third helps adolescents explore a more positive body image. The fourth chapter utilizes culturally appropriate ideas and activity ideas for working with Latino(a) young adults in group therapy. The fifth chapter, suitable for groups in an inpatient or outpatient treatment center, teaches teens interpersonal skills. The last two chapters in this section, targeted toward college-age populations, focus on increasing coping skills and crisis-intervention strategies.

The final section of this book, Interventions for Couple and Family Groups, offers tools for working with groups comprised of couples or family members. The first two chapters, focused on couples, assist with conflict mediation and resolution. The next three chapters present activities and handouts to use in parenting groups. Finally, the last chapter provides ideas to support the caregivers of a sick child.

Each chapter follows the same format: objective or purpose of the intervention, a brief rationale for use, detailed, easy to use instructions, suggestions for follow-up, contraindications, and resources for the group facilitator and client. Many of the chapters also include a clinical vignette.

References

Brabender, V. (2002). *Introduction to group therapy.* New York: John Wiley & Sons.

Buchele, B. J., & Price, J. R. (1995). Group psychotherapy: A managed care alternative for private practice. In L. VandeCreek & S. Knapp (Eds.), *Innovations in clinical practice: A source book* (Vol. 14, pp. 55-65). Sarasota, FL: Professional Resource Press/Professional Resource Exchange, Inc.

Fuhriman, A., & Burlingame, G. M. (1994). *Handbook of group psychotherapy: An empirical and clinical synthesis.* New York: Wiley.

MacKenzie, K. R. (2002). Effective group psychotherapies. In F. Kaslow (Ed.), *Comprehensive handbook of psychotherapy: Integrative/eclectic* (Vol. 4, pp. 521-542). New York: John Wiley & Sons, Inc.

McRoberts, C., Burlingame, G. M., & Hoag, M. J. (1998). Comparative efficacy of individual and group psychotherapy: A meta-analytic perspective. *Group Dynamics: Theory, Research, and Practice, 2*(2), 101-117.

Michalak, E. E., Yatham, L. N., Wan, D., & Lam, R. W. (2005). Perceived quality of life in patients with bipolar disorder. Does group psychoeducation have an impact? *Canadian Journal of Psychiatry, 50,* 95-100.

Tkachuk, G. A., Graff, L. A., Martin, G. L., & Bernstein, C. N. (2003). Randomized control trial of cognitive-behavior group therapy for irritable bowel syndrome in a medical setting. *Journal of Clinical Psychology in Medical Settings, 10*(1), 57-69.

Villeneuve, C. (2002). *Emphasizing the interpersonal in psychotherapy: Families and groups in the era of cost containment.* New York: Brunner/Routledge.

Yildiz, M., Veznedaroglu, B., Eryavuz, A., & Kayahan, B. (2004). Psychosocial skills training on social functioning and quality of life in the treatment of schizophrenia: A controlled study in Turkey. *International Journal of Psychiatry in Clinical Practice, 8*(4), 219-225.

Acknowledgments

I would like to acknowledge a number of people, without whom this project would have never gotten off the ground. First, I would like to express thanks to the remarkable authors who contributed to this book. These authors, seasoned professionals, educators, and students contributed insightful, timely, and well-written chapters, which made my job as an editor much easier. I would also like to acknowledge the encouragement and flexibility of Lorna Hecker, series editor, and the staff of The Haworth Press. I am privileged and honored to be a part of *The Therapists Notebook* series for a second time. Finally, I am grateful for the love and support of my family during this process. I particularly thank both of my children for napping so that I could proofread, edit, and write chapters.

SECTION I:
GETTING STARTED

Turning Group Theory into Group Practice: The Role of the Experiential Component in Group Facilitator Training

Donna Starkey
Laura Simpson

Type of Contribution: Activities

Objectives

These activities are intended to teach group facilitators fundamental skills. The goals of these activities are as follows:

1. Gain familiarity with the roles and functions of a group.
2. Become aware of the importance of the need for structure within the group to maximize efficacy.
3. Develop an appreciation for the purpose and meaning of risk, anxiety, vulnerability, and ambiguity.
4. Learn to identify group goals and dynamics as they occur.
5. Illuminate personal strengths and challenges as a future facilitator.

Rationale for Use

Traditional group theories, dynamics, and ethical standards provide a theoretical knowledge base without providing skills specific to the emerging group counselor (Furr & Barrett, 2000). Finding ways to help facilitators bond group theory to skills, and then link it from cognition to practice, is a challenge. Research indicates that minimum training guidelines have been inadequate in scope (Markus & King, 2003). In fact, Gladding (1999) postulates that the relatively recent focus on comprehensive training for group facilitators is in response to the need for competent and ethical practitioners in the counseling profession.

Education of a group facilitator is most comprehensively approached through the participation in a group experience and the inherent opportunity to view facilitation as a member. Previous literature reinforces the relationship between group class and group experience in the preparation of group leaders (Furr & Barrett, 2000). Yalom (1975) concluded that group facilitators develop greater insight into the potential group experiences of clients and a greater appreciation for the universality of the human experience through group membership. This impact on the de-

---

Parts of this chapter were previously published in the *Delta Education Journal* (Spring, 2004). Used with permission.

velopment of an effective group facilitator may best be illustrated with the model shown in Figure 1.1.

Anderson and Price (2001) report that students who participate in a group therapy experience as a group member claim experiential group activities are an "effective and necessary teaching method" (p. 177). Additional research further reveals that student facilitators-in-training reported intense emotive responses to a group experience (Murphy, Leszcz, Collings, & Salvendy, 1996). These results provide support for the authors' contention that experiential group activities create opportunity for enlightenment, understanding, and integration of theory and practice not available in a traditional didactic learning environment. With regard to a training continuum, this effort may be best served if the experiential component is completed after a theoretical foundation has been established to provide the group leaders with maximum benefit.

Instructions

This section will offer an array of activities intended to help develop rapport among group facilitators-in-training. While any one of these activities may serve as a catalyst for moving a group to the working stage, the experiences presented are categorized by level of perceived risk assumed by the group. Similar to the work of Ward (1985), this technique approaches the group experience as progressive and introduces activities beginning with individual thoughts, feelings, and perception, moving into interaction between group members, and ending with fully developed collaborative participation among members.

These activities can be used in many different settings, including a clinical training program and an agency or practice within a community. If the activities are used to train students in a training program, the instructor would take on the role of the group facilitator. If the activities are used in an agency or practice, the supervisor would act as the group facilitator.

Level I: Building Trust

This level serves to begin the process of learning about group dynamics. The exercises provided are geared toward the development of initial trust and are primarily cognitively based. They require minimal risk and vulnerability on the part of the participant. Each experience allows individuals within the group to identify and share personal thoughts and feelings.

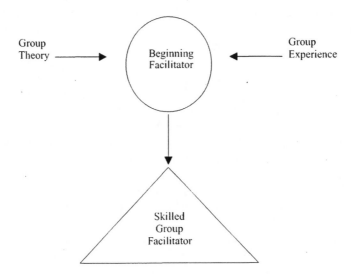

FIGURE 1.1. Influences on the Development of a Skilled Group Facilitator

Level II: Assuming Risk

Activities in this section are devoted to the group assessment of risk and the facilitation of self-disclosure. This level requires that group members participate on a more emotional level. It also involves interaction between group members.

Level III: Working Together

 This level of activity requires group members to participate in an emotionally intimate fashion. Safety needs have been met, and the exercises are geared toward the working stage of group development, encompassing the whole group as a unit.

Variation

While these exercises are presented here in a format to train group facilitators, the activities would also help build rapport, cohesiveness, and emotional expression in therapy groups. Level I activities would be suitable as icebreakers at the start of therapy groups, whereas Level II and III activities would be more appropriate during the working phase as the group begins to develop trust and meet stated objectives. When utilizing these activities with therapeutic groups, as with training groups, the group facilitator should pay particular attention to fully processing the activities and ensuring safety for group members.

Level I

The Dinner Party

Purpose: The purpose of this activity is to begin to integrate an understanding of interpersonal dynamics with the reality of how the perceptions of individuals and placement of group members affect the energy of a group.
Goals Addressed: 1, 2, 5
Materials Needed: 12 place cards for each group, 10 with names
Activity: Members are engaged in a discussion of the role of interpersonal dynamics in a group environment. Members should be encouraged to contrast previous group experiences that have been particularly engaging and insightful with those that have not been as successful. The facilitator will make an analogy between groups in general and the group dynamics of a dinner party. Discussing the energy and interests of attendees as well as the placement of individuals around the table, the group can focus on the power these factors bring to a group experience.
The facilitator will provide the group with twelve place cards. If the group is large, temporary subgroups may be created with each subgroup provided a set of cards. On the place cards, the facilitator will have written ten names. One method of name selection is to consider public figures in popular culture or to consider notable people from history. A sample list used in a recent exercise included President George W. Bush, Nelson Mandela, Madonna, Tiger Woods, and J. K. Rowling.
Although twelve place cards are provided, only ten names are used leaving two of the cards blank. The facilitator should provide a version of the following instructions to the students:

> Your task is to create the optimal group environment for a dinner party. Using the place cards provided, arrange the ten named cards in such a way as to set the stage for the best possible interaction. As a group, determine what two additional people would best fit the

stage your group has set, and place the new names accordingly. Use this time to process, as a group, how different personality types impact relating styles as you make your decisions.

During the activity, the facilitator should observe the interaction without unnecessary intervention. When the group has reached a consensus, allow the members to share what the process was like and how they arrived at the decisions they made.

Process: To meet the goal of increasing awareness of group dynamics, this session involves allowing group members to use their own dynamics to make decisions about the fictional group. The facilitator becomes aware of ways in which the group is beginning to relate to one another as they establish this model group. The session provides opportunities for parallels between the fictional group and the actual one by opening an overt dialogue to the evident analogous process. As the group gleans this new knowledge about itself, it can move toward increased openness and risk.

Spooning [adapted from Williamson (1993)]

Purpose: The purpose of this activity is to put group members at ease and encourage laughter as a bonding experience among members while illustrating the potential effects of embarrassment on interpersonal communication.

Goals Addressed: 2, 3

Materials Needed: One metal teaspoon and one paper towel per person

Activity: After giving each member a spoon and a towel, ask the members to make sure the spoon is clean and dry. Next, individuals should wipe the bridge of their nose with the towel, ensuring the area is free of moisture. While grasping the spoon on the handle, breathe into the concave portion of the bowl of the spoon. Finally, ask members to hang the spoon from the tip of their nose.

Process: As a group begins, members may feel unsure of themselves and self-conscious about expressing themselves. This experience allows each group member to recognize feelings of awkwardness that may prohibit an individual from interacting with others. While highlighting this important issue, the members are allowed an opportunity to have fun and laugh, resulting in a bonding experience with other group members. Facilitators must maintain awareness to ensure that no members are hurt or embarrassed by the actions of other group members. All members should participate in the activity at one time, thus eliminating the problem of specific members feeling as if all attention is focused on them.

Discussion among members following the activity should focus on the feelings experienced during the activity. The facilitators should then lead the discussion into the potentially harmful effects of insecurity on interpersonal dynamics, including withdrawal from others and social isolation.

Group Roles [adapted from Butler (2001)]

Purpose: The purpose of this activity is to clarify and recognize the various roles group members assume. Some behaviors and attitudes promote a cohesive and productive group, and time must be devoted to raising awareness of members own preferred roles and the subordinate styles they may have employed in previous experiences. It is critical to illustrate that members will benefit from the experience in direct proportion to how much they invest of themselves (Corey & Corey, 1997). Members are reminded through this exercise that the identity of a group is shaped by the roles of its members.

Goals Addressed: 1, 4, 5

Materials Needed: A container filled with group roles listed on cards

Activity: The facilitator initiates a discussion of specific group roles often found in groups. Examples include the *harmonizer,* who tries to keep peace at all costs; the *dominator,* who interrupts constantly; the *blocker,* who refuses to agree to anything; and the *self-confessor,* who manages to inappropriately reveal personal information with every contribution. Members should be challenged to consider the motivation behind particular roles and the purposes those roles may serve in a variety of settings. The group should share how outside roles may play out in a group environment.

The facilitator should then pass around a container full of group roles with brief definitions (for example, harmonizer-peacemaker or class clown–overly humorous). Members are instructed to select a role and reflect on the traits and characteristics assigned to that role while keeping the selection secret from the rest of the group. The facilitator will then explain that the activity will consist of the group discussing an assigned topic with each member interacting from the position of the role selected. Members are encouraged to be creative and to act and react from that assigned role. Following the activity, the group will process what it was like to interact from the selected roles.

Process: This activity offers an explicit link between theory and practice. Members are able to act out their interpretation of roles and receive feedback from others regarding the presence of such roles. This activity allows individuals to consider how they might relate to participants in group who take on roles that are often perceived as negative. The session provides members with opportunities to discover subordinate roles that may be less clear than their dominant functions. The facilitator has the opportunity and obligation to generate insights into role definition and group dynamics.

It is important not to explicitly link members by name to roles they exhibit (Kottler, 2000). It is more beneficial to put difficult behavior patterns into a context allowing individuals to build insight into what they may be doing that is not working well for them. This approach encourages other members to express themselves in response to dealing with others.

Level II

Fishbowl [adapted from Christian & Tubesing (1997)]

Purpose: This activity encourages participants to share personal concerns and fears.
Goals Addressed: 2, 3, 5
Materials Needed: One fishbowl, blank paper and writing utensils for each member
Activity: The fishbowl should be placed in a chair while the chairs of the participants should be arranged in a circle surrounding the bowl. Members are asked to write examples of areas in their life in which they feel exposed, self-conscious, or vulnerable. Beginning with the member that has a birthday closest to the first of the year, ask each participant to first express one concern about participating in a group experience. After every member has verbalized a concern, subsequent requests should focus on the ways members feel exposed or vulnerable in their personal lives. Members should be reminded that they are to share at a level at which they feel comfortable. The facilitator may encourage members to share as many times as needed.

After sharing, members place the papers with their written concerns inside the fishbowl. The fishbowl is left in place throughout the group experience as a reminder that every individual has vulnerabilities that should be respected.

Process: The facilitator must remind members that it is natural to feel uncomfortable or awkward, particularly in a new group where members do not know one another. As group work involves personal risk, members may feel nervous. The facilitator must attend to every member with respect and encouragement. Members have an opportunity to become more aware of specific personal feelings and the feelings of other members. At the conclusion of the exercise, the facilitator should attend to every member and verify emotional safety. The facilitator may take this opportunity to link characteristics members may have in common. Encouraging discussion and helping group members with intermember communication will enhance activity at the interpersonal level.

Peaks and Valleys [adapted from Christian & Tubesing (1997)]

Purpose: This activity provides a nonlinear look at the highs and lows in group members lives as an opportunity to reflect on the personal balance of positive and negative life experiences.
Goals Addressed: 2, 3
Materials Needed: Blank paper and writing utensils for each member
Activity: Each member is asked to draw a picture of a mountain landscape with a peak and a valley in it. As the participants draw the mountain, they are asked to reflect their own personal life journey and consider which experiences stand out as highs and lows. Near the top of the mountain, each member should list three experiences they consider the top in their life. Near the valley area, members should write down three experiences which they consider particularly difficult.
Process: The facilitator should invite members to share the experiences they have chosen as personal highs and lows. This exercise is intended to offer participants an opportunity to reflect on the positive and negative times of life and the relative balance between happy and difficult times. The facilitator may choose to pair up group members if the level of trust does not feel conducive to having members share openly among all the members. The facilitator may ask members to share what they have learned from these life experiences. This exercise is used to demonstrate the issue that positive and negative experiences can contribute to building strength to cope with life stressors.

Hot Seat

Purpose: To allow group members an opportunity to anonymously disclose a secret and explore the effects of shame on interpersonal relationships.
Goals Addressed: 2, 3, 5
Materials Needed: Blank paper and writing utensils for each member and a bowl or basket
Activity: Participants should be arranged in a circle, with designated hot seat somewhere in the circle. Every group member is given a piece of paper and asked to write down a personal secret they have felt reluctant to disclose. Members should be reminded that the issues will not be linked to any individual, and members will not be asked to disclose what they wrote. Members should challenge themselves to write any issues that have caused the individual to feel shame, embarrassment, fear of ridicule or judgment, or any emotion that contributes to feeling hesitant to disclose the event.
Members should then be instructed to fold the paper and place it in the basket where the responses can be well mixed. One at a time, members will sit in the hot seat and draw a response out of the basket and read it to the group. The individual reading the item will then be asked to respond to the following:

1. How do you feel at this moment?
2. How might this event cause shame?
3. What might you fear if faced with this situation?

Process: This activity is designed to promote empathy among members and encourage feedback between members. The facilitator must closely monitor the group to guard anonymity of the responses and promote an atmosphere of safety. The session has great potential to allow members with issues of shame to feel validated and comforted. Members are also offered an opportunity for interpersonal vicarious learning.

If any group members display inappropriate efforts to determine the identities of the disclosures, they should be removed. As with any group, the facilitator should intervene and process any comments that may be critical or debilitating. As members in the hot seat respond to the questions, the other group members may be encouraged to provide supportive feedback to help alleviate any anxiety they may experience.

Level III

Emotional Statues [adapted from Queen (1994)]

Purpose: This activity serves as a mechanism to promote expression of feelings and stories among participants. Through facilitative efforts, it allows group members to move from thinking about feeling to a more intimate emoting style.

Goals Addressed: 2, 3, 4

Materials Needed: Easel pad or other large surface for writing and markers

Activity: Begin the exercise by having students brainstorm a list of feeling words. Assist the members in ensuring that intense feelings are not excluded and duplication of feelings is minimized. Post this list where it is visible to the entire group. The facilitator should explain that, beginning with a volunteer, each person will be asked to select an emotion from which to create a statue. The following instructions should then be provided:

> In turn, each of you will select one of the emotions with which you closely identify. Thinking about a specific time you have experienced that emotion, create a frozen statue position that best depicts the intensity of the feeling you experienced. Remain in that position for a few moments to allow the group to gain an understanding of what you are trying to project. You will be told to unfreeze and can then join the group in the discussion of the feeling. Following this, you will be asked to share the story illustrated by your statue. Each of you will take a turn and feeling words will be crossed off of the list as they are used. We will process this experience at the close of the activity.

Process: This activity serves to challenge the group at an emotive level. The facilitator is challenged to create an atmosphere for acceptance of intense emotions. The understanding that feeling words describe concepts but do not describe individual experiences is illuminated through this exercise. Members should leave the activity enlightened as to the depth and intensity of emotional experiences held by fellow participants. The group has the opportunity to bond through shared experiences and through linking member stories.

Value Scenarios [adapted from Queen (1994)]

Purpose: This activity serves to encourage members to identify values that are of particular importance to them. In addition, it allows group members an opportunity to gain insight into the value systems of others.

Materials Needed: None

Goals Addressed: 2, 3, 4, 5

Activity: The facilitator will open a discussion about values with the focus on an exploration of the members personal values. Specific scenarios (such as the following samples) should be presented to encourage discussion among members about how to handle these issues. At the conclusion of interactions about the scenarios, members will be encouraged to describe life experiences that challenged their personal values. Group members are to be encouraged to respond to the descriptions offered by others. The facilitator must attend to each member's safety needs and watch carefully to intervene if any participant becomes critical or hurtful toward a member that is sharing. Conclude with adequate time to process the activity.

Scenario 1: While shopping you observe a frustrated women harshly disciplining her five-year-old child in a manner that includes verbal criticism. She also slaps him multiple times on the legs. What do you do?

Scenario 2: You are taking a class in advanced statistics and are concerned it will be the only blemish on your 4.0 GPA. A friend took it last semester and offers to give you copies of the homework and tests the professor uses each year. Do you accept?

Scenario 3: As you are purchasing your books for the semester at the bookstore, you observe a popular athlete on campus shoplifting. What do you do?

Process: Infusing values into this activity requires the group to get in touch with their own value structure and tendency toward judgment. The facilitator has the ability to assist the group in viewing values from multiple perspectives, thus encouraging dialogical thinking. The group can become aware of subgroups occurring based on shared experiences and value systems. If the climate is safe enough, this exercise offers the opportunity for participants to experience personal awareness, empathy, tolerance, and appreciation of others.

Who I Am?

Purpose: This activity requires members to get in touch with what makes them who they are, including how that has been manifested through acceptance and rejection by others. In addition to raising each member's awareness of the human experience, the activity should also serve as a catalyst for emotive expression related to feelings of inclusion and abandonment.

Goals Addressed: 3, 5

Materials Needed: None

Activity: The facilitator should begin the activity with a discussion of uniqueness. Addressing cultural and social forces, the group will be prompted to share what makes members who they are. Make the request that members share with the group some characteristics that make them unique and how that has helped and hindered them in their life experiences. To challenge members to explore significant life experiences, the following questions may be posed:

1. When has being you been difficult?
2. How were you received by others at this time?
3. What impact did that make on you and your life?

Close with time to process the universal themes revealed in the session.

Process: This activity has great potential to quickly move the group to an emotional level. Most individuals have experienced rejection or criticism, and the opportunity to view others' life experiences can promote insight while strengthening group cohesion. The facilitator must work to protect the safety of the group member sharing his or her concerns while allowing members to join each other in the rawness of emotion. As with any group experience, care should be taken to manage group members desirous of repressing the group through untimely humor or superficial concerns.

Suggestions for Follow-Up

There are three considerations related to follow-up: follow-up with the group and its members, follow-up for the present group facilitator, and follow-up for the facilitator-in-training or future group facilitator. For group members, as these exercises are meant to facilitate comfort with the group process, build structure, and help members appreciate risk taking, it will be important to assess if these goals are met. Group members should be offered the opportunity to process each experience fully to determine how well the exercise met the stated goals. In addition, group members should be offered the opportunity to revisit the exercise, or the processing of the exercise, at the next group meeting. Such an opportunity minimizes any unfinished business that might hinder the next activity. To help meet the intended goals of the activity, the exercises can be revisited throughout the training as needed.

With the group as a whole, as well as the individual members, present group facilitators need to continually assess the fit of an activity and its outcome. Are members more wary of one another? Did the activity increase the level of trust? How did members leave the group and what questions, concerns, or insights might they have? These types of questions serve as the foundation for discussing unfinished business within the group and allow the group facilitator to better identify group needs.

Perhaps more relevant to the topic of this chapter, group facilitators learn from each use of an activity with a group. As such, group facilitators-in-training may benefit from keeping logs of the use of these activities with subsequent groups including the following:

Type of group activity used
When in the group process it was introduced
Why it was selected by the leader
Initial reaction by the group
How it went
Process by group
Post-group process by leader (Was it the right time? What changes would I make to the use of this activity next time?)

This type of narrative reflection will serve as an invaluable tool for the group facilitator attempting to refine skills, make subsequent group decisions, participate in consultation, or receive supervision from colleagues.

Contraindications

The importance of risk, anxiety, vulnerability, and ambiguity within the group experience cannot be overemphasized when training group facilitators. The ability to create safety is largely contingent on the feeling of security and safety experienced by the group leader. As such, group facilitators who shy away from interpersonal risk, experience high levels of anxiety in group activities, or have a low tolerance for ambiguity should not attempt to use these exercises. It is expected that the group leaders' comfort with what may be perceived as a risky group experience will increase as they move through the three levels of activities. If, at any time, a leader is too uncomfortable to continue, the group should not persist in the activity.

Discomfort is subjective, however, and a leader's comfort is not a direct predictor of the members' comfort. Group leaders must rely on their intuitive skills to discern when the group is ready to move to an activity with a higher level of risk. In addition to intuitive skills, prudent group leaders maintain an open and active process dialogue with the group throughout the activities. This dialogue creates an open line of communication with regard to vulnerability and risk. The group facilitator is responsible for determining activities that would be contraindicated for specific group populations. For example, Hot Seat is ineffective with and potentially harmful to individuals with social anxiety or when particularly angry or malicious group members are allowed to be harshly critical of the person in the hot seat. Again, as with any group experience, it is the responsibility of the facilitator to mediate such attempts at group destruction.

Readings and Resources for the Professional

Association for Specialists in Group Work (2000). *Professional Standards for the Training of Group Workers.* Retrieved July 15, 2003, from www.asgw.org_standards.htm.

CACREP accreditation manual of the council for accreditation of counseling and related educational programs (1st ed.). (2001). Alexandria, VA: CACREP.

Corey, M. S., & Corey, G. (2001). *Groups: Process and practice* (6th ed.). Belmont, CA: Brooks/Cole Publishing Company

Donaldson, M. A., & Cordes-Green, S. (1994). *Group treatment of adult incest survivors.* Thousand Oaks, CA: SAGE Publications.

Dossick, J., & Shea, E. (1988). *Creative therapy: 52 exercises for groups.* Sarasota, FL: Professional Resource Exchange.

Dossick, J., & Shea, E. (1990). *Creative therapy II: 52 more exercises for groups.* Sarasota, FL: Professional Resource Exchange.

Dossick, J., & Shea, E. (1995). *Creative therapy III: 52 more exercises for groups.* Sarasota, FL: Professional Resource Exchange.

Eberhardt, L. Y. (1994). *Working with women's groups.* Duluth, MN: Whole Person Associates.

References

Anderson, R. D., & Price, G. E. (2001). Experiential groups in counselor education: Student attitudes and instructor participation. *Counselor Education & Supervision, 41,* 111-119.

Butler, C. A. (2001). *100 interactive activities for mental health & substance abuse recovery.* Plainview, NY: Wellness Reproductions & Publishing.

Christian, S., & Tubesing, N. (1997). *Instant icebreakers: 50 powerful catalysts for group interaction and high-impact learning.* Duluth, MN: Whole Person Associates.

Corey, M. S., & Corey, G. (1997). *Groups: Process and practice* (5th ed.). Belmont, CA: Brooks/Cole Publishing Company.

Furr, S. R., & Barrett, B. (2000). Teaching group counseling skills: Problems and solutions [Electronic version]. *Counselor Education & Supervision, 40*(2), 94-105.

Gladding, S. T. (1999). *Group Work: A Counseling Specialty* (3rd ed.). Upper Saddle River, NJ: Merrill.

Kottler, J. A. (2000). *The nuts and bolts of helping.* Needham Heights, MA: Allyn and Bacon.

Markus, H. E., & King, D. A. (2003). A survey of group psychotherapy training during predoctoral psychology internship [Electronic version]. *Professional Psychology: Research & Practice, 34,* 203-209.

Murphy, L., Leszcz, M., Collings, A. K., & Salvendy, J. (1996). Some observations on the subjective experience of neophyte group therapy trainees. *International Journal of Group Psychotherapy, 46,* 543-552.

Queen, S. (1994). *Wellness activities for youth.* Duluth, MN: Whole Person Associates.

Ward, D. E. (1985). Levels of group activity: A model for improving the effectiveness of group work. *Journal of Counseling and Development, 64,* 59-64.

Williamson, B. (1993). *Playful activities for powerful presentations.* Duluth, MN: Whole Person Associates.

Yalom, I. D. (1975). *The theory and practice of group psychotherapy* (2nd ed.). New York: Basic Books.

Tips on Running a Group

Christopher M. Faiver

Type of Contribution: Handout

Objectives

The following handout is intended for both seasoned clinicians and students-in-training as they consider designing a therapy group. The goals of this handout are to

1. Provide an overview to basic group process and components.
2. Provide the therapist opportunities for introspection on group design.
3. Review ethics and training.
4. Review group stages, leadership, and membership styles.

Rationale for Use

Novice and seasoned group therapists can benefit from taking time to plan as they contemplate the design of a new group. Milton Erickson suggested that one should follow the client and stay out of the way (Erickson & Rossi, 1976). Clients should not be made to fit into a group; groups should be designed after the needs of the client. Moreover, the therapist him or herself wisely reviews his or her philosophical stance, which impacts theoretical choice. Virtually all types of groups, whether individual, couples, and family, are impacted by the therapist's choice of theory and techniques, which emerge from his or her basic philosophy of humankind. In addition, the leader (Lewin 1948, 1958) and membership styles (Luft, 1970) of the therapist and group members, respectfully, influence the process and outcome of the group. Therefore, these considerations must be taken into account prior to starting a group.

Instructions

This handout reminds therapists that in order to plan for a group, which is a microcosm of society, that they must first strategize at the macrocosmic level. Hence, I recommend that the clinician needs to examine his or her philosophy of humankind, consequent theory of choice, and the techniques that emerge from this theory. An assessment of the practicalities of leadership and membership styles, group life stages, and ethics and training should then follow.

One could collapse the 300 or so therapeutic approaches into three therapeutic schools: psychoanalytic, cognitive-behavioral, and humanistic-existential (Corey, 2005; Yalom, 1995). For example, if you believe that people are inherently bad by nature and that their behaviors are determined, you may find a classic psychoanalytic approach as the best professional "fit." However, if you espouse the basic goodness and freedom of choice of persons, the theory of choice may be humanistic-existential. If you conclude that persons are simple analogous to pieces of clay, neither bad nor good by nature, and that they are determined by behavioral antecedents and consequences, the classic behavioral approach may be the most likely choice.

Techniques are derived from the therapeutic stance. For example, exploration of the past, addressing unconscious motivations and examination of transference are derived from the psychoanalytic approach, while the use of "homework," "thought stopping," cognitive restructuring, counting and charting behaviors, rewards and punishers, and token reinforcement systems are linked to the cognitive-behavioral approach. Finally, from the humanistic-existential approach, we find the use of role-plays, "active listening," the examination of meaning and values, and the reverence for the therapeutic relationship (Corey, 2000; Corey & Corey, 2002).

In addition to philosophical, theoretical, and technique examination, the therapist needs to be aware of leadership types as described by Kurt Lewin (1948, 1958), with an eye on her or his own leadership style. Do you tend to be authoritarian (directive), democratic (facilitative), laissez faire (more of a member), or a combination of the three? Research generally supports the democratic style; however, my experience indicates that one must be flexible. For example, during the initiation and termination of the group, I have found that I am somewhat authoritarian, setting and discussing ground rules at the beginning and insisting on processing feelings regarding the death of the group at termination and taking an assertive stand if any physical or verbal aggression occurs. However, when the members are hard at work, I find that I play a facilitative democratic role, encouraging the emergence of leadership within the group. And there are times when I can just sit back and watch the process, in my laissez-faire role.

Moreover, what membership styles emerge might emerge in your group—are there persons who hide information, persons who are blind to information, persons who operate with insight (open) or with none (unknown)? Ingham and Luft offer a unique way to examine these client styles in their "Johari Window" (after Harry Ingham and Joe Luft's window) (Luft, 1970). The Johari Window shows how a group member's window pane size is dependent upon that member's self disclosures as well as feedback from the therapist: the more *client self-disclosures* with concomitant *therapist feedback*, the larger the "open" (awareness and insight) pane becomes. This is a goal of treatment. In my practice, I have noticed that some group members react submissively to me as an authority, while others react aggressively or assertively. This appears to be a transference issue worthy of examination.

As a therapist, you must be cognizant of the life stages of a group. Tuckman (1965) describes the developmental stages of a group. During the "Forming" stage, members test and depend upon the leader for direction. The leader sets the stage for the group, delineating and discussing basic ground rules, including appropriate behaviors, attendance policies, and etcetera. There may be some intragroup conflict at the "Storming" stage as members resist the formation of a cohesive unit. The wise leader accepts the members' idiosyncrasies and resistances while setting a warm tone of structure and consistency. He or she "keeps cool."

The collection of individuals actually becomes a group at the "Norming" stage. During this stage, they enjoy being a part of an accepting whole. The leader often can work from the democratic leadership stance at this point, facilitating growth and positive interactions. The "Performing" stage allows members to work on their issues both within and outside the setting. The leader may encourage role plays, homework, and reporting back to the group for support and comments.

Members need to be encouraged to discuss their reactions to the death of the group at the "Adjourning" stage. Feelings of anger, sadness, and completion often emerge. A sense of closure is a goal here.

Lastly, you should adhere to your own professional code of ethics. Virtually all professional associations [American Counseling Association (ACA), American Psychological Association (APA), National Association of Social Workers (NASW), and the Association for Specialists in

Group Work (ASGW), among others] have codes of professional ethics, which address group work. Today, these codes are available on their respective Web sites (see Readings and Resources for the Professional). Individual state licensure laws and ethics codes mandate that those aspiring to do group work receive both academic training and experience in this important area of psychotherapy.

If you find your style does not fit the group (or a group member's style does not fit), you need to be flexible enough to change styles in order to accommodate the uniqueness group member. This follows Erickson's sage advice to follow the client and stay out of the way. Of course, this may be more easily said than done. In my experience, this ability to accommodate is predicated on both professional experience and consultation with knowledgeable colleagues and supervisors.

The Tips on Running a Group form (Handout 2.1) may be useful as a checklist as the group facilitator or therapist in training negotiates the process of designing and implementing a group. Certainly, it is a reminder to apply thoughtful consideration to the entire process in order to honor the clients.

Suggestions for Follow-Up

Once designed and initially implemented, the Tips on Running a Group handout could be reviewed by the group leader at the beginning or end of each group to ensure compliance and completion of the process of group formation. I might also suggest taking relevant group work courses as part of one's graduate education and/or continuing education. Most accrediting and licensing bodies now require group theories and techniques courses. Corey (2005) and Yalom (1995), among others, offer exceptional texts on group process and procedures.

Contraindications

As completing this handout requires introspection and may bring up transference or countertransference issues, a therapist will need to be aware of these issues and discuss with a supervisor or colleague as necessary.

Readings and Resources for the Professional

American Counseling Association: www.counseling.org
American Group Psychotherapy Association: www.agpa.org
American Psychiatric Association: www.psych.org
American Psychological Association: www.apa.org
Association for Specialists in Group Work: www.asgw.org
Jacobs, E., Masson, R., & Harville, R. (1998). *Group counseling strategies and skills* (3rd ed.). Newbury Park, CA: Brooks/Cole.
National Association of Social Workers: www.naswdc.org

Bibliotherapy Sources for the Client

Yalom, I. (2002). *The gift of therapy: An open letter to a new generation of therapists and their patients.* New York: HarperCollins.
Yalom, I. (1989). *Love's executioner and other tales of psychotherapy.* New York: HarperCollins.

References

Corey, G. (2000). *Theory and practice of group counseling* (5th ed.). Newbury Park, CA: Brooks/Cole.

Corey, G. (2005). *Theory and practice of counseling and psychotherapy* (7th ed.). Pacific Grove, CA: Brooks/Cole.

Corey, G., & Corey, M. S. (2002). *Groups: Process and practice* (6th ed.). Pacific Grove, CA: Brooks/Cole.

Erickson, M. & Rossi, E. (1976). *Hypnotic realities*. New York: Irvington.

Lewin, K. (1948). *Resolving social conflicts: Selected papers on group dynamics*. G. W. Lewin (Ed.). New York: Harper & Row.

Lewin, K. (1958). Group decisions and social change. In E. E. Maccobby, T. M. Newcomb, & E. L. Hartley (Eds.), *Readings in social psychology* (pp. 330-344). New York: Holt, Rinehart & Winston.

Luft, J. (1970). *Group processes: An introduction to group dynamics* (2nd ed.). Palo Alto, CA: National Press Books.

Tuckman, B. (1965). Developmental Sequence in Small Groups. *Psychological Bulletin, 63,* 384-399.

Yalom, I. (1995). *Theory and practice of group psychotherapy* (2nd ed.). New York: Basic Books.

HANDOUT 2.1. GROUP GUIDELINES:
TIPS ON RUNNING A GROUP

1. Be aware that your *philosophy of life and humankind* affects your approach to other people, including your small group.

2. Your philosophy determines which one of the *three basic theoretical approaches* to group work you may "buy" into:
   a. psychoanalytic
   b. behavioral
   c. humanistic-existential
(The wise group leader will read up on these. I suggest Corey [2005] *Theory and Approaches to Group Counseling*.)

3. Following a logical process, one's theoretical approach influences his/her *techniques* for conducting a group. For example,
   a. psychoanalytic— exploration of the past, addressing the unconscious, etc.
   b. behavioral—use of homework, counting and charting behaviors, etc.
   c. humanistic—existential—use of role-plays, "active listening," etc.
(Again, the wise leader needs to thoroughly explore the various techniques for group work. A start would be Corey & Corey [2002] *Groups: Process and practice*.)

4. You should also be aware of *leadership styles* (Lewin, 1948):
   a. authoritarian
   b. democratic
   c. laissez-faire
   d. combination of above

5. Your members may also have their own *membership styles* (a la Faiver):
   a. submissive
   b. aggressive
   c. appropriate
(Another way to look at *membership styles* is the "Johari Window" [Luft, 1970].)

6. If your "collection of individuals" develops into a group, this group will move through *developmental stages* (Tuckman, 1965):
   a. testing and dependence—forming
   b. intragroup conflict—storming
   c. development of cohesion—norming
   d. functional role relatedness—performing
   e. termination—adjourning

7. You also need to be aware that various professional groups (e.g., ACA, APA, NASW, ASGW, etc.) have *codes of ethics* to which a wise leader abides.

8. Finally, the wise group leader continues to update his/her skills through *continuing education*.

Faiver, C.M. (2007). Tips on running a group. In D. R. Viers (Ed.), *The group therapist's notebook: Homework, handouts, and activities for use in psychotherapy* (pp. 15-19). Binghamton, NY: The Haworth Press.

3

Creating a Disclosure Statement for Group Work: Best Practices in Action

R. Valorie Thomas
Meredith W. Neill

Type of Contribution: Handout

Objective

The objective of this handout is to provide clinicians with an outline of the elements necessary for a comprehensive professional disclosure statement when practicing ethical group work. Disclosure statements inform clients about the group therapy process, as well as educate them regarding the parameters of their participation in group treatment. Clear communication regarding the benefits and limitations of group therapy can help prevent client distress and address liability concerns, as well as facilitate a positive working relationship between the client and the therapist. In addition, disclosure statements help clients comprehend informed consent so they can discern voluntary participation.

Rationale for Use

Group therapists who conduct groups for individuals, couples, or families should be aware of their ethical responsibility to prepare a disclosure statement when planning a group. According to the Association for Specialists in Group Work (ASGW) Best Practices Guidelines in Group Work (1998), clinicians conducting groups are ethically bound to provide their clients with a professional disclosure statement that encompasses information pertaining to "confidentiality and exceptions to confidentiality; theoretical orientation; information on the nature, purpose(s), and goals of the group; the group services that can be provided; the role and responsibility of group members and leaders; Group Workers' qualifications to conduct the specific group(s); specific licenses, certifications and professional affiliations; and address of licensing/credentialing body" (p. 239).

Clients have the right to be informed about what they can and cannot expect to occur as a result of their participation in a group. This information should be discussed in the screening process. In this way, potential group participants can ask questions and clarify their expectations regarding the nature of the group experience. A disclosure statement allows clients to collaboratively (along with the therapist) decide if they will agree to participate in the group and abide by the parameters set forth in the informed consent (Corey, Corey, & Callanan, 2003). In addition, clinicians should be aware of their state statutes when creating disclosure statements, because they are accountable to applicable laws and regulations governing the protection of their clients. Moreover, professional codes of ethics hold clinicians to a higher standard of care (reflecting ideal principles) to which they should adhere. For example, in some states therapists have no statute requiring a duty to warn an individual of intended danger given a threat from a client. The ACA Code of Ethics, on the other hand, holds therapists to a higher standard of care, suggesting that they have an ethical responsibility to protect third parties from intended harm.

Instructions

Therapists engaged in group practice should design a comprehensive disclosure statement in the planning stages of their targeted group. Disclosure statements need to be specifically designed to address the goals and unique population to be served. For example, a group designed for married heterosexual couples desiring to enhance their communications skills might include goals such as (a) learning how to use I-messages, (b) identifying and expressing feelings with their partner, and (c) learning problem-solving skills. By contrast, a group targeted for individuals experiencing panic attacks might focus on the goals of (a) learning positive self-talk, (b) challenging irrational belief systems, and (c) practicing relaxation techniques.

The Best Practice Guidelines in Group Work (ASGW, 1998, p. 239) suggests the following elements be included when creating a comprehensive disclosure statement. The authors have elaborated on each element in order to provide guidelines for practitioners:

- *Information on confidentiality and exceptions to confidentiality.* Define confidentiality and how it will be implemented. Be sure to address the unique considerations that group work presents and how they impact your group members. For example, confidentiality is an ethical concept safeguarding the release of information from a clinician to a third party unless given written consent by the client or under certain conditions mandated by law. In group work, the clinician has the responsibility to educate group participants about the tenuous nature of this shared responsibility. In other words, it should be emphasized that responsibility lies with each group member to keep confidential the discussions that occur in group and that the breach of this confidence has probable consequences. Confidentiality, thus, has limitations when applied to group work. In addition, when the group is an open group, in which new members fluctuate in and out of treatment, it is important to reiterate the definition and limitations of confidentiality in each group session. Finally, the legal concept of privilege (prohibiting mental health practitioners to disclose information at the request of the client in legal proceedings) "does not apply to group discussions (unless provided by state statute)" (ASGW, 1998, p. 240). Group workers have a responsibility to clearly communicate this unique feature as it pertains to their clients' rights to privacy while participating in group treatment.
- *Theoretical orientation.* Include information on the theory(ies) that informs your clinical group practice. What theories guide your understanding about what helps people make changes in groups? Provide a brief overview of the theory.
- *Information on the nature, purpose and goals of the group.* Describe how your group will be conducted. What is the reason for your group? How will participants benefit from it? What can clients expect? How will they know they are making progress?
- *Group services to be provided.* Indicate the type of group you are offering. Is it a psychoeducational group, a counseling group, or a therapy group? Is it open to new members throughout the duration of the group or closed after the first session? What is the duration of the group? How long is each session? Do you have a coleader? Will you be consulting with other professionals or supervisors? How will documentation be handled? What are the fees for attending group? What method of payment do you accept? If insurance is used, how is it handled?

- *Role and responsibilities of group members and leaders.* Define your responsibility to your group members. How will you help them meet their goals? What techniques might they anticipate? What do you expect of the participants in your group? Outline group members responsibilities to the group (for example, maintaining confidentiality, interacting respectfully, coming to group on time, following policies prohibiting substance abuse, entering and exiting the group, and group members' relationships outside of sessions).
- *Therapist's qualifications (licenses, certifications and professional affiliations and address of licensing/credentialing body).* State your credentials and experience as it pertains to group work. Be sure to include specific qualifications and training relevant to the particular group you are leading as well as any prior experience you have in leading a group.

Be aware that when you are creating your disclosure statement, there is a delicate balance between stating too much and not covering all the essential elements (Corey et al., 2003). A sample disclosure statement is provided (Handout 3.1) to serve as a template for clinicians in everyday practice. Be aware that disclosure statements should be specific to the particular group you are offering and should be reviewed with potential clients in their screening appointment.

Suggestions for Follow-Up

Group therapists should review the disclosure statement in the first group meeting. In follow-up sessions, some elements can be brought to the attention of participants as the group develops. It is important to remember that some aspects of a professional disclosure statement, such as confidentiality and informed consent, are an ongoing process (Corey et al., 2003).

Contraindications

There are no groups or group members for which a well-written disclosure statement would not be helpful.

Readings and Resources for the Professional

Association for Specialists in Group Work (1998). ASGW Best Practice Guidelines. *Journal for Specialists in Group Work, 3,* 237-244.
Association for Specialists in Group Work: www.asgw.org
Best Practices in Group Work: www.asgw.org/best
Rapin, L. S., & Conyne, R. K. (1999). Best practices in group counseling. In J. P. Trotzer (Ed.), *The counselor and the group: Integrating theory, training and practice* (3rd ed., pp. 257-276). Philadelphia: Accelerated Development.

References

Association for Specialists in Group Work (ASGW) (1998). ASGW Best Practice Guidelines. *Journal for Specialists in Group Work, 23,* 237-244.
Corey, G., Corey, M. S., & Callanan, P. (2003). *Issues and ethics in the helping professions* (6th ed.). Pacific Grove, CA: Brooks/Cole Publishing.

HANDOUT 3.1. SAMPLE DISCLOSURE STATEMENT
FOR CLINICAL GROUP PRACTICE

This sample is designed for use in group practice with individual participants experiencing significant anxiety and/or panic attacks and may be modified for use with couples and families.

Meredith Thomas, PhD
Licensed Marriage and Family Therapist
Licensed Mental Health Counselor
300 North Winter Avenue, Suite 5
Winter Park, Florida
(704) 555-0404

Welcome to the Anxiety and Panic Management group designed for individuals who hope to learn ways to manage anxiety and panic in their everyday lives. The following information is provided for you in order to help you understand and consent to group treatment. I look forward to building a trusting counseling relationship with you and to helping you learn productive ways for managing anxiety.

Group Counseling

The following information is provided to help you understand what group counseling involves. Participating in a group can increase self-awareness, improve communication, reduce interpersonal and internal conflict, and alter distressing moods. Likewise, while participating in a group, you may also experience unpleasant feelings. You are encouraged to discuss these feelings in your group. While benefits are expected in group counseling, specific results are not guaranteed. Consider the benefits and risks of group participation. You are encouraged to discuss any concerns regarding the group you are considering with your therapist.

Your Therapist's Qualifications

I received my PhD in marriage and family therapy from the University of Florida in Gainesville. I am licensed by the State of Florida to practice as a Marriage and Family Therapist and Mental Heath Counselor. I am also a Certified Group Psychotherapist and a Clinical Member of the American Association for Marriage and Family Therapy. I have fifteen years of clinical experience in group work with individuals, couples, and families, and have served as the coordinator of group services at Winter Park Family Counseling Services for ten years. I have conducted a variety of psychoeducational, counseling, and therapy groups for people experiencing anxiety, depression, self-esteem issues, eating disorders, parenting difficulties, family conflict, and couple communication issues. In addition, I have specialized training in conducting anxiety and panic management groups.

Credentialing Agency Address:
Counselor Licensing Board
Department of Health
Division of Medical Quality Assurance
PO Box 6320
Tallahassee, Florida 32314-6320
www.myflorida.com

Thomas, R. V., & Neill, M. W. (2007). Creating a disclosure statement for group work: Best practices in action. In D. R. Viers (Ed.), *The group therapist's notebook: Homework, handouts, and activities for use in psychotherapy* (pp. 21-26). Binghamton, NY: The Haworth Press.

Theoretical Orientation

I draw from several theoretical orientations when practicing group work. Foremost, I utilize a brief solution-focused approach when working with clients. Thus, group participants identify and utilize their personal strengths as well as draw from past successes in order to find workable solutions to their problems. Group therapy is time limited and averages six to eight sessions. In addition, I adhere to a cognitive-behavioral approach to group practice when conducting anxiety/panic management groups. This approach challenges participants to examine their thought process and belief system while working toward successful behavioral change. A cognitive-behavioral approach is supported in the literature and has been beneficial to individuals coping with anxiety and panic issues. Finally, I draw from systems theory to help clients explore how messages from their family of origin impact their current coping style.

Nature, Purpose, and Goals of the Group

The intent of this group is to provide psychoeducation, support, and resources to persons experiencing significant levels of anxiety and panic attacks that impair their functioning in day-to-day life. Specifically, this group will teach participants how to reduce and manage their anxiety and panic.

Personal goals and individual treatment plans may be identified in the screening process. General goals for this group's members include the following:

1. To understand the role and nature of anxiety and panic from a nonreactive cognitive perspective
2. To explore the many causes of anxiety and panic, including messages from received from one's family of origin
3. To learn appropriate coping skills to decrease anxiety or eliminate panic
4. To increase awareness of negative self-talk and to learn how to challenge it
5. To learn and to practice relaxation techniques
6. To utilize appropriate resources and support persons

Group Services to Be Provided

The anxiety and panic management group is a closed psychoeducational group designed to help participants learn specific skills to manage anxiety and panic as well as receive support and encouragement from other group members. It is both educational and therapeutic. The group will meet for eight consecutive weeks from 5:30 p.m. to 7:30 p.m. beginning Monday, March 3rd. The group will be composed of no more than eight participants. The group is designed for men and women over the age of eighteen who have been screened by the group therapist and who have completed the required pretesting.

Fees and Payment

Group fees are $500 for the eight-week session and are due prior to the first group meeting. This fee is inclusive of a screening appointment and assessment materials. Please be aware that insurance is not accepted for this group service. In the event that you leave the group prior to completion, your fee will be adjusted accordingly.

Thomas, R. V., & Neill, M. W. (2007). Creating a disclosure statement for group work: Best practices in action. In D. R. Viers (Ed.), *The group therapist's notebook: Homework, handouts, and activities for use in psychotherapy* (pp. 21-26). Binghamton, NY: The Haworth Press.

Roles and Responsibilities

Being on time for group and completing any homework assignments given to you in group allows for a successful group experience. In addition, sharing your experiences, knowledge, support, and feedback with other group members while respecting individual differences contributes to a productive group. Confidentiality must be maintained at all times. Each group participant will be required to sign an Informed Consent for Treatment and Confidentiality Statement prior to the first session.

Be mindful that attending this group is voluntary, which means that you may discontinue group participation in collaboration with your therapist.

I will provide copies of written handouts and a one-page bibliography for use by the group. In addition, I will offer formal instruction and demonstrate anxiety and panic reduction techniques to the group.

Confidentiality and Privileged Communication

In order to develop and maintain a trusting environment, it is essential for each group member to maintain confidentiality. Group participants feel safer and more comfortable expressing their thoughts and feelings when each member agrees that what is discussed and experienced is kept within the group and not discussed or reported to another person. You do not violate confidentiality, however, when you talk about what YOU learned or experienced in a group session.

What is said in the group stays in the group unless one of the following conditions is met:

1. you give your written consent or authorization to release information only as it applies to you; or
2. suspicion of neglect or abuse of a child, elderly, or disabled person exists; or
3. a judges order indicates a report is required; or
4. it is thought that you intend to harm yourself or others.

Since providing a safe environment is one of the purposes of a group and each member shares this responsibility, the therapist cannot be held accountable for individual violations of the confidentiality agreement on the part of group members. In addition, it is important that you understand that the legal concept of privilege, which prohibits mental health practitioners to disclose information at the request of a client in legal proceedings, does not apply to our group discussions.

Consent for Group Treatment

By signing below, I agree that I have read and understand the above agreement and consent to group treatment with my therapist. I understand my rights and responsibilities as a group participant and acknowledge that I am voluntarily choosing to participate in the anxiety and panic management group.

_____   _____
Client's Signature and Date   Therapist's Signature and Date

Thomas, R. V., & Neill, M. W. (2007). Creating a disclosure statement for group work: Best practices in action. In D. R. Viers (Ed.), *The group therapist's notebook: Homework, handouts, and activities for use in psychotherapy* (pp. 21-26). Binghamton, NY: The Haworth Press.

SECTION II:
INTERVENTIONS FOR ALL GROUPS

4

Play Ball! The Name Is the Game

Shirley R. Simon

Type of Contribution: Activity

Objective

This activity is an icebreaker to facilitate quick, initial, energetic interaction among all group members. It also helps group members learn to identify and recall one another's names.

Rationale for Use

This simple exercise facilitates the quick engagement of participants with one another. The initial stages of a group are often fraught with caution and tentativeness (Wickham, 2003; Toseland & Rivas, 2005) or, as identified in Garland, Jones, and Kolodny's (1973) well-known model of the stages of group development, approach-avoidance. New members are typically unsure about their commitment to the group. Issues of trust, safety, fit, and acceptance are all appropriate and anticipated considerations (Brandler & Roman, 1999). Even members who attend of their own volition experience the push-pull of whether to actually commit to the group. To decrease this natural ambivalence and encourage engagement, the inclusion of an easily mastered, low risk, participatory experience during the first session is often recommended. This activity fits these criteria.

It is important during the beginning stage of a group's development that activities are engaging but not too challenging or frustrating (Garland et al., 1973). The opportunity for all members to participate and feel included in the process is essential. Participation typically increases the likelihood of a member's commitment to and identification with the group (Knowles & Knowles, 1972). During the first session, members are busy exploring and assessing the group and its members—who the other people are in the group, how do they fit in with one another, will they be accepted by the group, etc. Much of this checking out takes place surreptitiously, with quick glances from an appropriately polite distance. Indirect communication predominates (Berman-Rossi, 1993). This name game facilitates members' exploration by requiring that the entire group look at and interact with one another. The goal is to encourage the members to own the group as quickly as possible. Hence, activities which prompt interaction and participation are vital beginning inclusions.

One of the most significant representations of an individual's identity is his or her name. Being accurately addressed by name confirms one's importance and conveys respect. Name recognition facilitates the personalization of the group experience and interaction. Addressing others by name early in the group experience fosters the development of cohesion and group identity. Cohesion, as Yalom (1995) asserts, is the single most important therapeutic factor in determining the effectiveness of groups. Thus, activities that build cohesion and mutual respect are highly desirable. By promoting the early mastery of group members' names in a fun, interactive process, this name game encourages group bonding and identification and allows the group to begin on a personal and energetic note.

Instructions

Materials: Soft ball—a foam ball, a child's toy, or even a ball of yarn could be used.

Environment: Room should accommodate the participants standing in a circle and seeing each other. Ideally, there should be no impediments, such as posts or room dividers, that could inhibit members from freely tossing the ball to one another.

Participants: 5 to 25

Time: 5 to 20 minutes, depending on size of group

Process: Have the members stand in a circle facing one another. Ask one member to toss the ball to another member while saying his or her own first name. The person who catches the ball then tosses it to another member of the group and says his or her own name. This continues for a while. Inevitably members begin to identify anyone who has not yet received the ball and, without being told, will toss the ball to these members. At this point in a group's development, participants are very careful to be inclusive and often, after attempting to include everyone, even ask if there is anyone who has not had a turn. Names and nicknames are readily clarified via the informal sharing. When everyone has had a turn or two, ask the participants what the next step might be. Typically they say, "Now we have to throw the ball to someone and say their name." This is, of course, accurate, but including their suggestions also increases ownership and respect. Members might be nervous about remembering others' names, so it is important to normalize the anxiety and give permission to make mistakes. It is often helpful to emphasize that the goal is not to be correct, but rather to have a better overall sense of the participants and their names. Giving permission to ask for assistance when one is unsure of someone's name is also reassuring.

Once the ball has gone around a couple of times, ask members to switch positions in the circle, thereby disrupting the memorization by location process, and reinforcing the actual learning of members' names. During the game, there is likely to be laughter, as members miss or drop the ball, as well as eye contact and genuine interaction among participants, all of which tend to facilitate initial commitment to the group. The game can be continued with different topics such as favorite foods, movies, colors, or other topics. Once the game has ended, it is frequently productive to ask how members felt about the experience. This can lead naturally to an interactive discussion about members' feelings and responses, the essence of most group experiences.

Suggestions for Follow-Up

This game is often repeated at the beginning of the next group session. This provides an opportunity to review the earlier group interaction while experiencing the comfort of a familiar process. Because members are frequently surprised and a bit nervous by how much they have forgotten since the first session, it is helpful to ask if they would like to begin by having each person state their own name while tossing the ball in the first go around. Typically, this follow-up experience takes less time than the initial activity, and the majority of time is spent on the recall portion of the interaction.

This exercise can be used again when the group is reconstituted or when new members enter the group. If it is an open group, with different constituencies each session, the ball toss activity could be a regular part of the beginning structure of the sessions. The name portion of the exercise could also be adapted to address topics specifically relevant to the purpose of the group, e.g., participants could identify current places of employment, internships, motivations for coming to this group, or even the individuals' goals for participating in this group.

Additional icebreakers, some with similar objectives and components, can be found in Readings and Resources for the Professional.

Contraindications

It is important to consider the physical and cognitive abilities of potential participants when using this exercise. If members have physical challenges affecting mobility and coordination, this interaction may not be suitable or may need to be modified. One modification that can facilitate implementation with such groups simply requires the ball to be rolled instead of tossed. If one member of the group has a physical limitation, such as being confined to a wheelchair, the exercise can still be utilized. Members typically will go out of their way to include others and will walk over and hand the ball to the member in the wheelchair or offer assistance in other ways. With cognitive difficulties, such as memory limitations, this exercise may also be contraindicated. It can, however, be used to encourage recall and learning with appropriate groups.

Finally, this exercise may not be appropriate for groups having members with behavior disorders or anger management issues, since the ball can become a type of missile or weapon. Using a soft ball counteracts much of this; nevertheless, such circumstances warrant consideration.

Readings and Resources for the Professional

Barlow, C., Blythe, J., & Edmonds, M. (1999). *A handbook of interactive exercises for groups.* Boston: Allyn & Bacon.

Carrell, S. (2000). *Group exercises for adolescents: A manual for the therapist* (2nd ed.). Newbury Park: Sage Publications.

Haslett, D. C. (2005). *Group work activities in generalist practice.* Belmont, CA: Brooks/Cole.

Johnson, D. W., & Johnson, F. P. (2003). *Joining together: Group theory and group skills* (8th ed.). Boston: Allyn & Bacon.

McManus, R., & Jennings, G. (Eds.). (1997). *Structured exercises for promoting family and group strengths.* Binghamton, NY: The Haworth Press.

Nell Warren Associates (1992). *The warm-ups manual, volume II: More tools for working with groups.* Toronto, Ontario, Canada: Nell Warren Associates.

Pfeiffer, J. W., & Ballew, A. C. (1988). *Using structured experiences in human resource development.* San Diego, CA: University Associates, Inc.

Schwartz, R. M. (2002). *The skilled facilitator: Practical wisdom for developing effective groups* (2nd ed.). San Francisco, CA: Jossey-Bass Publishers.

Yalom, I. D. (2002). *The gift of therapy: An open letter to a new generation of therapists and their patients.* New York: Harper Collins Publishers.

References

Berman-Rossi, T. (1993). The tasks and skills of the social worker across stages of group development. *Social Work with Groups, 16*(1-2), 69-81.

Brandler, S., & Roman, C. P. (1999). *Group work: Skills and strategies for effective interventions* (2nd ed.). Binghamton, NY: The Haworth Press.

Garland, J. A., Jones H. E., & Kolodny, R. L. (1973). A model for stages of development in social work groups. In S. Bernstein (Ed.), *Explorations in group work: Essays in theory and practice* (pp. 17-71). Bloomfield, CT: Practitioners Press.

Knowles, M., & Knowles, H. (1972). *Introduction to group dynamics* (2nd ed.). New York: Cambridge, The Adult Education Company.

Toseland, R. W., & Rivas, R. F. (2005). *An introduction to group work practice* (5th ed.). Boston: Allyn and Bacon.

Wickham, E. (2003). *Group treatment in social work.* Toronto, Canada: Thompson Books.

Yalom, I. D. (1995). *The theory and practice of group psychotherapy* (4th ed.). New York: Basic Books.

5

Learning How to De-Stress

Elwood R. Hamlin II
Michael Kane

Type of Contribution: Activity

Objective

The goal of this activity is to teach muscle relaxation exercises in a group setting that can be used to counter or minimize tension, anxiety, and stress. These exercises are often included in stress management programs and will assist individuals to gain control over stresses in their life that lead to emotional and/or physiological discomfort.

Rationale for Use

Stress is subjective and inevitable. Some people, from time to time, experience stress that they believe is unmanageable. We know stress taxes one's physical and emotional state of health and is counterproductive in the workplace. Levi (1996) found stress related to several negative effects on the community, specifically low productivity and absenteeism in the workplace. Often people attempt to cope with stress by making external adjustment to either flee the event that they perceive as stressful or struggle with the stressful situation in an attempt to overcome it. Sometimes this comes at a cost to one's emotional and physical health.

The relaxation response, according to Benson (1975), is a restorative process that allows the body to cure itself in response to stress, pain, or injury. Relaxation training is one of a number of procedures used by cognitive-behavioral therapists. A distinction may be made between the goals of relaxation techniques and hypnotherapy. Relaxation techniques seek to bring awareness to the individual group members of the detrimental effects of stress and tension, while hypnotherapy seeks to bring individuals to levels of deeper concentration (Barker, 1999), often using induction techniques such as relaxation. One type of relaxation training involves teaching group members to self-induce relaxation of muscles while learning how to perform breathing exercises. According to McGuigan (1994), by learning muscle relaxation with focus on breathing, individuals are better able to assume control over their tension and emotional behaviors.

Relaxation training follows the principle of counterconditioning. Counterconditioning, in essence, refers to the use of learning new behaviors to substitute one type of response (relaxation) for another (tension, anxiety) (Wolpe, 1982). The group members learn how to identify muscle tension and use relaxation techniques to counter the tension. Relaxation procedures are used singly or in conjunction with other cognitive-behavioral interventions in many clinical settings with a variety of client populations.

Relaxation procedures within stress management programs have been helpful, to individuals experiencing a wide range of medical problems, in reducing pain and depression (Smarr et al.,

1997). In the health care field, there is evidence that learning muscle relaxation may be helpful in stress inoculation training with patients undergoing surgical procedures (Blythe & Erdahl, 1986), irritable bowel syndrome, (Shaw et al., 1991), hypertension (Johnston, 1991), and diabetes (McCrady, Bailey, & Good, 1991). It is suggested that relaxation procedures may reduce the need for pain medication and clinic visits, and decrease length of stay in hospitals (Caudill, Schnable, Zuttermeister, Benson, & Freidman, 1991; Alberts, Lyons & Moretti, 1989). Hough and Kleinginna (2002) reported on the efficacy of relaxation training with spinal cord injury patients in reducing depression and pain.

In the field of mental health, relaxation training has been used in conjunction with other treatment interventions very successfully. With children, relaxation training has been effective in conjunction with anger management interventions (Goldstein, Glick, Reiner, Zimmerman, & Coultry, 1987), in combination with other cognitive-behavioral interventions (Schrodt, 1992), in treating mood disorders (Field et al., 1992), separation anxiety disorders (Thyer, 1991), and tic disorders (Ollendick & Ollendick, 1990). Stress management using relaxation training has also been successful with individuals with severe mental health problems (Starkey, Deleone, & Flannery, 1995) and post-traumatic stress disorder (Taylor, Thordarson, Maxfield, Fedoroff, & Lovell, 2003).

Instructions

For this activity, the therapist begins by opening discussion with group members about the subject of stress, how they handle stress, and the effects of stress on their psychological and physiological well-being. Relaxation is introduced as a concept that can be helpful to individual members in coping with or eliminating harmful effects of stress. Group members are given information about the benefits of relaxation and encouraged to talk about ways in which the group members relax. The therapist suggests that group members may feel better, physically and emotionally, by learning relaxation techniques that they can use when they feel the need. The therapist obtains consent to teach group members relaxation exercises.

For purposes of this group activity, we will focus on instructing group members on a modified progressive muscle relaxation procedure (Jacobson, 1974). Group members are helped to understand how they might benefit from using this procedure. It is suggested that stress is related to excessive tension, and tension is experienced by our bodies in the form of muscle tightness. Often we do not recognize muscle tension until it is too late or results in muscle pain or aches. This discussion helps group members make the connection between stress (mind) and physiological tension (body).

Next, we discuss with group members the potential benefits derived from learning to self-induce muscle relaxation. It is suggested to members that they cannot be relaxed and tense at the same time. That comment normally causes them to pause a minute and reflect on its implications. Group members are taught the importance of focusing on their body as they consider the mind/body connection or how one's emotions and thoughts affect their body. Conversely, when their body is not feeling well, it can adversely affect their emotional well-being.

Guided Visual Imagery

The group session prior to conducting the muscle relaxation procedure is devoted to introducing the topic of relaxation, the means by which stress affects our thinking, emotions, and behaviors, and helping group members enter a relaxation state using guided imagery.

Guided visual imagery involves the therapist asking individuals in a group to think about the most relaxing and soothing scene or place that they can imagine. Each individual will have a favorite place to return to or scene they can vividly imagine as peaceful, serene, and calming. The therapist asks each member to close his or her eyes and visualize the scene for about forty-five seconds to one minute. Following this exercise, the therapist asks group members to share their relaxing and calming scene or place with other members. The therapist requests that members describe their pleasurable images in vivid detail using their senses of sight, smell, touch, taste, and sound. For example, if the pleasurable scene consists of a valley of flowers, the member may describe the scent of the flowers, the feel of green grass beneath her or his feet, the sound of the wind as it whistles through the valley, and the taste of wild blackberries nearby. If the scene is on a beach in a tropical climate, the member may describe the sounds of the pounding waves as they wash up on the beach, the taste of salt air, and the enveloping grains of sand. This exercise allows individuals to mentally prepare for the progressive muscle relaxation procedure by allowing them to erase stressful images as a prelude to relaxation.

Following the visual imagery procedure, the therapist discusses with group members the importance of breathing. Members should take a deep breath, hold it for a few seconds then exhale. The therapist suggests to group members that proper breathing can help induce a relaxation state during the time that they will be tensing and relaxing muscles.

Teaching Muscle Relaxation

Words are used to create images. It is recommended to use words associated with relaxation as you talk the group through the procedure. For example, when you ask in a soft voice tone for the group to tighten or flex a muscle, you might describe the sensation of tightness, stiffness, and discomfort. Conversely, as you ask the group to release that muscle, you may draw to their attention to how that release of muscle tension might be experienced, such as a warm and soothing feeling, as their tension is evaporating. In short, you are helping the group to consistently focus on each muscle and how it feels to them when each muscle is tense and how it feels when the muscle is relaxed.

The following relaxation procedure is a modified version of the Jacobson relaxation method (Jacobson, 1974). Preparation of the room is important in setting up a relaxing environment. If possible, lights may be dimmed, chairs should be comfortable, and distractions limited.

The therapist requests that group members sit comfortably in their chairs. The group members are asked to place both feet on the floor and arms comfortably in their lap or on the handles of their chair. The group members are also requested to loosen tight fitting clothing such as neckties. Following the comfortable position in the chairs, group members are asked to take a deep breath by inhaling through their nose, hold it for five seconds, and then to slowly exhale through their nose. The nose controls breathing. This exercise is repeated two to three times, allowing group members to feel comfortable and attend to their breathing. Following this, group members are asked to visualize their favorite calming scene. Next, the group members are requested to tighten a specific muscle for approximately five seconds and then to relax that muscle. During both the tightening (tensing) and relaxation cycles of the muscle, the therapist continually points out to the group members how uncomfortable and painful the tensed muscle feels. Conversely, it is suggested to group members that relaxing of the same muscle brings a soothing and pleasurable sensation. The teaching point here for the group is to focus on specific muscles, one at a time, and become consciously aware of the discomfort associated with the tensed muscle as well experience the relief and pleasurable sensation associated with the same muscle when in a relaxed state.

Several muscles that are the focus of attention, in sequential order, are the toes, calves, stomach, biceps, back, shoulders, neck, mouth, forehead, and eyebrows. We begin with the toes and ask members to "tighten your toes by curling them and push both feet against the floor. Notice the uncomfortable feeling in your toes as they are squeezed. Now release the curl and feel the soothing sensation in your toes." Following the toes, we focus on the calves. "Tighten your right calf by lifting your leg and flexing your foot toward your body. Hold it and notice how tight it feels. Now release the flex and place your foot back on the floor. Notice how comfortable your calf muscle feels, as if tension is draining from your leg." (Do same for the left calf). Next, we move to the stomach muscles. "At this time, while both feet are on the floor, tighten your stomach by pulling in your stomach and tightening to the muscles. Make it feel like your stomach is in a knot. Notice how uncomfortable it feels. Continue tightening for a few more seconds. Now release it and take a deep breath, breathing through your nose. Notice how relaxed your stomach muscles feel as you release all the tension."

Now we move to the upper body and focus on the arms, specifically, the biceps. "Make a fist with both hands and bring your arms toward your chest as if you are showing off your muscles. Tighten your fists and biceps and hold it there for a few more seconds. Feel the tension in your arms and hands. Now release your fist, drop your arms to your sides and notice the tension draining from your arms." Another example includes the back muscles. The therapist requests that group members focus on their back muscle and provides the following instructions: "Now I want you to focus on your back muscles. I am going to ask you to arch your back, sticking your chest and stomach out. Notice how tight your lower back muscles feel. Keep that position for a few more seconds. Now relax your back and sit comfortably. Notice the relief you feel in your back and lower torso." The shoulders are the next muscle to focus on. "Raise your shoulders toward your ears as if you are shrugging your shoulders. Keep that position for a few more seconds. You will notice how uncomfortable and tight that position feels. Now relax and feel the weight and tension draining from your shoulders." Next we focus on the neck. "Rotate your neck from side to side. Now place your head on your left shoulder and keep it there for a few seconds. Change to the right shoulder and keep it there for a few more seconds. Notice the tightness in your neck. Now relax your neck and feel the tension dissipating from your neck."

Now we move to the mouth. "Open your mouth wide for a few seconds. Notice the tension and stinging sensation around the corners of your mouth and the top of your lips. Now relax your mouth and feel the tension evaporating." Following the mouth exercise, we move to the forehead and eyebrows. "Let's begin by wrinkling or furrowing our eyebrow as if we are angry. Keep it there for a few more seconds. Notice the tightness and tension in your forehead. Now relax your eyebrows and your forehead muscle and notice the soothing feeling around your eyebrows and your forehead. The tension is gone."

The therapist provides instructions and demonstrates the exercises (tensing and relaxing) for each muscle with the group members. In each muscle rotation, the therapist emphasizes the tension and uncomfortable feelings associated with tightness of the target muscle followed by the soothing, warm sensation associated with the relaxation of the same muscle.

Suggestions for Follow-Up

Following the muscle relaxation exercise, a debriefing is conducted where group members describe what the experience was like for them. Group members will routinely report that they are now more aware of which muscle group they feel most tension in when under pressure or stress. Typically members report neck, forehead, and stomach muscles as stress or tension points. Following this discussion, members talk about how they might prepare themselves when anticipating stressful situations. A tape recording of the relaxation exercise can be given to each group member, and members should be encouraged to practice the exercises at home and prior to stressful events. In subsequent group sessions, it is suggested that the group therapist begin the session with muscle relaxation exercises. Once group members become familiar with the exercises, they can be completed in ten to fifteen minutes at the beginning of each group session.

Contraindications

Stress management using relaxation procedures with breathing and visual imagery exercises must be used with the consent of group members. It is advisable that group members who are experiencing health issues relating to muscle or joint problems consult their physician before participating in stress-reduction exercises. In addition, relaxation procedures are not a substitute for dealing with severe personal problems or situations that have created a crisis in ones life. These procedures need to be combined with other interventions to address personal or crisis issues. It is helpful to advise group members that when they are asked to tighten specific muscles, you would not expect them to work so hard that they strain the muscle. In other words, they are advised to flex or tighten muscles only to the point of consciously feeling tension in that specific muscle.

Readings and Resources for the Professional

Beck, J. (1995). *Cognitive therapy: Basics and beyond.* New York: The Guilford Press.
Benson, H. (1975). *The relaxation response.* New York: Morrow.
Jacobson, E. (1974). *Progressive relaxation.* Chicago: University of Chicago Press.

Bibliotherapy Sources for the Client

Charlesworth, E., & Nathan, R. (2004). *Stress management: A comprehensive guide to wellness.* New York: Random House.
Davis, M., Eshelman, E., & McKay, M. (2000). *The relaxation and stress reduction workbook* (5th ed.). Oakland, CA: New Harbinger Publications.

References

Alberts, M., Lyons, J., & Moretti, R. (1989). Psychological interventions in the pre-surgical period. *International Journal of Psychiatry in Medicine, 19*(1), 91-106.
Barker, R. (1999). *The Social work dictionary* (4th ed.). Washington, DC: NASW Press.
Benson, H. (1975). *The relaxation response.* New York: Morrow.
Blythe, B., & Erdahl, S. (1986). Using stress inoculation to prepare a patient for open-heart surgery. *Health and Social Work, 11,* 265-273.
Caudill, M., Schnable, R., Zuttermeister, P., Benson, H., & Freidman, R. (1991). Decreased clinic use by chronic pain patients: Response to behavioral medicine intervention. *Clinical Journal of Pain, 7,* 305-310.
Field, T., Morrow, C., Valdeon, C., Larson, S., Kuhn, C., & Schanberg, S. (1992). Massage reduces anxiety in child and adolescent psychiatric patients. *Journal of the American Academy of Child and Adolescent Psychiatry, 31,* 125-131.
Goldstein, A., Glick, B., Reiner, S., Zimmerman, D., & Coultry, T. (1987). *Aggression replacement training: A comprehensive intervention for aggressive youth.* Champaign, IL: Research Press.
Hough, S., & Kleinginna, C. (2002). Individualizing relaxation training in spinal cord injury: Importance of injury level and person factors. *Rehabilitation Psychology, 47,* 415-425.
Jacobson, E. (1974). *Progressive relaxation.* Chicago: University of Chicago Press.
Johnston, D. (1991). Stress management in the treatment of mild primary hypertension. *Hypertension, 17*(Suppl. 4), 11163-11168.
Levi, L. (1996). Spice of life or kiss of death? In C. Cooper (Ed.), *Handbook of stress medicine and health* (pp. 1-10). Boca Raton, FL: CRC Press.

McCrady, A., Bailey, B., & Good, M. (1991). Controlled study of biofeedback-assisted relaxation in Type 1 diabetes. *Diabetes Care, 14,* 265-360.

McGuigan, F. (1994). Stress management through progressive relaxation. *International Leadership and Organization Development Journal, 13,* 27-32.

Ollendick, T., & Ollendick, D. (1990). Tics and Tourette syndrome. In A. Gross & R. Drabman (Eds.), *Handbook of clinical behavioral pediatrics* (pp. 243-252). New York: Plenum.

Schrodt, G. (1992). Cognitive therapy of depression. In M. Shafii & S. Shafii (Eds.), *Clinical guide to depression in children and adolescents* (pp. 197-217). Washington, DC: American Psychiatric Press.

Shaw, G., Srivastava, E., Sadlier, M., Swann, P., James, J., & Rhodes, J. (1991). Stress management for irritable bowel syndrome: A controlled trial. *Digestion, 50,* 36-42.

Smarr, K., Parker, J., Wright, G., Stucky-Ropp, R., Buckelew, S., Hoffman, R., O'Sullivan, F., & Hewett, J. (1997). The importance of self-efficacy in rheumatoid arthritis. *Arthritis Care and Research, 10,* 18-26.

Starkey, D., Deleone, H., & Flannery R. (1995). Stress management for psychiatric patients in a state hospital setting. *American Journal of Ortho-psychiatry, 65,* 446-450.

Taylor, S., Thordarson, D., Maxfield, L., Fedoroff, I., & Lovell, K. (2003). Comparative efficacy, speed, and adverse effects of three PTSD treatments: Exposure therapy, EMDR, and relaxation training. *Journal of Consulting and Clinical Psychology, 71,* 330-338.

Thyer, B. (1991). Diagnosis and treatment of child and adolescent anxiety disorders. *Behavior Modification, 15,* 310-325.

Wolpe, J. (1982). *The practice of behavior therapy.* New York: Pergamon Press.

6

The Magic Wand

Shirley R. Simon

Type of Contribution: Activity

Objective

To empower group members, via fantasy and imagination, and to symbolically experience change and envision growth. Through the use of this simple tool, members have an opportunity to visualize new experiences and articulate dreams and wishes.

Rationale for Use

A magic wand is associated with fairy tales, magic, and imagination. It conjures up images of power, dreams, and hope. From Merlin the Magician, to Cinderella's Fairy Godmother, to the escapades of Harry Potter's world, the magic wand is a long-standing, easily recognizable symbol of empowerment. This simple visual representation can recall and capture a wide variety of familiar, yet uncommon emotional experiences.

As a therapeutic tool, the magic wand gently implores group members to engage their imaginations and fantasies in the process of change. As Walsh, Richardson, and Cardey (1991) state, ". . . the intrinsic appeal of pretend evokes spontaneous responses across the age-span" (p. 61). The presence of a symbolic magic wand subtly alters the group climate and requests that participants engage in a slightly different, less overtly clinical process. As such, the magic wand can be an effective tool for group therapists in a variety of applications.

Instructions

Begin by identifying the goal of the exercise. It is important to design the instructions to address the specific objective of the experience. The therapist should be clear that the objective is not to change someone else or to expunge a mistake or past hurt. Rather, it is an opportunity to feel or experience a potential change in a safe, supportive environment. It is an opportunity to utilize this nonverbal tool to stimulate risk and growth.

The wand itself can be as simple as a wooden stick or broom handle. It can be a party favor or a home-decorated paper towel roll. Fancier versions can be purchased with colored shapes and glitter shining through the wand's tubing. Group members can also design and name their own magic wands, thereby experiencing the wand's creativity and energy from the beginning.

Typically, the wand is passed around the circle, with each member taking a turn to speak on the designated topic. Time limits should be addressed. If a brief statement by each participant is anticipated, this should be articulated. If a longer statement and explanation is desired, determine in advance whether there are any restrictions on the length of contributions. Also clarify whether cross talk by others in the group is invited. Be certain there is sufficient time for all group members to not only express their responses but to experience them on an affective level.

The magic wand can be used to empower members, deepen and broaden conversation, tap into members' fantasies and wishes, imbue order and procedure, or just add a sense of whimsy and play to the group process. In addition, as with most programmed activities, the therapist has the opportunity to observe and assess client behavior in nontraditional interactions, thereby providing further information for diagnosis and treatment (Brandler & Roman, 1999; Toseland & Rivas, 2005). Therapists can integrate the magic wand according to the needs and the purposes of the group. Its versatility and simplicity make the wand a particularly useful tool in ones therapeutic repertoire.

Some of the clinical objectives that can be facilitated by the use of the magic wand include personal growth or change, motivation, experiencing new roles and behaviors, feedback, instilling order and procedure, and facilitating closure and separation. These are discussed separately in the following sections.

Personal Growth or Change

As a vehicle to stimulate personal growth, each member can hold the magic wand and empower herself or himself to make a desired change. An individual might say, "With the power given to me with this wand, I will now take the first step in losing weight and attend Overeaters Anonymous," or "I will now begin an exercise program by walking for a half hour tomorrow morning. In a couple or family group, the wand can empower a member to visualize and describe a change she or he could make that would benefit the couple or family. The member can hold the wand and say, "With the magic wand's help, I plan to . . . give my spouse two compliments a day," or "turn off all electronic devices and talk to my parents for ten minutes once a day," or "pick up my dirty clothes and place them in the hamper everyday." Whatever the content of the statement, the affective experience generated by the magic wand, of having the power to change, can be therapeutically significant.

Motivation

In a discussion about the purposes of program activities, Brandler and Roman (1999) indicate that activities can be used to help clients engage ". . . an area in which particularly problematic or painful material creates resistance" (p. 139). By evoking pretense and fantasy, the magic wand can diminish resistance and facilitate problem resolution. If, for example, the goal is to increase the members' desire to break a negative pattern, such as an addiction or obsession, the wand can be used to empower members to experience what their lives might be like without this interference. Members can be instructed to wave the wand and imagine what a typical day might be like without the intrusion of the addiction or obsession and focus on what they would be doing or feeling instead. Frequently, troubled individuals have not taken the time to consider the impact of the problem on their daily activities. In this way, the magic wand exercise can provide a safe opportunity to experience the difference and, potentially, motivate a change.

Experiencing New Roles and Behaviors

The opportunity to engage in play and fantasy can bring out the child in all of us. Via fantasy, members are afforded the chance to experiment with new roles and unexplored aspects of their personalities (Brandler & Roman, 1999). The magic wand can be used to allow group members to try out new ways of interacting, such as by role-playing a character or by simply expressing interests and desires that are frequently repressed in the routines of daily life. The straight-laced businessman may find himself unexpectedly enchanted by the prospect of being a jazz musician. The housewife, who is constantly cleaning and organizing, may be ecstatic when envisioning herself as an artist working in a paint smeared smock. Given permission, through the power of the magic wand, to be different than we are in day to day activities is freeing and could potentially lead to growth. The wand can allow an individual to temporarily experience a new persona and thereby, facilitate the emergence of unexplored feelings, energies, and abilities. Care, of course, should be taken to use this power with appropriate populations who have a clear grasp of the difference between fantasy and reality.

Feedback

Much has been written about the importance of feedback in therapeutic groups (Corey, 2004; Toseland & Rivas, 2005; Yalom, 1995). One way to elicit constructive feedback is through the use of the magic wand. The imaginary power of the magic wand can be the instrument to facilitate a member's sharing of a wish or a hope for another member of the group. The timing of this exercise and the directions given should be carefully considered so as to elicit thoughtful, nonjudgmental feedback that is well received by the group members. The instructions to the group can be phrased as follows: "Using the magic wand, grant a group member the power to change something about her/his interpersonal behavior. Be sure your wish is constructive and realistic. The goal of this experience is to provide helpful, positive feedback." The therapist can then follow these directions with examples of appropriate feedback.

Order and Procedure

As a talking stick, the wand can give an individual permission to speak in the group. Possessing the wand gives the group a clear indication of an individual's authority to speak. If needed, it is easy to remind the group about who can speak by asking them, "Who has the talking stick?" This is especially helpful in groups with monopolizers, interrupters, or other dominating personalities. With active children's groups, the talking stick can provide a concrete reinforcement of order and procedure.

Facilitating Closure and Separation

The magic wand can be used toward the end of a group's time together to facilitate transition and acceptance of the loss of the group. Members can take turns holding the wand and identifying the magical things they will take with them as they leave the group. Members can also empower themselves with strengths and memories as they prepare to move on. Finally, members can put voice to their hopes and fears as the group's termination draws near. These statements can then lead to an open discussion about the meaning and impact of the group's ending, a vital therapeutic component of a healthy termination (Corey & Corey, 1992; Wickham, 2003).

Suggestions for Follow-Up

The magic wand exercise can be repeated in a follow-up session in order to reinforce the concept of personal empowerment. However, one should be cautious not to over use this tool. Its magic wears thin with over use! Follow-up discussions and references to members' experiences with the wand are highly desirable and reinforcing. As with most program experiences, processing the interaction is critical (Haslett, 2005). Immediately after the group members complete their turns with the wand, an open discussion focusing on the affective nature of the experience is often fruitful. Members can share how it felt to have the power to change, what internal messages they gave themselves during the exercise, what they plan to do as a result of this experience, what responses they had to others' statements, or simply whether engaging in a nontraditional interaction was valuable. Such a conversation can then lead to additional self-disclosure and insight.

Contraindications

When using the magic wand, it is important that participants are able to distinguish between fantasy and reality. Participants who do not have a clear grasp of reality would not be well served by the imaginary empowerment of the magic wand. In addition, care must be taken if the wand is to be used with aggressive or acting out clients. The wand can become a weapon or an imaginary sword or club and can lead to aggressive interactions. Close monitoring is essential if such behaviors are likely.

Readings and Resources for the Professional

Carrell, S. (2000). *Group exercises for adolescents: A manual for the therapist* (2nd ed.). Newbury Park, CA: Sage Publications.

Garvin, C. D., Gutierrez, L. M., & Galinsky, M. (Eds.). (2004). *Handbook of social work with groups.* New York: The Guilford Press.

Johnson, D. W., & Johnson, F. P. (2003). *Joining together: Group theory and group skills* (8th ed.). Boston: Allyn & Bacon.

McManus, R., & Jennings, G. (Eds.) (1997*). Structured exercises for promoting family and group strengths.* Binghamton, NY: The Haworth Press.

Middleman, R. R. (1968). *The non-verbal method in working with groups.* New York: Association Press.

Nell Warren Associates (1992). *The warm-ups manual, volume II: More tools for working with groups.* Toronto, Canada: Nell Warren Associates.

Schwartz, R. M. (2002). *The skilled facilitator: Practical wisdom for developing effective groups* (2nd ed.). San Francisco, CA: Jossey-Bass Publishers.

Yalom, I. D. (2002). *The gift of therapy: An open letter to a new generation of therapists and their patients.* New York: HarperCollins Publisher.

References

Brandler, S., & Roman, C. P. (1999). *Group work: Skills and strategies for effective interventions* (2nd ed.). Binghamton, NY: The Haworth Press.

Corey, G. (2004). *Theory and practice of group counseling.* Belmont, CA: Brooks/Cole-Thomson Learning.

Corey, M. S., & Corey, G. (1992). *Groups: Process and practice* (4th ed.). Pacific Grove, CA: Brooks Cole Publishing Company.

Haslett, D. C. (2005). *Group work activities in generalist practice.* Belmont, CA: Brooks/Cole.

Toseland, R. W., & Rivas, R. F. (2005). *An introduction to group work practice* (5th ed.). Boston: Pearson Education, Inc.

Walsh, R. T., Richardson, M. A., & Cardey, R. M. (1991). Structured fantasy approaches to children's group therapy. *Social Work with Groups, 14*(1), 57-73.

Wickham, E. (2003). *Group treatment in social work: An integration of theory and practice* (2nd ed.). Toronto, Canada: Thompson Educational Publishing, Inc.

Yalom, I. D. (1995). *The theory and practice of group psychotherapy* (4th ed.). New York: Basic Books.

7

Group Sculpting

Elwood R. Hamlin II
Michael Kane
Dawn Viers

Type of Contribution: Activity

Objective

Sculpting is an activity designed to allow family members to use spatial relationships to symbolize one's perception of family relationships, events, or situations at a moment in time. As a result, this activity enables family members to reflect and discuss their relationships or perceptions of an event or situation as well as to share how they would view an improvement in their relationship, event or situation. This activity uses group members as substitute family members in a sculpting exercise.

Rationale for Use

Family sculpting is an expressive activity that has theoretical roots in the experiential model of family therapy. Proponents of the experiential model focus on the present and use observations of interactions between family members to enhance self-growth by encouraging self-expression (Satir & Baldwin, 1983). Uncovering or deciphering symbolic factors, including factors found in dreams, fantasies, and conversations, help family members understand and accept a variety of perceptions of oneself and others in the family (Whitaker & Keith, 1981). Growth is identified through increased self-awareness by individuals within a family, a sense of togetherness along with a healthy differentiation of self, and positive self-esteem.

Sculpting, a technique developed in the 1960s and early 1970s at the Boston Family Institute by Fred Duhl, David Kantor, and Bunny Duhl, has been shown to be useful in facilitating understanding and communication between family members. Sculpting serves as a means to encourage family members to reflect, communicate, and understand how each of them might view situations, relationships, and events differently. The technique acts as a vehicle that encourages family members to get in touch with unexpressed feelings about situations, events, and relationships. It uses space and physical activity to convey feelings and perceptions among family members. This activity is especially useful for younger or less verbal individuals who often have a difficult time verbalizing their feelings about or perceptions of an event, relationship, or situation (Duhl, Kantor, & Duhl, 1973). Sculpting is also seen as a less threatening activity to convey one member's perception of an event, relationship, or situation within the family. Mealey (1977) suggests "a major advantage of sculpting is that it cuts through intellectualization, defensiveness, and projection of blame" (p. 121). Sculpting has since become a popular technique with family therapists following many theoretical modalities.

The use of sculpting in a group system, as opposed to a family system, is a natural progression of this exercise. Group members are free from family alliances, secrets, and preconceived notions which may prohibit family members from fully acting out their assigned roles. This can help the actors offer the sculptor a different take on the scene and situation. Logistically, groups provide more actors and opportunities to sculpt a past memory, the current situation, or the family of the future. Further, sculpting can serve to promote cohesiveness and bonding among group members as well as help each member individuate and grow (Papp, Silverstein, & Carter, 1973).

Although this activity uses group members as substitute family members, it can be expected that the activity would approximate a family sculpting experience. Duhl, Kantor, and Duhl (1973) state "in what seems a magical way, sculptors...often choose people whose qualities and experiences are similar to the characters to be portrayed" (p. 54). Indeed it has been the experience of one of the authors (D. V.) that sculptors often pick actors to play the same roles these actors played in their own family of origin. Sculpting has been used with student training groups (Lordan, 1996; Mealey, 1977), couple groups (Lawson, 1989), and groups with members with schizophrenia (Julius, 1978).

Instructions

Sculpting may be employed at various times during group assessment and treatment. It is used as an assessment tool to understand an individual's perception of his or her family. It can also be beneficial during the treatment phase to overcome an impasse such as an individual's reluctance or inability to verbally express himself or herself about something. This technique can be useful as a joining exercise and can help group members understand transgenerational patterns that may be affecting their current situation.

The group facilitator would introduce sculpting as an activity that will involve one group member placing the others in nonverbal, fluid poses that reflects a scene from the individual's memory of his or her family of origin. The facilitator further elaborates on the activity by describing the roles of monitor, sculptor, actors, and audience. The facilitator notes that he or she will play the role of the monitor. The monitor assists the sculptor (group member) in establishing a particular situation, event, or relationship that the sculptor wishes to portray and moderates the sculpting activity. The sculptor arranges her or his family members using distance, space, and body gestures in relation to one another, as if drawing a portrait or making a living sculpture of their family. The actors, including the sculptor, are the remaining family members. Finally, the audience is the rest of the group members, who act as observers to the sculpting. If there are too few group members to act as family members, the monitor, sculptor, or inanimate objects such as chairs may take the place of the remaining actors (Duhl, Kantor, & Duhl, 1973).

The monitor and the sculptor identify a situation, event, or relationship within the family of origin that the sculptor will portray. The sculptor then picks actors from the group to play each family member in the sculptor's family. With the assistance of the monitor, the sculptor begins to physically arrange family members including himself or herself in poses/positions that express the sculptor's perception of the situation, event, or relationship. The monitor assists the sculptor in arranging each group member in the different positions. As the sculptor works, the monitor asks for details of the scene, event, or relationship being portrayed. The monitor asks questions or makes comments about preferred facial expressions, body positions, or fluid movements and proximity of the actors in relation to each other. Each actor can also ask his or her own questions to get a sense of the role.

As group members take different poses/positions in relation to one another following the direction of the sculptor, it is not uncommon for the sculptor to request individuals to change poses to more accurately portray what the sculptor wishes to convey. Once the family is sculpted, the monitor asks the sculptor, "Is this the sculpture/picture you want to communicate?" If there are no further changes, the monitor requests each member to act within his or her pose for a couple of minutes and think about where he or she is in relation to other family members.

Following the sculpting activity, the monitor asks each member to share what it felt like for her or him to be placed in the position. This allows the members to be physically aware of their position, talk about themselves in relation to the position, and talk about their position in relation to other members' positions. Expressions may range from how physically demanding it is to hold this position to symbolic expressions such as, "I didn't realize I am so overbearing." Generally, each member will have a unique view and thoughts based on their position in the sculpture. Audience members are also encouraged to share their observations about the scene.

After each actor and audience member is debriefed, the sculptor discusses her or his intentions for placing members, including himself or herself, in the positions. At the conclusion of the activity, group members are given an opportunity to share what, if anything, they learned from this experience. This question supports self-expression and gives each member permission to share observations of the family being sculpting and their own family.

Brief Vignette

Beth, age thirty-five, Anne, age thirty-four, Emma, age twenty-three, Carol, age thirty, and Mary, age thirty-two, were in a twelve-week women's issues group focusing on self-esteem. Each group member was in individual and/or couples counseling and was referred to the group by their therapist as a way to receive support while addressing issues affecting their relationships with others. Several of the group members had trouble expressing emotions and would often retreat rather than discuss painful topics. Beth, on the other hand, expressed a lot of anger and would often express barbed comments regarding her husband and family of origin, sometimes to the consternation of other group members.

While focusing on transgenerational issues, the cofacilitators of the group introduced sculpting. Beth immediately volunteered to be the sculptor. With the cofacilitators acting as monitors, Beth decided to sculpt a predinner scene after Beth's father had returned from work. The actors were Beth at age fifteen, her brother at age twelve, her father, and her mother. Beth first chose Emma, the youngest and most reserved in our group, to be her father. Beth placed Emma at an imaginary kitchen table reading the newspaper with her back to the room. With the monitors asking questions regarding the details of the scene, Beth directed Emma to hunch her shoulders and have a scowl on her face.

Next, Beth chose Anne to act as her mother. She placed Anne at a stove with her back to Emma. Beth told Anne to stir soup in an imaginary pot. Beth then selected Carol, the most outgoing in the group, to act as her brother. Beth described her brother as hyper and directed Carol to dart in and out of the space dribbling a basketball. Finally, Beth put herself at the kitchen table working on homework, across from her father and with her back to her mother. Mary, the last member of the group, acted as the audience. When Beth agreed that the scene was accurate, the monitors asked each player to act out their poses. After about one minute, one of the monitors asked the actors to leave their roles and resume the group.

One of the monitors asked the actors to describe what it was like to act in these roles. Emma, who acted as Beth's father, spoke first. She stated that her shoulders and head hurt from holding this position and that she felt as though she had the weight of the world on her shoulders. She also said that she felt isolated and wanted to join the family but did not know how. Next, Carol, playing Beth's brother, described how she felt exhausted from all of her activity. She said she felt as if she had to keep moving because the scene was so quiet and she felt pressure to liven it up. Lastly, Anne, acting as Beth's mother, also said she felt tired from stirring the soup and feeling the need to take care of the family alone. Anne reflected that she felt like a martyr in the family as she didn't receive help but didn't ask for it either. She also stated she was distracted by Carol and had to laugh at "her son's" antics.

During this process, Beth looked surprised by some comments and nodded in agreement at others. One of the monitors invited Beth to share her reasons for sculpting each actor in their respective positions and for her own thoughts about the sculpture. Beth described her family as very traditional as her father was the breadwinner working outside the home while her mother worked inside the home. She agreed with Emma's statement that her father had the world on his shoulders but was surprised that he felt isolated. Emma and Beth continued to dialogue this point. Emma said although she was closest in position to Beth, she felt that even Beth shut her out. This, again, surprised Beth as Beth stated that she thought she had the closest connection with her father.

Beth concurred that her brother was the clown in the family. He often distracted people, especially her mother, but his antics allowed him to get away with more than she did, which often made Beth angry with him. Beth stated that her mother played a long suffering role of a martyr; she was often tired from taking care of the family on her own but got angry at others when they helped, because they did not do things her way. As for her part, Beth stated she felt removed from the scene and immersed herself in her homework. She stated that she played the role of the good girl while growing up by getting good grades and staying out of trouble. Mary, the audience member, asked Beth if she realized that she kept looking at her mother and father. Beth stated she did not realize this, but reflected she often worried about their silence and, as a result, would distance herself while thinking that she did not want a relationship like theirs.

At the conclusion of the debriefing, the monitors asked the actors what they learned about the sculpture, the family, and themselves. Each actor reflected on the similarities between the roles they portrayed in the sculpture, the roles they assumed in their own family of origin, and their own personalities. Each also concurred that they felt isolated and exhausted in these roles. Beth expressed how the roles in her family of origin were comparable to her current family, including her husband and three children. She said she always felt angry at her husband for not helping out and for being able to be the fun parent with their children, but realized through this sculpture that she helped shut him out, thus recreating the same roles her own parents played.

At the end of the group meeting, Emma privately approached the group facilitators. She stated she had previously felt very uncomfortable with Beth but, through the sculpture, saw Beth in a different light. During the remainder of the group sessions, the facilitators noticed less distance between Beth and the rest of the group members. Beth, for her part, also seemed a little less angry and more reflective in later group sessions.

Suggestions for Follow-Up

In subsequent sessions, the facilitator may request each group member take the role of the sculptor in order to understand the different perceptions that each member may have about a situation, event, or relationships with his or her own family. This can help the sculptors and actors understand their families and one another. This exercise can also be used to sculpt one's current family, circle of friends, or other groups that a group member wishes to sculpt.

This activity can help members act out a variety of perspectives on a given situation, event, or set of relationships. If, for example, the sculptor portrayed the family as he or she perceives it now, the facilitator may in a subsequent meeting request the same individual sculpt his family as he or she would like it to be in the future. By doing so, the group can pick up on the contrast between how the family is perceived now and the preferred state of functioning. This would provide a guide for treatment planning and suggestions on how to help achieve this state.

Contraindications

Individuals or groups, who after receiving information about the activity and choose not to participate, should have the option not to participate in this activity. Sculpting should only be used once the group develops rapport and trust. Terribly upsetting events and situations may have occurred within the life of the family that are too sensitive to examine using sculpting. Likewise, family secrets may emerge during a sculpting session. The monitor should pay close attention to these issues and ensure safety for all members. Groups whose members are extremely antagonistic or sarcastic would not be appropriate for this activity.

Readings and Resources for the Professional

Duhl, F., Kantor, D., & Duhl, B. (1973). Learning, space, and action in family therapy: A primer of sculpture. In D. Bloch (Ed.), *Techniques of family psychotherapy: A primer* (pp. 47-63). New York: Grune & Statton.

Duhl, B., & Duhl F. (1981). Integrative family therapy. In A. Gurman & D. Kniskern (Eds.), *Handbook of family therapy* (pp. 483-513). New York: Brunner/Mazel.

Nerin, W. (1986). *Family reconstruction: Long day's journey into light.* New York: W. W. Norton & Co.

Satir, V., & Baldwin, M. (1983). *Satir step by step: A guide to creating change in families.* Palo Alto, CA: Science and Behavior Books.

Bibliotherapy Sources for the Client

Rosenberg, M. (2003). *Nonviolent communication: A language of life.* Encinitas, CA: Puddle Dancer Press.

Rosenthal, N. (2003). *The emotional revolution.* New York: Citadel Press.

References

Duhl, F., Kantor, D., & Duhl, B. (1973). Learning, space, and action in family therapy: A primer of sculpture. In D. Bloch (Ed.), *Techniques of family psychotherapy: A primer* (pp. 47-63). New York: Grune & Statton.

Julius, E. K. (1978). Family sculpting: A pilot program for a schizophrenic group. *Journal of Marital and Family Therapy, 4*(3), 19-24.

Lawson, D. M. (1989). Using family sculpting in groups to enrich current intimate relationships. *Journal of College Student Development, 30,* 171-172.

Lordan, N. (1996). The use of sculpt in social groupwork education. *Groupwork, 9,* 62-79.

Mealey, A. (1977). Sculpting as a group technique for increasing awareness. *Perspectives in Psychiatric Care, 15,* 118-121.

Papp, P., Silverstein, O., & Carter, E. (1973). Family sculpting in preventative work with well families. *Family Process, 2,* 197-212.

Satir, V., & Baldwin, M. (1983). *Satir step by step: A guide to creating change in families.* Palo Alto, CA: Science and Behavior Books.

Whitaker, C., & Keith, D. (1981). Symbolic-experiential family therapy. In A. Gurman & D. Kniskern (Eds.), *Handbook of family therapy* (pp. 187-225). New York: Brunner/Mazel.

8

Striving for Meaningfulness and Self-Acceptance: An Existential-Humanistic Group Therapy Activity

Glenn W. Lambie
Shari M. Sias

Type of Contribution: Activity

Objectives

The existential-humanistic theoretical constructs of congruence, self-acceptance, existential meaningfulness, personal responsibility of choice, and growth are related to an individual's overall functionality and well-being. The objectives of the this group activity include

- emphasizing the importance of congruence (both personal and occupational),
- emphasizing the here-and-now phenomena,
- seeking meaningfulness in life (search for meaning),
- understanding the role of personal choice in life (personal responsibility), and
- increasing self-awareness of what it means to be a human being.

Rationale for Use

An existential-humanistic perspective matches the values of the majority of therapists (Kelly, 1995). Humanistic therapeutic models are positively related to supporting a client's level of functionality (Lambie, 2006). Historically, humanistic psychology and existential philosophy began as a reaction to the mechanized reductionistic view of people put forward by psychoanalytic and behavioral theories (DeCarvolho, 1990). For example, theorists like Maslow (1968), Frankl (1963), May (1953), and Rogers (1951) rejected the idea that a client be reduced to a collection of drives or discrete behaviors, advocating instead that a therapist empathize with a client's experience of the world and work to facilitate a safe environment supporting the client in moving toward self-actualization and growth (Hansen, 1999; Lambie, 2006). Thus, clients (group members) will be better able to cope with the problems they currently face as well as future challenges.

A founding theoretical construct within the humanistic philosophy is congruence (genuineness or realness). Incongruence is the condition whereby individuals are not authentic and genuine, but rather wear a facade or mask that they feel will please others and meet others' expectations. Living incongruently leads to feelings of dissatisfaction with one's life and with oneself (Corey, 2005; Lambie, 2006). A congruent or genuine individual possesses a high level of self-acceptance and therefore would be at a lower level of susceptibility to dysfunctionality. On the other hand, an incongruent or fake individual, having a lower degree of self-acceptance, would experience a higher degree of dysfunctionality because of his or her effort to please others in an attempt to gain acceptance.

An underlying element of congruence is self-acceptance. An individual with a higher level of congruence possesses greater flexibility, autonomy, self-acceptance, and moves toward self-actualization. These qualities run counter to the characteristics positively correlated with persons who are at greater risk for dysfunctionality (Lambie, 2002), including

- lower levels of ego development,
- a lack of assertiveness,
- poor self-esteem,
- intolerance,
- need for approval,
- perfectionism,
- difficultly with ambiguity,
- external locus of control,
- inability to deal with anger and frustration,
- fear of failure,
- impatience, and
- impulsiveness.

Furthermore, research suggests an individual's characteristics (such as his or her needs systems), unrealistic expectations that are unchallenged, and personal philosophy contribute to his or her level of functionality and/or dysfunctionality (Jones & Emanuel, 1981). Therefore, clients who work and challenge themselves to become congruent (genuine) are likely to have a greater level of self-acceptance and understanding, and as a result experience greater functionality. Consequently, an effective group strategy for therapists is to encourage and support congruence among their clients through the constructs of humanistic philosophy.

Within humanistic therapeutic models, therapists work collaboratively with clients (group members), supporting their innate ability to grow and develop. It is as if the therapist and group members are dancing—the group members are leading while the therapist continuously flexes and responds based on the group's lead (Lambie, 2004). In addition, empathy is a foundation of this group therapeutic approach (Corey, 2004; Gladding, 2003). Research has found that therapist empathy accounts for two-thirds of the variance in supporting clients' positive behavioral change (Miller & Rollnick, 2002). This therapeutic approach promotes group members' feelings of self-efficacy and responsibility, while supporting the therapeutic change process.

Instructions

Effective use of this activity requires preparation. First, the therapist needs to understand and appreciate the existential-humanistic model. This model emphasizes the therapeutic relationship and the importance of the group facilitator being genuine in communicating unconditional, positive regard and acceptance to the group members within an empathic group climate (Johnson & Johnson, 2003; Rogers, 1995). Within this existential-humanistic therapeutic approach, the relationship is paramount and therapeutic techniques are secondary. Therefore, it is important for group facilitators to continuously promote and support a safe and trusting therapeutic climate during the application of this group activity.

This activity should be implemented once trust has been established within the group. To promote a safe group climate, it is suggested that the therapist facilitate various group formation activities that foster the establishment of trust among the members. With this safe and trusting group climate, group members will feel comfortable sharing and being genuine.

To begin the activity, the group members are asked to construct a personal meaningfulness statement, similar to a personal epitaph or obituary. Elaborating further, the group leader provides clarification by asking, "when you die, what would you want your obituary to say about you?" The group members are given the freedom to create their personal statements in any fashion, including writing a narrative, drawing important elements in their lives, or creating an interpretative illustration, with the understanding that they will have to present their statements to the group. The group leader supplies colored markers, crayons, colored pencils, and paper. The group members are given approximately 20 minutes to reflect and construct their personal meaningfulness statements.

Once each person has constructed a personal meaningfulness statement, the group is asked to reconvene and present their statements. The group facilitator explains that all members will present their statements and asks for a volunteer to start the process. Group members are permitted to comment on each other's statements and ask for clarification.

During the next step of the activity, the therapist asks the group members to reflect and write down what they feel are the greatest sources of stress in their lives. The group members next present their sources of stress to the rest of the group. Following this discussion, the group members are asked to examine their personal meaningfulness statements and their sources of life stress together. In essence, the therapist asks the group members if they are being true to what is most important to them in their lives, which is the theme of their statements. The therapist then facilitates a discussion relating to the group members' identified incongruences and works to generate possible approaches that may be taken to support greater congruence. After this discussion, the group leader summarizes the common themes that emerged in the group discussion, linking the commonality among the group members. Lastly, the therapist closes the group by recommending that members work to become cognizant of the incongruence within their lives. Thus, the therapist challenges all group members to appreciate the role their personal choices have within their feelings of distress and encourages all members to strive for greater congruence, thereby decreasing their level of stress and potential dysfunctionality.

Throughout the striving for meaningfulness and self-acceptance activity, the therapist supports the group members in expressing and discussing their feelings and thoughts relating to the activity. Inaddition, the group therapist employs the group counseling facilitating technique of linking (emphasizing the common shared themes and concerns among the group members) to call attention to the fact that the stressors and struggles of each group member are often normal and universal among people (decreasing their feeling of isolation).

Brief Vignette

The following case example was implemented with a university counseling group. The group was composed of one male and eight females who were graduate-level counseling students ranging in ages from twenty-three to fifty-three. The group met weekly for an hour and half. This activity was conducted during the sixth group session.

The session began with a check-in with each group member. Following the check-in, the facilitator provided a general orientation to the activity. Next, the group leader asked the members to construct a personal meaningfulness statement, elaborating that this statement is similar to a personal epitaph or obituary. To provide further clarification, the therapist asked, "When you die, what would you want your obituary to say about you? In other words, what do you want to be remembered for and/or as?" At this point, the group facilitator distributed paper, colored pencils, colored markers, and crayons to group members, explaining that they may construct their personal meaningfulness statement however they feel most comfortable. The group members were given approximately 20 minutes to complete their personal meaningfulness statement and once finished, each presented their statement to the group.

Group members constructed their personal meaningfulness statement in many different fashions, from listing roles that were most meaningful to them, to constructing a metaphoric epitaph, to creating a picture that they interpreted. Common themes that emerged from the group members' responses included

- family was a priority,
- religion and spiritually were important,
- being a good partner and friend was significant, and
- being a good person was essential.

None of the nine group member responses listed their work as one of their top three priorities; however, "helping others" was listed.

During the next step of the activity, the group therapist asked the group members to reflect and write down what they felt were the greatest sources of stress in their lives. The group members then presented their sources of stress to the rest of the group. The life stressors shared among the members were very similar. The common life stressors related to work, including unrealistic systemic expectations, work bureaucracy, "challenging" clients, and members' feeling that the occupational climate was inconsistent with what they felt it means to be a professional. The "challenging" clients seemed to be more of a concern to the group members who appeared to have increased feelings of responsibility for their work outcomes.

Following this discussion, the group members were asked to examine their personal meaningfulness statements and reflect to see if they felt their lives were congruent with the message conveyed in their statements. In other words, were they being true to what was most important to them in their lives, which was the theme of their statements. All the members conveyed that they were trying to be congruent but struggling. When asked if they were putting the majority of their energy and time into the most important component of their lives, they all said "no." Next, the therapist facilitated a discussion relating to the members' incongruences and worked to generate possible approaches they may take to support greater congruence.

This discussion launched a dialogue between the group members on how they were trying to achieve balance in their lives, with each of them sharing and supporting the other members. Interestingly, all the members expressed that they had never thought about their life values in relation to their stress and happiness in this way. The discrepancies between the group members' personal meaningful statements and their current behaviors and perspective of their stressors seemed consistent among all the group members. In addition, all the members expressed that this exercise made them think and increased their self-awareness about their current life, happiness, and areas of stress. The group members' support for one another appeared to enhance this process.

During the group's final session, the facilitator asked the group members about their life congruence. All the group members expressed that they remembered the striving for meaningfulness and self-acceptance activity and were consistently working on being true to themselves; however, they noted that it was hard work.

Suggestions for Follow-Up

The striving for meaningfulness and self-acceptance activity can be an effective therapeutic strategy in helping group members become acquainted and establish trust, build empathic listening skills, and begin to identify issues that require further exploration. In addition, within an existential-humanistic therapy model, the group experience is a therapeutic process that continuously evolves. Therefore, it is suggested that therapists explore the issues raised in this activity (congruence, self-awareness, life meaningfulness, and personal responsibility) throughout the therapeutic process. This group activity may also be implemented using other group therapeutic models, such as an expressive arts approach or psychodrama (Moreno, 1964).

Contraindications

Prescreening of prospective group members is always necessary prior to initiating group therapy. In addition, therapy groups and their goals should match potential group members' therapeutic needs, abilities, and level of functioning. The striving for meaningfulness and self-acceptance activity is an existential-humanistic therapeutic approach. Therefore, it is abstract in nature and some therapists and group members may not feel comfortable with the nondirective and unstructured nature of this approach. Consequently, it is suggested that this activity not be implemented with groups whose members are experiencing an acute crisis, such as those who have suicidal/homicidal ideations, untreated clinical depression, substance-abuse related disorders, post-traumatic stress disorder (PTSD), and/or thought disorders. In addition, because some elements of this therapeutic strategy are abstract in nature, it is suggested that this activity should not be used with cognitively low functioning groups. Finally, as with all therapeutic approaches, it is important for the therapist to have an awareness and appreciation of potential cultural limitations relating to his or her theoretical and/or technical orientation.

Readings and Resources for the Professional

Bugental, J. F. T. (1978). *Psychotherapy and process: The fundamentals of an existential-humanistic approach.* Reading, MA: Addison-Wesley.

Cain, D. J., & Seeman, J. (Eds.). (2002). *Humanistic psychotherapies: Handbook of research and practice.* Washington, DC: American Psychological Association.

Frankl, V. (1963). *Man's search for meaning.* New York: Beacon House.

May, R. (1953). *Man's search for himself.* New York: W. W. Norton & Co.

May, R., & Yalom, I. (2000). Existential psychotherapy. In R. J. Corsini & D. Wedding (Eds.), *Current psychotherapies* (6th ed., pp. 273-302). Itasca, IL: F. E. Peacock.

Rogers, C. R. (1951). *Client-centered therapy.* Boston: Houghton Mifflin.

Rogers, C. R. (1970). *Carl Rogers on encounter groups.* New York: Harper & Row.

Rogers, C. R. (1995). *A way of being.* New York: Houghton Mifflin Company.

Van Deurzen, E. (1998). *Paradox and passion in psychotherapy: An existential approach to therapy and counseling.* New York: John Wiley & Sons.

Yalom, I. D. (1980). *Existential psychotherapy.* New York: Basic Books.

Yalom, I. D. (1995). *The theory and practice of group psychotherapy* (4th ed.). New York: Basic Books.

Bibliotherapy Sources for the Client

Simon, S. B. (1993). *In search of values: 31 strategies for finding out what really matters most to you.* New York: Warner Books, Inc.

Simon, S. B., Howe, L. W., & Kirschenbaum, H. (1995). *Values clarification: A practical action-directed workbook—new revised edition.* New York: Warner Books, Inc.

Smith, H. (2000). *What matters most: The power of living your values.* New York: Franklin Covey Co.

References

Corey, G. (2004). *Theory and practice of group counseling* (6th ed.). New York: Wadsworth Publishing.

Corey, G. (2005). *Theory and practice of counseling and psychotherapy* (7th ed.). New York: Wadsworth Publishing.

DeCarvolho, R. (1990). A history ᶠ the "third force" in psychology. *Journal of Humanistic Psychology, 30,* 22-44.

Frankl, V. (1963). *Man's search for meaning.* Boston: Beacon Press.

Gladding, S. T. (2003). *Group work: A counseling specialty* (4th ed.). Upper Saddle River, NJ: Merrill Prentice Hall.

Hansen, J. T. (1999). A review and critical analysis of humanistic approaches to treating disturbed clients. *Journal of Humanistic Counseling, Education and Development, 38*(1), 29-38.

Johnson, D. W., & Johnson, F. P. (2003). *Joining together: Group therapy and group skills* (8th ed.). Boston: Allyn & Bacon.

Jones, M. A., & Emanuel, J. (1981, October). *Preventing burnout through counselor training.* Paper presented at the annual meeting of the North Central Association for Counselor Education and Supervision, Milwaukee, WI.

Kelly, E. W. (1995). Counselor values: A national survey. *Journal of Counseling and Development, 73*(6), 648-653.

Lambie, G. W. (2002). The contribution of ego development level to degree of burnout in school counselors. (Doctoral dissertation, The College of William & Mary, 2002). *Dissertation Abstracts International, 63,* 508.

Lambie, G. W. (2004). Motivational Enhancement Therapy: A tool for professional school counselors working with adolescents. *Professional School Counseling, 7*(4), 268-276.

Lambie, G. W. (2006). Burnout prevention: A humanistic perspective and structured group supervision activity. *Journal of Humanistic Counseling, Education and Development, 45*(1), 32-44.

Maslow, A. (1968). *Towards a psychology of being* (2nd ed.). Princeton, NJ: Van Nostrand.

May, R. (1953). *Man's search for himself.* New York: W. W. Norton & Co.

Miller, W. R., & Rollnick, S. (2002). *Motivational interviewing: Preparing people to change addictive behavior* (2nd ed.). New York: The Guilford Press.

Moreno, J. L. (1964). *Psychodrama: Vol. 1* (3rd ed.). Beacon, NY: Beacon House.

Rogers, C. R. (1951). *Client-centered therapy.* Boston: Houghton Mifflin Company.

Rogers, C. R. (1995). *A way of being.* New York: Houghton Mifflin Company.

9

What's in a Name?

Paul Springer
George W. Bitar
Robert Gee III

Type of Contribution: Activity

Objective

The purpose of this activity is to build group cohesiveness and insight on the part of group members by exploring the various meanings behind each member's name.

Rationale for Use

Names have significant power and meaning in culture, family, and individual lives. Seeman (1983) speaks to this power in the following passage:

> Personal names serve many purposes, both for the namer and the named. They are con-ferred, at least in part, in honor of someone who has gone before. Cultural traditions dictate the extent of commemorative name-giving. Names inform about genealogy and geogra-phy, and about the circumstances of birth. The etymological and linguistic associations of names are grasped intuitively without conscious knowledge of semantic roots. These un-conscious associations frequently emerge in nicknaming and in dreams. Passage from one life stage to another may accompany a change of name, as may religious conversion or new ideological affiliation. Because so many inferences can be drawn from the choice of a given name, it is no wonder that, in some cultures, the personal name is kept secret, a pro-tection against betrayal. (p. 237)

Meanings attributed to names, therefore, are rich windows into intrapsychic and interper-sonal realms of group members' lives. Exploring the meanings behind members' names can thus be used as the catalyst for enhanced cohesiveness, insight, and growth.

Instructions

This activity should be done with an established group, where the members feel comfortable or, at the very least, demonstrate respect for each other. This is due to the fact that this activity of-ten creates space where individuals can be vulnerable and express family of origin issues that are difficult to share. If introduced prematurely, this activity will not have the impact it could have had otherwise.

At the beginning of a session, the group facilitator can introduce the What's in a Name? activity by explaining that names have different but significant meanings for many people. The facilitator can continue by stating that names provide a window into who we are and, often, the way we behave. The following questions can be asked throughout the course of this activity:

1. How was your name chosen?
2. What is the family significance of your name?
3. Who else in your family bears your name?
4. What is the actual meaning of your name?
5. What is the country/cultural origin of your family name?
6. What does your name mean to you in the present?
7. What do you like about your name?
8. What do you dislike about your name?
9. What nicknames do you have as a result of your name?
10. If you could choose your own name, what would it be?

The group facilitator may choose to model the exercise and tell the group about his or her name, or the facilitator can ask a group member to start the exercise. If the facilitator believes that the group may struggle with the insight required in the activity, the facilitator may chose to disclose the significance of his or her own name first. Having the facilitator begin the exercise has the advantage of illuminating the significance of one's name. This can be an important first step since many people do not generally realize the impact and meaning of names on their lives. In addition, as the facilitator displays vulnerability by beginning the activity, group members may be more likely to also respond without fear of showing vulnerability. As with any disclosure, the facilitator must be sure that his or her own vulnerability adds to the therapeutic context and does not distract.

During the exercise, the group facilitator may also choose to ask clarifying questions and use reflective comments during the group members' disclosure. Each member is given a chance to share. After each group member shares, the facilitator may choose to connect similarities or themes within the disclosures and ask the group members if they identified with any particular group member or disclosure.

Depending on the target audience for the group (individual, couple, or family), the group facilitator may choose to ask additional questions or complete activities based on their names. These are highlighted in the following sections.

Additional Questions for Couple Groups

1. If you decided to keep your maiden name, why and how was this decision made? What did your partner think and feel about the decision? [To partner] What did you think and feel about this decision?
2. If you decided to change your maiden name, why and how was this decision made? What did your partner think and feel about the decision? [To partner] What did you think and feel about this decision?
3. If you plan on having children, what will you name the child? What are the meanings behind the names that you will choose?
4. If you do not plan on having or adopting children, what does that decision mean for your family name?

Additional Questions/Activities for Family Groups

1. Why and how did you decide on your child/children's name(s)?
2. Based on the name(s) you gave your child/children, what legacy are you attempting to impart?
3. Have the families break into groups and write a statement about what their family name currently means to them and what they would like their name to mean to them in the future. Each family then shares what they wrote with the larger group.
4. Have the families design and draw a family crest based on their family name. Each family then shares their crest with the larger group.

Brief Vignette

The following is an example of how this activity can be applied to a couple group dealing with alcoholism.

GROUP FACILITATOR (GF): Let's begin by having the group share what they like and dislike about their full names. Who would like to begin?

GREG: I will. I can easily start with what I dislike; it's harder for me to discuss what I like. I have the same name as my father, who was also an alcoholic. My name reminds me of him, and it also reminds me of how I have become a lot like him with my own alcoholism.

GF: [To Wendy (Greg's spouse)] How do you think your husband feels about his name by what he has just said?

WENDY: I think he feels a lot of shame and guilt about becoming like his father.

GF: [To Greg] Is that accurate?

GREG: Yeah. I promised myself that I would be different from my dad, but as I got older, I found myself dealing with problems the same way. Drinking seems to be a big piece of my family legacy. That's why I have my close friends call me by my middle name, Michael.

GF: So what is it about your middle name that you prefer?

GREG: Well, my middle name is not a family name, so I feel that I have some distance from my dad when I use it.

GF: So why don't you go by Michael with everyone instead of Greg?

GREG: I don't really know. I guess 'cause my wife and family know me on a different level and they have seen all of the bad stuff that I've done. At least with my friends, I can pretend to be someone different from who I am.

GF: Wendy, what thoughts or feelings do you have about what Greg has said so far?

WENDY: I'm surprised to hear Greg talk about his name this way. I knew he wasn't close to his dad, but I wasn't aware of why he used his middle name with some of his close friends.

GF: Greg, it seems that you have a desire to escape your father's legacy, by using the name Michael, but the hope of escaping is overwhelmed by the shame over who you have been.

GREG: Yeah. When I try to do better, it's like my past is never far behind.

GF: I appreciate what you both have said so far. [To the group] Who can identify with what Greg is saying about his name?

At this point, another group member discussed her struggles with the first name that she shared with her mother, who was emotionally abusive and also struggled with alcoholism. As the session progressed, the group facilitator connected and established themes among the group members' disclosures, thus enhancing a sense of cohesiveness in the group. The session concluded with group members sharing what they liked about their names and how their names provided them with a sense of strength.

Suggestions for Follow-Up

The follow-up is dependent on what emerges in the previous session. If focus in the previous session was on the negative aspects of people's names, the next session may want to focus more on the positive. For example, in a following session, the group facilitator can introduce the topic of how group members can create a positive family legacy for their children through their names.

Contraindications

This activity may be more applicable for presenting problems that have a strong intergenerational component. For example, groups whose members have presenting problems such as alcoholism, depression, and sexual and physical abuse may receive more benefit from this activity. Groups that struggle with trust and vulnerability or that lack insight may not find this activity as helpful.

Reading and Resource for the Professional

Seeman, M. V. (1983). The unconscious meaning of personal names. *Names, 31,* 237-244.

Reference

Seeman, M. V. (1983). The unconscious meaning of personal names. *Names, 31,* 237-244.

Behavioral Scaling As a Group-Guided Approach to Self-Management

Nancy G. Calley

Type of Contribution: Handouts

Objectives

This activity is designed to promote a solution-focused perspective to group therapy and expedite the group process. There are two primary learning objectives for this handout:

1. Increase self-management skills through the use of self-assessment.
2. Increase individual group member's sense of self-awareness by receiving behavioral feedback from other group members.

Indirect benefits of the activity include the promotion of client empowerment as a result of increased self-management skills and the illumination of therapeutic group factors to maximize the group process.

Rationale for Use

The exercise draws largely from solution-focused theory; however, behavior therapy must also be credited with the self-assessment nature of the exercise. The learning objectives listed previously integrate a solution-focused treatment philosophy with the primary tenets of behavior therapy.

More often than not, clients seek counseling as a result of being unable to identify a solution as a result of being overwhelmed by a specific problem. Movement toward the elimination of this problem-saturation state then becomes one of the initial therapeutic tasks for the client and clinician. Part of the constructivist family, the approaches contained under the umbrella of solution-focused theories (de Shazer, 1985; O'Hanlon & Weiner-Davis, 1989) provide the framework for transitioning from a problem focus toward a solution focus.

To promote understanding of the solution-focused approach, several assumptions have been articulated (de Shazer, 1985; de Shazer, 1988; O'Hanlon & Weiner-Davis, 1989; Walter & Peller, 1992). Some of these assumptions include:

1. focusing on the positive, on the solution, and on the future facilitates change in a positive direction;
2. focusing on what is right and working, as opposed to what is wrong and the problem, facilitates movement away from problems and toward solutions;

3. exceptions to problems suggest solutions, and therefore, must be identified in order to facilitate movement toward solutions;
4. small change leads to bigger change; therefore, the change process must be incremental, with success marked by celebration;
5. change is always happening as nothing stays the same; therefore, change is attainable;
6. treatment is organized around goals, so that treatment implies a forward focus (future) opposed to a backward focus (past); and
7. therapeutic group membership is based on shared goals and equal investment in the change process.

Drawing from these assumptions, the group process is guided by establishing a therapeutic framework that promotes a solution focus while enlisting the support of group members in each other's treatment.

Self-assessment is utilized in this exercise through the use of a self-monitoring tool. This type of self-monitoring is based on behavior therapy, emphasizing a self-control approach while ensuring that goals (solutions) occupy a central place in the therapeutic domain (Spiegler & Guevremont, 1998). Further, assessment is viewed as a continuous process that is integral to the therapeutic process and, as such, becomes a focal point of each therapy session. In this vein, group members check-in with one another to learn about each group member's self-report of progress.

The tool requires that members identify where they believe they are in regard to reaching their desired solution, and that they indicate precisely what supporting evidence exists that they are on the path to a solution. This type of evidence-based approach resonates with the scientific approach of behavior therapy in which conclusions must rely on observation as opposed to personal beliefs (Spiegler & Guevremont, 1998). It is in this manner that self-assessment is used to promote self-evaluation, to illuminate the self-directedness of the approach, to promote the continuous degree of client involvement necessary for achievement of solutions, and, ultimately, to improve the individual's self-management skills through the adoption of new tools.

Building on the self-assessment process, group members provide assessment feedback to one another regarding their perception of each other's progress toward solutions. This type of other assessment of self allows each group member to compare and contrast self-perception with the perception of others. Loosely related to the group factor of interpersonal learning, "group members, through feedback from others and self-observation, become aware of significant aspects of their interpersonal behaviors..." (Yalom, 1995, p. 42). Because of the safety provided within the group and the guidance provided by the facilitator, the client is able to compare one's self-assessment with the assessment from others to gain a more accurate picture of where one is with regard to progress toward identified solutions.

Through this process of self-monitoring, sharing with the group one's progress and evidence of such progress, and receiving feedback from the group regarding other's perceptions of one's progress, the group process is able to more quickly move toward the working stage. Group work then can be expedited as a result of the facilitated give and take experienced by group members that is inherent in this activity. It is in this vein that the group may begin to establish cohesion as members begin to acknowledge the need to provide and receive support from one another. Cohesion, related to the feelings of comfort experienced by group members, the sense of belonging to the group, the notion that one is valued by the group, and that the group is of value to each member (Bloch & Crouch, 1985) is integral to the productivity of the group. Thus, the use of exercises designed to promote such mutuality and support among group members contributes to the group's progress.

While this type of scaling exercise can also be used in individual therapy, the group modality presents opportunities to the clinician and client that are otherwise unavailable in individual work. As a result, this exercise is used to promote group member feedback to individual clients, further promoting exploration of self-perception versus other's perception of the self.

Instructions

The Scaling Exercise (Handout 10.1; see also completed sample in Handout 10.2) is introduced to all group members during the first session, following orientation to the group and the establishment of initial group rules. Each group member is asked to identify a current issue (problem) that they are facing. They then use the vertical scale to identify what would be happening when the problem is at its worse and what would be happening when the problem no longer exists (when the solution has been achieved). For instance, Hank defines a 1 (problem at its worse) as his wife leaving the house, no longer speaking to him, following another argument that he initiated and his feelings of utter self-loathing as a result of his continued inability to control his actions (that is, begin an argument). He defines a 10 (having reached a solution) by he and his wife being able to enjoy time together eating dinner, taking a walk, and sitting down after work to talk about their days without initiating an argument or saying something belittling or critical to his wife. This type of processing promotes a behavioral perspective by prompting the client to provide evidence of the actual behaviors, feelings, and/or actions related to the status of the problem thereby "operationalizing" the issue. By viewing both polarities of the issue in action-oriented terms, the problem and the solution come alive, thereby making success more tangible and the change process less mysterious.

Next, group members use the horizontal scale to identify their current status in relation to the problem and provide evidence in behavioral terms to support this in the space provided. Again, through the use of action-oriented language, personal ownership of the problem and solution are promoted. Each group member's personal behaviors are illuminated while group members are able to examine the relationship between personal behaviors, feelings, and results. Group members then identify where they would like to be within one week (future focus) with regard to the problem, scaling the problem upward, and provide evidence as to what will be happening as indicative of progress. In keeping with the philosophy inherent in solution-focused practices that small changes lead to bigger changes, it is important here that group members are reminded to attempt incremental change, not striving for too much too soon, as progress is what is sought, not the immediate rectification of the problem. Finally, group members identify the strategies that will be employed to achieve the desired solution. Identification of specific strategies provide the action steps toward goal attainment, promoting client ownership in reaching personal solutions, and thus, making progress (outcomes) easy to measure.

Each subsequent week, specific group members use the Scaling Exercise handout to report on their individual progress and provide supporting evidence. Other group members provide feedback as to where they perceive the specified client to be in relation to the client's solution and provide their own supporting evidence, in behavioral terms. The group leader promotes the group as a social microcosm (Yalom, 1995) by prompting group members to examine the interpersonal dynamics occurring within the group for evidence of individual progress or lack of progress (for example, Hank lashed out a group member and called the member an idiot). As a result of this within-group focus, an evidence-based climate is again used to promote personal responsibility. Group discussion centers on differences and or similarities between self- and other feedback, exploring such differences and/or working together to come to an agreement with regard to the individual group member's progress. Together the group determines where on the scale the reporting client should strive to reach by next week and what strategies should be used. It is through this collaboration and a unified approach to treatment that the cohesion of the group begins to develop, as the "we-ness" of the group becomes reinforced.

As self-growth is viewed as a continuous process, once solutions are reached, new issues can be identified and the process can begin again.

Variation

Although the instructions and following vignette illustrate the use of this handout with individual group members, it can also be used with couple and family groups. Couples and family members should be encouraged to identify a presenting problem and solution together, scale their progress toward a solution, and provide supporting evidence of their progress. The use of the handout in couples and family therapy can be used to promote a systems perspective within the therapeutic environment by the identification of a shared problem/shared goal rather than focusing on an individual's problem or solution. While scaling the progress toward the solution, each family member is enlisted to reach the solution, promoting further familial alliance in problem solving, thus, strengthening the family unit. As with individual groups, other group members (if participating in multifamily group therapy) and the therapist, would be encouraged to provide feedback about the couple's or family's progress and help develop strategies for moving up the scale.

Brief Vignette

Gerri had initially identified her inability to accept help or support from others as an issue with which she was currently struggling. Gerri realized that she was in need of assistance for specific tasks; but she was often unable to ask for assistance. At times, however, the assistance that Gerri described was a need to talk to someone when she had a problem and "let it out" (in her words).

Gerri identified the behavior when the problem was at its worst as her sense of frustration and the feeling that she was stuck. As a result of this behavior, she became immobilized and unable to move forward; she was carrying her problem around as opposed to seeking the help needed. Gerri believed that she would know the problem no longer existed if she immediately sought help or support when she recognized that she was in need of such support. As a result, she would not spend time berating herself for not having accessed some other outlet. As she put it, she would quickly take care of herself first and then keep pressing forward.

During the fourth week of group, Gerri reported that she had not made any progress toward her solution. She had been struggling for the past five days over a conflict with her boss that she wanted to share with someone. While she recognized the extent to which the issue was on her mind and her desire to discuss it with a friend, she could not bring herself to do so. Group members were asked to assess where they thought Gerri was with regard to her work on this issue. Shaundrea stated that although Gerri did not take immediate action by discussing her problem with a friend, the fact that Gerri was able to present the issue to the group was indicative of Gerri's progress. Janet further stated that Gerri's statement to the group (earlier in the same session) that she was feeling overwhelmed with the demands of the group provided additional support for her progress toward seeking support when needed.

As a result of the continued group discussion, Gerri was able to reconsider and revise her initial self-assessment that she had not made progress toward her goals. The group worked together to identify Gerri's next weekly goal and the supporting evidence that would show she was meeting this goal. Using the momentum created by the group, Gerri was encouraged to take the same risk outside that she had been able to demonstrate within the group, to achieve support when needed.

Suggestions for Follow-Up

This exercise is designed to teach self-management skills and to emphasize the importance of checking-in with others to determine if one's self-analysis is consistent with the evaluation of others. By introducing the tool within the context of group, clients are able to self-determine their abilities and systematically work toward desired solutions. In the spirit of both solution-focused theory and behavior therapy, independent continuous use of the tool both inside and outside of the group, as a means to engaging in further self-directed growth, is encouraged.

Contraindications

While the use of brief-oriented therapeutic exercises may be attractive due to their alignment with outcomes-driven practice, it is imperative that the development and nurturing of the therapeutic relationship remain at the center of the group therapist's efforts. The therapeutic relationship is no less critical to solution-focused therapy as to other therapeutic approaches as positive treatment outcomes have been found to correspond to the powerful working alliance formed between the client and therapist in solution-focused work (McKeel, 1996). Along these same lines, brief-oriented tools should only be used in conjunction with a supporting solution-oriented conceptual framework built on the promotion of trust and mutuality in the therapeutic relationship, and self-directedness as a means to achieving success. As this group exercise is dependent on problems largely being interpersonal in nature, thus, taking advantage of the social microcosm created by the group process (Yalom, 1995), the exercise lends itself best to groups formed around interpersonal challenges. Finally, the exercise is not recommended for individuals unable to engage in self-directed work.

Readings and Resources for the Professional

Bohart, A. C., & Tallman, K. (1999). *How clients make therapy work: The process of active self-healing.* Washington DC: American Psychological Association.

de Shazer, S. (1985). *Keys to solutions in brief therapy.* New York: W. W. Norton & Co.

de Shazer, S. (1988). *Clues: Investigating solutions in brief therapy.* New York: W. W. Norton & Co.

Miller, S. D., Hubble, M. A., & Duncan, B. L. (Eds.). (1996). *Handbook of solution-focused brief therapy* (pp. 251-271). San Francisco: Jossey-Bass.

O'Hanlon, W. H. (1999). *Do one thing different.* New York: Harper-Collins.

O'Hanlon, W. H., & Weiner-Davis, M. (1989). *In search of solutions: A new direction in psychotherapy.* New York: W. W. Norton & Co.

Walter, J. L., & Peller, J. E. (1992). *Becoming solution-focused in brief therapy.* New York: Brunner/Mazel.

Yalom, I. D. (1995). *The theory and practice of group psychotherapy* (4th ed.). New York: Basic Books.

Bibliotherapy Source for the Client

Watson, D. L., & Tharp, R. G. (1993). *Self-directed behavior: Self-modification for personal adjustment.* Pacific Grove, CA: Brooks/Cole.

References

Bloch, S., & Crouch, E. (1985). *Therapeutic factors in group psychotherapy.* New York: Oxford University Press.

de Shazer, S. (1985). *Keys to solutions in brief therapy.* New York: W. W. Norton & Co.

de Shazer, S. (1988). *Clues: Investigating solutions in brief therapy.* New York: W. W. Norton & Co.

McKeel, A. J. (1996). A clinician's guide to research on solution-focused brief therapy. In S. D. Miller, M. A. Hubble, & B. L. Duncan (Eds.), *Handbook of solution-focused brief therapy* (pp. 251-271). San Francisco: Jossey-Bass.

O'Hanlon, W. H., & Weiner-Davis, M. (1989). *In search of solutions: A new direction in psychotherapy.* New York: W. W. Norton & Co.

Spiegler, M. D., & Guevremont, D. C. (1998). *Contemporary behavior therapy* (3rd ed.). Pacific Grove, CA: Brooks/Cole.

Walter, J. L., & Peller, J. E. (1992). *Becoming solution-focused in brief therapy.* New York: Brunner/Mazel.

Yalom, I. D. (1995). *The theory and practice of group psychotherapy* (4th ed.). New York: Basic Books.

HANDOUT 10.1. SCALING EXERCISE

Identify a current issue with which you are faced and which you would like to see changed.

_____

In behavioral terms identify what would be happening when the problem is at its worse (1) and state what would be happening when you know you have reached your solution (10). Identify various other points on the scale as desired.

1. _____
2. _____
3. _____
4. _____
5. _____
6. _____
7. _____
8. _____
9. _____
10. _____

Circle where you are currently in relation to the problem and provide evidence on the space provided below.

    1   2   3   4   5   6   7   8   9   10

Evidence: _____

Circle where you would like to be within one week and state what will be happening to inform you that you reached your goal.
(1 = problem at its worse; 10 = reached solution)

    1   2   3   4   5   6   7   8   9   10

Evidence: _____

Using behavioral terms, identify the strategy(ies) that you will use to achieve your goal.

_____

_____

_____

Calley. N G. (2007). Behavioral scaling as a group-guided approach to self-management. In D. R. Viers (Ed.), *The group therapist's notebook: Homework, handouts, and activities for use in psychotherapy* (pp. 59-66). Binghamton. NY: The Haworth Press.

HANDOUT 10.2. SCALING EXERCISE SAMPLE FOR "PAUL"

Identify a current issue with which you are faced and which you would like to see changed.

Procrastination, never finishing my homework

In behavioral terms identify what would be happening when the problem is at its worse (1) and state what would be happening when you know you have reached your solution (10). Identify various other points on the scale as desired.

1. Failing grades for not doing homework
2. Grounded because of grades
3. _____
4. _____
5. _____
6. _____
7. _____
8. Being in control
9. Completing all homework
10. Feeling good about school

Circle where you are currently in relation to the problem and provide evidence on the space provided below.

1   2   ③   4   5   6   7   8   9   10

Evidence: Was with friends, did not do two out of three assignments, coach is going to bench me from game if I don't do my homework

Circle where you would like to be within one week and state what will be happening to inform you that you reached your goal.
(1 = problem at its worse; 10 = reached solution)

1   2   3   4   ⑤   6   7   8   9   10

Evidence: Doing my homework, feeling more informed in class

Using behavioral terms, identify the strategy(ies) that you will use to achieve your goal.

Will do my homework after dinner before I do anything else

Will ask my brother to make sure I finish my homework

Calley, N G. (2007). Behavioral scaling as a group-guided approach to self-management. In D. R. Viers (Ed.), *The group therapist's notebook: Homework, handouts, and activities for use in psychotherapy* (pp. 59-66). Binghamton, NY: The Haworth Press.

11

Activities for Termination

Randyl D. Smith
Maria T. Riva
Jeffrey A. Rings

From the end spring new beginnings.

Pliny the Elder, 50 AD

Type of Contribution: Activities/Handout

Objective

The goals of termination activities for group members include the successful transition to life without the group, careful consideration of how group members will continue to take the gains made within the group and apply them to other areas of their lives, and management of appropriate and complete good-byes. Because the end stage of a group can generate intense and conflicting emotions, it is important for group leaders to structure terminations according to the type of group and the characteristics of members within the group. This chapter will address strategies and techniques that can increase the effectiveness of this stage.

Rationale for Use

Termination is not just a final session of a group; rather, it is the final stage in the development of the group. As a stage, termination is both unavoidable and potentially very powerful, yet it has been underemphasized in both theory and research literature. Corey and Corey (2001) state that termination gives group members an opportunity to review and clarify their experience in the group, to discuss what they have accomplished, and to decide how they will generalize and continue their progress after the group has ended. Of course, termination will depend on the type of group (e.g., support group, theme centered, or inpatient), the length of time the group has met, the cohesiveness of the group, and the age of the group members, to name just a few considerations. The purpose of this chapter is to discuss the impact of a planned termination on group members, outline the goals of this stage, and describe some specific techniques that group leaders may find helpful in consolidating what has occurred during the group counseling process.

In time-limited groups, the process of termination begins, in some sense, at the outset of group. Because, in most cases, the number of sessions in a group is predetermined, there is always a defined framework. This allows the group leader to use time purposefully, to examine group progress in terms of how much time has elapsed and how much time remains, and to pace the therapeutic processes according to a predefined timetable (MacKenzie, 1997). The concept of time and the approaching ending must be raised continuously by the leader as the group progresses, so that members are aware of the finality of group and can begin to prepare for the inevitable ending.

The process of termination is accompanied by many emotions, not only for group members but also for group leaders. Group members often feel ambivalent about ending group counseling. Some will indicate their concern about ending group sessions by what they say. "How will I make it without the support of the group?" or "I have a new concern that I have not had the chance to discuss in group," are common statements members make toward the end of group. Some may indicate how difficult ending counseling is by what they *do not* say, such as "I'm really fine about leaving group. I don't really have any feelings about it at all." Others may demonstrate their discomfort by getting angry at other members or at leaders to make it easier to leave the group, by disengaging from any meaningful work in group, or by disappearing from group altogether.

As termination approaches, the group leader needs to be alert for termination anxiety. Corey (2004) states that during the final phase of group treatment, members may feel anxiety over the reality of separation. This view is supported by at least one research study that found that even in successful groups, members showed an increase in anxiety levels during the termination stage (Kacen, 1999). It seems reasonable then that one goal for termination would be to address and normalize this anxiety, along with helping group members gain confidence in their newly obtained skills.

Group leaders need to acknowledge, and even predict, that some members may find it easier to leave group before the scheduled ending. Group members may plead for more time or drop the proverbial "bomb" of explosive new information in an effort to extend the group. By addressing feelings of disappointment (for example, members' feelings that not enough time is available or not enough attention was given to particular issues) the group leader can help reduce anxiety and contribute to members' understanding of their own reactions.

Endings can also raise intense feelings for group leaders, who may experience a mixture of sadness at the loss of the group, guilt that not enough has been accomplished, relief that the hard work is over, and/or joy at the strides made by group members. It is not uncommon for group leaders, like group members, to resist termination. Some leaders may feel compelled to extend the final group date, while others may forget to address the approaching ending. Although it may be tempting to extend the number of group sessions, leaders must carefully weigh the benefits and drawbacks of this strategy. In fact, it may be much more important for members to experience a healthy ending, since it is an opportunity to say good-bye without feeling abandoned. A vital role of the leader is to acknowledge, accept, encourage, and explore these feelings and contribute to a healthy and positive termination.

In addition to positive feedback, review, and application of changes to everyday life, group leaders can facilitate a healthy termination process by modeling skills that bring about closure (Gladding, 2003). Included here are actual good-byes that may be done on the group level (for example, with a closing sentiment about the group as a whole or the use of a metaphor such as weather conditions to describe the group's involvement or movement over the course of the sessions) or on the individual level (such as a handshake or a farewell message to each individual). Regardless of the choice of good-bye behavior, leaders need to be able to model endings that are positive, genuine, and complete. For many members, this may be the first such experience.

Instructions

Preparing for Termination

Because of the complicated feelings often associated with terminations, it is important for group leaders to put careful thought and effort into planning the ending stage of a group. Group termination requires more than a cursory handshake or a fleeting "good-bye and good luck!" There are important goals and tasks that must be addressed to facilitate a productive termination. These tasks will vary depending on the characteristics of the particular group and even the characteristics of particular members within a group. Jacobs, Masson, and Harvill (2002) suggest that termination work focus on assisting members to

- Assess their growth and change,
- Review and summarize the group experience,
- Provide feedback to one another,
- Apply change to everyday life outside of the group,
- Plan for continued problem resolution, and
- Manage good-byes.

In addition, group leaders may want to facilitate discussions or activities that encourage members to

- Reflect on the meaningfulness of relationships that have developed and
- Acknowledge feelings related to loss of the group as a continuing source of structure, support, and guidance.

Though the primary responsibility for encouraging the group to address termination goals falls on the group leaders, it is sometimes valuable to elicit ideas and activities from group members. While group members do not generally make decisions regarding *when* to terminate, it may be extremely helpful for members to invest in the process of *how* to terminate. Reflecting on the development and accomplishments of the group must be a conscious and planned process but need not be planned without the input of group members.

It is often helpful to ask members to talk about how they see themselves as having grown or changed as a result of the group. Revisiting the goals that were set by members at the start of the group will allow them to more realistically discuss their progress. While it is important for members to recognize gains in their own behavior, it is also of tremendous value for them to acknowledge the progress of others. Exchanging feedback about other group members can generate a lively and sometimes surprising discussion, filled with comments like, "I remember when you wouldn't even talk in group...," "Before I got to know you, I used to think you were such a know-it-all...," and so forth. A group feedback session, then, allows members, as well as leaders, to comment on the growth and change they have observed in others and to hear what others have observed in them. This can be a very powerful group phenomenon and a valuable consolidation of individual learning. One cautionary note is that group leaders need to be purposeful as to the type of feedback given to individual members. Depending on the group composition, it may even be prudent for leaders to avoid engaging in specific comments to each member, since that may invite unnecessary social comparisons by the members (MacKenzie, 1997). In such cases, general supportive comments, such as letting others in the group know how their involvement was valued and reviews of group process as a whole, are meaningful methods of closure.

Corey (2004) states that one group leadership skill that is especially important is "the capacity to assist members in transferring what they have learned in the group to their outside environments" (p. 119). Likewise, Yalom (1995) describes the need for the "adaptive spiral," which refers to how changes that occur within the group spiral out to members' lives away from the group (that is, in the family, at work, in school). Acknowledging the ways that group members plan to generalize their newfound group skills to their everyday lives is an important discussion for the final sessions. This discussion provides a bridge that extends within-group changes to a much larger context, and group members can see that, even though the group is coming to an end, the gains made in group can and should continue.

Termination can raise a multitude of reactions. Feelings of accomplishment and pride at termination may be accompanied by fear and dejection. Members often imagine that they will never again find such a trusting environment or such supportive company. It is often helpful to remind the group that trust and support were established through their own hard work and commitment, and that these same factors work on the outside, as well. The termination process itself can be used as yet another example of how change in group can be applied to everyday life, as members are, in effect, practicing ending relationships in a thoughtful, caring, mature, and open way. The group leaders can help members recognize that the skills and attitudes they have acquired in the group will serve them well as they form new relationships and take on new roles in life.

Evaluation of the Group

Written evaluations are becoming more common. Instead of bemoaning their invasion into the therapeutic process, we may want to think about them as a sort of ritual of termination, the way that intake forms are a sort of ritual of beginnings in treatment (Gutheil, 1993). If we recognize the value of written evaluations in termination, we can make deliberate and meaningful use of them, so that they enhance rather than detract from the termination process. Asking group members for formalized feedback about the group experience is not just a means of collecting useful data for implementation in future groups. It is also a means for encouraging immediate reflection, which may enable the group members to engage more readily in a discussion of highs and lows of group, the gains they have made, and what it was like to participate in the group process. If the treatment site or agency does not have a required form, group leaders can create their own or use the Group Evaluation Form (Handout 11.1) included at the end of this chapter. Because members have become adept, by this point, at working together, the evaluation can be facilitated as a group activity. Following are some useful and thought-generating questions:

- What did you find most helpful about this group?
- What did you find least helpful?
- If you were able to change one thing about the group, what would you have changed?
- What is one event or discussion that will stick with you after the group has ended?

This last question often leads to a review of critical incidents in the life of the group and may result in laughter and/or tears as members recount the most powerful or memorable moments of their group involvement.

Termination Activities

The final session of a group calls for a fair amount of structure. The exact nature of that structure is best determined by recognizing the needs and characteristics of both the group as a whole and the members in it. Because of the variability in group needs, capacities, and desires related to termination, several activities are offered. They can be used individually or in combination, and with creativity on the part of the leader and group members, each option has many variations.

My greatest hope/greatest fear for you is . . . Members take turns saying what they hope and fear for the others in the group. Rather than focusing on the past and what has transpired during the weeks, months, or years in the life of the group, this exercise encourages members to think about the future, which can be instrumental in translating within-group change to real-life change. It is a good exercise to use to avoid strictly positive and artificially optimistic feedback, since it requires members to address their doubts and concerns as well (Corey & Corey, 2001). Typically, members find it easy to provide feedback to one another that sounds like, "You've come a long way, baby," but more challenging to provide take-home messages about continued work and growth.

This exercise can produce statements like, "My greatest hope for you is not that you'll find Mr. Right, but that you'll remember that you don't need Mr. Right to be whole" or "My greatest fear for you is that, without the regular support of this group, you'll begin relying on alcohol again in social situations." Such comments suggest the need for ongoing mindfulness so that members can retain the gains they have made in group. This exercise also leads naturally to a discussion about how members can take the group with them by encouraging members to imagine what other group members would say when they engage in a certain behavior.

Reunion Fantasy. It is not uncommon, during the termination stage of a group, for members to plan reunions, exchange telephone numbers and e-mail addresses, or schedule dates for future get-togethers. Group leaders cannot restrict the autonomous plans of the group but can be helpful in getting members to think about the pros and cons of such reunions. Members need to see past the illusion that the group will go on as it has been and get back to the important focus of termination.

One way to do this is to recognize the wish for a reunion and to put that wish to good use in a reunion fantasy. The group leader can remind the members that termination is unavoidable and that the group as they know it is ending. However, through the reunion fantasy, each member is asked to project five years into the future, imagining what he or she will tell the other members about his or her life and the achievements made since group ended (Jacobs et al., 2002). This is a thought-provoking exercise that, like "My greatest wish/greatest fear for you is . . . ," focuses on the future and how new skills learned in group might impact it.

Rituals, Graduations, Celebrations. Rituals can enhance the termination process, especially for children and adolescents. Tokens or keepsakes of the group experience, such as a photograph of group members or a certificate of progress, can be given to each member. As members receive their tokens, they tell the others what they will remember most about being a part of the group. Sometimes, a graduation ceremony or party is appropriate and will reinforce for members that they have progressed and grown as a result of the group experience. Celebrations serve as a transition to the less-structured social interactions of life outside the group and bring the group to a ceremonial, festive ending.

Brief Vignette

A twenty-week process group with a focus on relationship issues was nearing its final session. The group leaders asked the seven members, all women in their twenties, for their input about how to end the group. As is often the case, the members jumped on the idea of a party. When they were asked, however, to think about whether there were feelings other than joy about their accomplishments that might also need to be addressed, several of the members acknowledged sadness, anxiety, and a sense of looming loss. One of the group leaders suggested that, while a party would be fun, maybe there was something more lasting than a piece of cake that could be given, shared, and taken away from the final group. The members agreed on a need to summarize, to wrap up the gifts of their interactions with one another. The leader provided several options or strategies for doing so and the group chose the "My greatest hope/greatest fear for you is ..." exercise. The members had a week to think about what they might say to one another, which contributed to the meaningfulness and depth of their statements.

The parting gifts that the women gave to each other were words that may stay with them for years and years. Most were upbeat and optimistic, such as the message to a group member who had become aware, with the group's help, of an uncomfortable shift in her identity as a result of a major knee surgery in college: "My greatest hope for you is that, even though you can't be a gymnast anymore, you'll be able to see yourself as strong and beautiful." Some messages were more pointed and challenging, as in the case of a statement to Lisa, who had expressed, early in the life of the group, her (unreciprocated) attraction toward another member. "My greatest hope for you," Lisa was told, "is that you'll be able to see people for who they *are* and not who they could be to *you*." This seeming indictment of Lisa's interpersonal relations, done in the context of a very cohesive group, was a reiteration of some revelations that had previously been made in the group. This statement was then followed with, "My greatest fear is that you'll be so afraid of repeating some of your patterns with people that you won't give others a chance to know you like we've all gotten to know you."

Another member, who had stayed largely on the periphery of the group's interactions, came to the final session with notes, precisely folded and tied with a tiny ribbon, for each of the other members. On each folded piece of paper was her "My greatest hope/greatest fear for you is …" comment, which she shared orally as well. When asked about the notes, she said, "I wanted to give you something tangible, something you could hold on to, since you've all given me so much." Though the final group session did involve cake and a celebratory atmosphere, it went far beyond what might be expected of a farewell party.

Suggestions for Follow-Up

The termination considerations and activities described in this chapter are meant as ways to end the group. In most situations, follow-up is not necessary, practical, or even appropriate. Yet there are occasions when a group leader, particularly one who is behaviorally oriented, may schedule follow-up meetings. These meetings can serve both as booster sessions to address inevitable setbacks that members may experience and as opportunities for members to share how they have maintained changes and experienced success after the group's termination (Corey, 2004). While occasional future group sessions may encourage some accountability in members and provide positive reinforcement to continue the work begun in group, the benefits of follow-up meetings must be weighed against the potential for scheduled get-togethers to undermine the process of termination.

Another important aspect of follow-up is the group leader's incorporation of the written and verbal feedback gleaned during termination. Whether or not group members completed a formal evaluation, the leader should be mindful of the feedback received and consider modifying, intensifying, or otherwise adjusting therapeutic practices when structuring the next group.

Contraindications

The options outlined in this chapter are meant neither as a conclusive list nor as a prescribed formula. They are ideas to be mixed and matched and used in accordance with the needs of the group and the personal preference, style, and comfort of the group leaders. While group termination should not be about giving everyone a pat on the back, the ideal termination will avoid reopening old wounds or creating new ones. No activities should be done without careful thought as to organization and cohesiveness of the group, the potential risks and benefits to its members, and the time required during and after the activity for the group to process.

Readings and Resources for the Professional

Brabender, V., & Fallon, A. (1995). Termination in inpatient groups. *International Journal of Group Psychotherapy, 46,* 81-98.

Ross, S. (1991). The termination phase in groupwork: Tasks for the groupworker. *Groupwork, 4*(1), 57-70.

Shapiro, E. L., & Ginzberg, R. (2002). Parting gifts: Termination rituals in group therapy. *International Journal of Group Psychotherapy, 52*, 319-336.

References

Corey, G. (2004). *Theory and practice of group counseling* (6th ed.). Belmont, CA: Brooks/Cole.

Corey, M. S., & Corey, G. (2001). *Groups: Process and practice* (6th ed.). Florence, KY: Wadsworth Publishing.

Gladding, S. T. (2003). *Group Work: A counseling specialty* (4th ed.). New Jersey: Prentice Hall.

Gutheil, I. A. (1993). Rituals and termination procedures. *Smith College studies in social work, 63*(2), 163-176.

Jacobs, E. E., Masson, R. L., & Harvill, R. L. (2002). *Group counseling: Strategies and skills* (4th ed.). Pacific Grove, CA: Brooks/Cole.

Kacen, L. (1999). Anxiety levels, group characteristics, and members' behaviors in the termination stage of support groups for patients recovering from heart attacks. *Research on Social Work Practice, 9*, 656-672.

MacKenzie, K. R. (1997). *Time-managed group psychotherapy: Effective clinical applications.* Washington, DC: American Psychiatric Press, Inc.

Yalom, I. (1995). *The theory and practice of group psychotherapy* (4th ed.). New York: Basic Books.

HANDOUT 11.1.
GROUP EVALUATION FORM

I joined this group because _____

_____

_____

_____

One thing that surprised me about being in a group was _____

_____

_____

_____

What I found most helpful about this group was _____

_____

_____

_____

What I found least helpful about this group was _____

_____

_____

_____

If I could have changed one thing about the group, it would be _____

_____

_____

_____

One event or discussion that I will remember from this group was _____

_____

_____

_____

Other comments: _____

_____

_____

_____

Smith, R. D., Riva, M. T., & Rings, J. A. (2007). Activities for termination. In D. R. Viers (Ed.), *The group therapist's notebook: Homework, handouts, and activities for use in psychotherapy* (pp. 67-74). Binghamton, NY: The Haworth Press.

SECTION III:
INTERVENTIONS
FOR POPULATION-SPECIFIC
GROUPS

12

Nine Steps to Anger Management

Floyd F. Robison

Type of Contribution: Handout/Homework/Activity

Objective

This handout (Handout 12.1) applies cognitive-behavior modification principles to assist persons in managing their anger more successfully over a short treatment period. It is appropriate for groups of individuals, couples, and families. The brevity of the handout makes it particularly suitable for use with group members who would benefit from an anger management intervention during groups that are not conducted specifically for that purpose.

Rationale for Use

The handout is grounded in cognitive-behavioral theories (Beck, 1976, 1999; Meichenbaum, 1995), which posits that persons behave according to messages they tell themselves in particular situations. This is also called self-talk (Nisbett & Wilson, 1977). From this perspective, persons who do not manage their anger appropriately tend to engage in negative self-talk through which they tell themselves in various ways that they are being attacked and must act aggressively to stop it (Beck, 1976). In daily life, angry thoughts include self-talk such as, "He's trying to take advantage of me; nobody does that to me and gets away with it" or "Any woman who would spend money as she does is a stupid bitch! I work hard for a living, and I won't stand for my money to be spent like that!" If people successfully identify angry thoughts and consistently change them to self-statements that do not construe the situation as a personal attack, then they can apply behaviors that enable them to manage their angry feelings and change their behavior to be consistent with their new thoughts.

The group activity described is grounded in Beck's (1976, 1999) proposed relationships between cognitions and behaviors, that is, persons change their behavior when they change their thoughts about the situation. Through the activity, persons effect behavior change when they engage in the following process:

1. Identify cognitions (self-talk) that maintain undesired behaviors.
2. Create new self-talk, that would enable them to behave differently.
3. Identify and learn new behavior consistent with their new self-talk.
4. Stop their old self-talk when it occurs, replace it with their new self-talk, and use the behavior they have committed to in combination with their new self-talk.

In addition, this program includes a preliminary step that assists participants in identifying physical cues (such as chest tightness, flushing, and dizziness) of escalating anger. Awareness of these cues often assists angry persons in recognizing more quickly that they are becoming angry and need to act in order to manage it (Meichenbaum, 1995). Variations of this approach have been described by several writers (see, for example, Hershorn, 2002).

Instructions

The anger management program described in the handout consists of nine steps. At the first meeting during which the program will be conducted, the facilitator distributes the handout, in its entirety, to the participants. As the group progresses through each step in the program, participants individually complete the section of the handout relevant to that step then discuss their responses with the group in order to receive feedback and support. Participants are also asked to take the handout with them after each meeting, in order to reflect further on their responses and apply changes to their self-talk and behavior in anger-evoking situations that may arise between meetings. Thus, the handout serves as both as a series of structured activities during group meetings and a series of homework assignments between meetings.

To begin the anger management program, the group facilitator distributes the handout and gives the following instructions:

> In this program, you will learn a nine-step process to (a) identify the cues that let you know when you are becoming angry, (b) identify your angry attitudes and angry self-talk, (c) decide how you will talk to yourself in ways that allow you to control your anger, and (d) take action in ways that are not aggressive.
>
> The entire anger management process includes nine steps. The first four steps involve learning what you do when you are angry and creating new thoughts and behaviors to enable you to manage your anger. The remaining five steps of the process are action steps. They enable you to actually stop your angry self-talk before you lose control and apply your new thinking and behavior in a situation where you have become angry. This procedure is called SWaTAT (Stop, Walk, Think, Access, Talk). The steps are as follows:

1. Learning your physical anger cues
2. Identifying your angry attitudes, angry self-talk, and angry behaviors
3. Creating new angry self-talk and behavior
4. Decide to act
5. Stop what you are doing and saying
6. Walk away from the situation
7. Think about what to do
8. Access a designated friend
9. Come back and talk it out

Instructions for completing each of the steps are printed in the handout. Step 1 through Step 4 may be conducted in a single meeting or extended over several meetings, according to participants' success in completing each step. Step 5 through Step 9 (the actual anger control process) is typically covered in a single meeting. Beginning with Step 5, participants are asked to maintain a journal or diary that describes their behavior in anger-provoking situations and includes:

1. the circumstances of the situation during which they felt angry,
2. their anger cues and angry self-talk,
3. the manner in which they implemented Step 5 through Step 9 of the SWaTAT model,
4. the outcome of the situation, and
5. their evaluations their responses (what worked and what did not work).

Participants are asked to bring the handout and their journals with them to each meeting, in order to discuss their successes and problems in using the steps. When necessary, participants may review the outcomes of their work on the first four steps if they find themselves partially or completely unsuccessful in managing their anger outside the group using the latter five steps.

When working through each step in the process, the facilitator encourages the exchange of feedback with the group in order to help members clarify their thinking and accompanying behaviors in situations during which they become angry and fail to manage it appropriately. The group format is particularly useful for this activity in several ways. First, members can assist one another in clarifying their recall and interpretation of recent situations during which they became angry. This feedback can help recipients better grasp the nature of the events that led to their angry reactions and to clarify the content of their thoughts. Second, as a social microcosm, the group can serve as a setting where participants may actually become angry, engage the anger management process, and receive immediate feedback from the group. Third, participants who are denying their anger management problems may benefit from the consistent and direct confrontation of their denial that a group can provide.

Brief Vignette

Paul was an electrician who joined the group for help in managing his short fuse. He told the group that, for the past several days, he had been wiring a house under construction in a local neighborhood. The job was complicated, and he had spent many hours running cable, wiring the circuit breaker box, and checking connections. He was almost finished and was relieved because he had to move on to another house very soon in order to meet his commitments. This morning, however, the construction manager told Paul that the homeowner wanted some changes in the wiring. These changes required Paul to redo a substantial amount of the work he had done for the past few days and required him to delay the start of his next job. The construction manager insisted that the changes must be made. Paul went off on the manager, calling him names and throwing a screwdriver, burying it in a nearby wall. He then walked off the job site. The manager called him later that day to tell him that he had until "quitting time tomorrow" to make the changes and repair the wall he had damaged or, "you can pick up your check in the morning and be out of here."

Paul returned a few hours later and made the repairs. He told the group, "If the manager had still been on site, I might have decked him." This was the latest of several outbursts Paul had made in response to requests that he make adjustments to his work. He admitted to the group that, although he felt some pressure because another job was to start the next day, he had gone off on supervisors and co-workers in other situations when he had been criticized about his work but was under no particular time pressure.

Using a role-play of this situation during the first meeting, the group helped Paul identify and write in his handout (Step 1) the physical cues he experienced when he was becoming angry. Those cues included tightness in his chest and flushing in his cheeks. With their encouragement, he also was able to verbalize and write in his handout (Step 2) his self-talk during this situation, as follows, "I've been an electrician for nineteen years and my work is second to none. The homeowner is questioning my work, saying it's no good, eh? And the manager is agreeing with him. Why doesn't he just say I can't wire these circuits? Well, no one slams my work and gets off free with it!" Feedback from the group helped Paul understand that, with these kinds of thoughts, he would be likely to go into a rage in response to the site manager's feedback.

Paul then wrote his angry behaviors on his handout (Step 2). He agreed to reconsider what he told himself when he was asked to correct or modify his work. After some reflection during the following week, he decided that better self-talk would be, "Hold on now, the boss isn't getting on me. He has to please the homeowners. It's the homeowners' house and they sometimes change their minds about how they want things done." He had written these thoughts on his handout (Step 3) prior to the second group meeting. During the second meeting, he decided that the appropriate behavior to accompany these new thoughts would be to either agree to redo aspects of the job or, if time was limited, to negotiate either modifications that could be accomplished in his available time or a revised timeline for completing the work at the next job site. He made a commitment to the group to attempt to apply his new thoughts and behavior the next time he encountered a situation in which he became angry and further documented his decision to act by circling YES on his handout (Step 4). At this point, the facilitator reviewed Step 5 through Step 8 of the anger management process with the group and illustrated their application in a role-play. In the role-play a participant acted out the part of an angry person who used the steps to avoid behaving aggressively toward a store clerk who did not have an item in stock that the participant badly needed. Paul also agreed to keep a journal of any situation that evoked anger in him during the following week in order to review with the group the outcomes of his anger management efforts.

The following week, Paul informed the group that he had been asked to modify work by the manager at another site where he had been working. He reported that he had felt his cheeks flush and realized he was beginning to lose his temper. He was able to pinch himself on the left wrist, as he had agreed to do in an earlier group session, then simply said "okay" to his boss and quickly walked to another location on the job site. He walked around the site for ten minutes, reading from an index card the self-talk he had developed during the earlier group meeting. Then, he called a colleague on his cell phone and talked with him for a few minutes about his situation. The colleague reassured Paul that his positive self-talk was accurate. He was able to return to his work area and inform his boss that the job modifications could be completed by noon the next day, a timeline the manager agreed to. The group provided support and reinforced Paul's success in using the anger management process.

Suggestions for Follow-Up

After participants have learned the nine anger management steps, they will need time outside the group to try out their newly developed thoughts and behaviors. Different participants will require different amounts of practice to master their anger. The progress of individual participants in being able to successfully use the steps should be reviewed during several subsequent group meetings.

Contraindications

This activity is based on an assumption that participants are not managing anger due primarily to a lack of awareness of anger cues and thoughts and inadequate knowledge on managing it. Clinical experience has revealed that the activity should not be used as the sole treatment strategy for anger management with group members who present one or more of the following conditions:

1. neurological disorders that may contribute to ineffective anger management, such as seizure disorders or neurological trauma due to head injury
2. schizophrenia and other psychotic disorders
3. intermittent explosive disorder, moderate and severe bipolar disorders, and PTSD
4. Cluster A (paranoid, schizotypal, schizoid) and Cluster B (antisocial, narcissistic, histrionic, borderline) personality disorders
5. certain pervasive developmental disorders, such as autistic disorder and Asperger's disorder
6. mental retardation

These persons require more extensive medical, socialization, and psychotherapy services, of which this activity may be one component.

Reading and Resource for the Professional

Kassinove, H., & Tafrate, R. C. (2002). *Anger management: The complete treatment guidebook for practitioners.* Atascadero, CA: Impact Publishers.

Bibliotherapy Resource for the Client

Hershorn, M. (2002). *Sixty second anger management: Quick tips to handle explosive feelings.* Far Hills, NJ: New Horizon Press.

References

Beck, A. T. (1976). *Cognitive therapy and the emotional disorders.* Boston: International Universities Press.

Beck, A. T. (1999). *Prisoners of hate: The cognitive basis of anger, hostility, and violence.* New York: HarperCollins Publishers.

Hershorn, M. (2002). *Sixty second anger management: Quick tips to handle explosive feelings.* Far Hills, NJ: New Horizon Press.

Meichenbaum, D. (1995). Changing conceptions of cognitive-behavior modification: Retrospect and prospect. In M. J. Mahoney (Ed.), *Cognitive and constructive therapies: Theory, research, and practice* (pp. 200-238). New York: Springer.

Nisbett, R. E., & Wilson, T. D. (1977). Telling more than we can know: Verbal reports on mental processes. *Psychological Review, 84,* 231-259.

HANDOUT 12.1. NINE STEPS TO ANGER MANAGMENT

STEP 1: LEARNING YOUR PHYSICAL ANGER CUES

What kinds of physical feelings (e.g., tightness in chest, lump in throat, hot flashes) do you feel as you become angry? How do those sensations change as you get more angry? As you get uncontrollably angry?

Try to recall the feelings you had the last time you became angry. Write them below. You will use them as cues that you're becoming angry and to know when to go to the next step in the program.

_____

_____

_____

_____

_____

_____

_____

_____

_____

Robison, F. F. (2007). Nine steps to anger management. In D. R. Viers (Ed.), *The group therapist's notebook: Homework, handouts, and activities for use in psychotherapy* (pp. 77-86). Binghamton, NY: The Haworth Press.

STEP 2: IDENTIFYING YOUR ANGRY ATTITUDES, ANGRY SELF-TALK, AND ANGRY BEHAVIORS

Determine what you are telling yourself that is making you uncontrollably angry in situations where you lose control. Bring to mind one or two recent (within the past two weeks) situations where you exhibited poor management of your anger. Write them below—be specific:

_____

_____

_____

_____

Next, use the lines below to write down what you did after you had the angry self-talk you recalled above. Again, be specific!

_____

_____

_____

_____

Robison, F. F. (2007). Nine steps to anger management. In D. R. Viers (Ed.), *The group therapist's notebook: Homework, handouts, and activities for use in psychotherapy* (pp. 77-86). Binghamton, NY: The Haworth Press.

STEP 3: CREATING NEW ANGRY SELF-TALK AND BEHAVIOR

Now think about what you could have said to yourself instead that would have led to your remaining in control in each of those situations. These alternate thoughts cast the situation in a more positive way. Please write down your alternate, more positive thoughts on the lines below.

_____

_____

_____

_____

Now, think of the action or actions you would take if you told yourself the things you have written above, rather than what you usually tell yourself.

_____

_____

_____

_____

Robison, F. F. (2007). Nine steps to anger management. In D. R. Viers (Ed.), *The group therapist's notebook: Homework, handouts, and activities for use in psychotherapy* (pp. 77-86). Binghamton, NY: The Haworth Press.

STEP 4: DECIDING TO ACT

Would you be willing to "force" yourself to think these new, alternate thoughts and use the new behaviors the next time you're angry at something or someone? (circle)

YES   NO

If your answer is yes, then write these alternate thoughts and behaviors on a 3 × 5 index card as soon as possible. Keep the card in your pocket, wallet, or other convenient place at all times. Refer to it at least five times throughout the day between rising and retiring, whether you are angry or not, but at least three times when you are not angry.

If your answer is no, you may stop here. This program will not work for you.

Robison, F. F. (2007). Nine steps to anger management. In D. R. Viers (Ed.), *The group therapist's notebook: Homework, handouts, and activities for use in psychotherapy* (pp. 77-86). Binghamton, NY: The Haworth Press.

USE THE FOLLOWING STEPS THE NEXT TIME YOU ARE ANGRY . . .

STEP 5: STOP WHAT YOU ARE DOING AND SAYING

Simply stop. If necessary, keep a rubber band on your wrist and snap it when you feel the physical sensations that let you know you're getting angry enough to lose control. Others, if they and you wish, can help you stop by providing you with a cue word, that is, a word or phrase (e.g., "you're losing it") that will remind you to stop.

STEP 6: WALK AWAY FROM THE SITUATION

Simply turn around without another word and leave the scene. You'll come back later to work things out. If someone, such as the person with whom you in conflict, tries to follow you, you must firmly but calmly tell that person that you need a few minutes to be alone. If they continue to follow or you simply cannot leave the situation completely, it is your responsibility to avoid going back to your usual way of thinking and behaving when you're angry. Proceed to Step 7 anyway.

When possible, it is very helpful to explain to persons with whom you are often angry that you are practicing an anger management program and describe the program's steps. Ask them to help you by allowing you to leave when you realize you are becoming angry. Explain to them that allowing you to work through your anger alone helps you select better ways to work out your conflict when you return. In fact, the person with whom you are in conflict may help you by reminding you to leave and work through the program if he or she realizes that you becoming angry before realize it!

If you need help talking to persons close to you about this program, your counselor will, with your written consent, be willing to discuss the program with them.

STEP 7: THINK ABOUT WHAT TO DO

Walk for a minimum of ten minutes. At first, do a slow burn, cuss under your breath, whatever. But walk it off. Then, as you walk, read the alternate thoughts you wrote on the index card in your pocket (it is in your pocket, isn't it?). Read them repeatedly and think about the commitment you made to follow them.

STEP 8: ACCESS A DESIGNATED FRIEND

Have in mind a friend who will talk with you during times when you are angry. After ten minutes, go to a phone and call that buddy. Talk to this person for a minimum of five minutes about anything the two of you wish. **Remember, no drinking or drugs during this time!**

STEP 9: COME BACK AND TALK IT OUT

When you think you are ready, return to the scene of your anger and try working things out, using your alternate thoughts about the situation (See Step 3).

Robison, F. F. (2007). Nine steps to anger management. In D. R. Viers (Ed.), *The group therapist's notebook: Homework, handouts, and activities for use in psychotherapy* (pp. 77-86). Binghamton, NY: The Haworth Press.

13

A Little Worn and Wrinkled, but Still Valuable

Susan A. Adams

Type of Contribution: Activity/Homework

Objective

The goal of this activity is to help clients recognize that they have an intrinsic value no matter what life circumstances they have been through. It is important that clients recognize that they have value. By using a single dollar bill, they can symbolically understand that although they can get "damaged," this does not change their worth as a person.

Rationale for Use

Adults who grow up in dysfunctional families incorporate a kaleidoscope of painful childhood memories into all their relationships. From birth, we have a need for a bonding relationship with others, and we need others to desire a relationship with us (Bowlby, 1969; Cassidy & Shaver, 1999; Karen, 1994). As infants, babies learn to monitor the voices and nonverbal interactions with their primary caregivers and feel shame when they displease them. Children develop the template for emotional connections with others, known as *interpersonal bridges* (Kaufman, 1992), based on initial interactions within the home. When these bridges are damaged and become bound to shame, then a negative pattern extends to other interactions as well.

Shame is one of the nine innate emotions and is universal across cultures and ethnicities (Kaufman, 1992). It is a valuable emotion and not damaging when it is ". . . temporary in length, moderate in intensity, and points people toward what they need to do in order to feel pride and wholeness" (Potter-Efron & Potter-Efron, 1999, p. 2). Potter-Efron and Potter-Efron (1999) and others (Bradshaw, 1988; Kaufman, 1992; Wilson, 1990) suggested that the primary origin of bridge-damaging binding shame comes from a deluge of internalized negative messages in the family of origin because children have limited capacities to interpret or refute faulting messages. "To live with shame is to feel alienated and defeated, never quite good enough to belong. And secretly we feel to blame. The deficiency lies within ourselves alone. Shame is without parallel a sickness of the soul" (Kaufman, p. 12).

Individuals internalize this sickness, often without others being aware of the process, until it becomes a basic cornerstone of their identity and they can "autonomously activate and experience shame in isolation" (Kaufman, 1992, p. 74). This creates a shame spiral that solidifies within the person's emerging identity. Kaufman further suggested this sets a process in motion that creates a downward spiral of shame and a "real likelihood of renewed or additional shame internalization emerges" (p. 115) which creates a debilitating overload of shame.

This overload of shame has been labeled *shame-based identity* by Potter-Efron and Potter-Efron (1989) and *shame bound* by Kaufman (1992). This overload of shame keeps people from liking themselves or making healthy connections with other people. Potter-Efron and Potter-Efron (1989) suggested that people who are shame based have at their inner core the "painful belief in one's basic defectiveness as a human being" (p. 2). Bradshaw (1988) argued that it is this shame overload (known as *toxic shame*) that binds us and "is the basis for both neurotic and character disordered syndromes of behavior" (p. 10).

According to Potter-Efron and Potter-Efron (1999), at the very core of this shame overload are three primary fears. The *fear of abandonment* is indicative of a break in the interpersonal bridge formed from birth when infants are totally dependent on others. The second is *fear of losing yourself,* which is about abandoning one's true self in order to conform or fit in with those around you. The third fear is the *fear of incompetence* and is quite common in the United States because we often measure worth by accomplishments. This fear surfaces because we want to avoid the shame of comparative failure.

Although shame and guilt may frequently be linked together or used interchangeably, McCullough, Pargament, and Thoresen (2000) and others (Potter-Efron & Potter-Efron, 1989; Tangney & Dearing, 2002) outlined distinct differences between them. Shame is about a person's being, shortcomings, and fear of abandonment. Guilty people focus on what they did, are more concerned about transgressions, and fear punishment. Potter-Efron and Potter-Efron (1989) argued that "shame can be more difficult to heal than guilt because it is about the person rather than specific actions" (p. 4).

As an emotion, shame is not bad. It raises our level of awareness, and a world without shame "can create wounds rather than heal them" (Brothers, 2005, p. 6). However, it is important to understand shame's significance in relationship to "self-esteem, identity, and intimacy; and exploring the varied phenomena of addiction, abuse, and so-called dysfunctional family systems" (Kaufman, 1992, p. x). There are many ways that a person attempts to cover this toxic or shame-based defect. There are socially destructive addictions (for example, alcoholism, physical and sexual abuse), socially unacceptable addictions (for example, eating disorders, relationship addictions), and socially acceptable addictions (for example, workaholism, perfectionism, excessive spending) that are used to cover up this sense of defectiveness (L'Abate, Farrar, & Serritella, 1992). There is an attempt to cover defectiveness because "if I tell you who I am, you may not like who I am, and it is all that I have" (Powell, 1998, p. 24). Therefore, a thousand fears keep people locked in the solitary confinement of silence, struggling with toxic shame. It is this type of shame that often brings clients into therapy. As a clinician, "I must try to hear what they are *not* saying, what they perhaps will never be able to say" (Powell, p. 99).

Transactional Analysis (TA) provides a theoretical perspective that illuminates this faulty shame spiral and empowers clients to alter this negative pattern. According to Berne (1964), everyone has three primary ego states: Child, Adult, and Parent. The Child ego state is the first to develop and is subdivided into the Adapted Child and the Natural or Free Child. The Adapted Child houses the rules learned as a child through initial interactions with the primary caregivers and is compliant. The Free Child is that spontaneous, fun-loving part of our identity that embraces life with impulsivity and little or no thought about the consequences of such behavior. The Adult ego state is not subdivided and functions without emotion. It simply processes data, tests reality, and mediates between the Parent and Child ego states. The Parent ego state is also composed of two subdivided ego states. The Nurturing Parent comforts and praises the child, and the Critical Parent ego state finds fault.

It is the Critical Parent that repetitively delivers harsh, damaging messages that are absorbed by the Adapted Child with little or no mediation by the Adult; this lack of intervention is due to an underdeveloped and silent Adult state. The Adult is muted because it lacks the strength and skills to act as a referee to dispute these harsh, faulty messages. This permits the Adapted Child to accept these accusations, whether true or not. Therefore, these shameful messages establish a pattern of dysfunctional internal interactions between the Critical Parent and the Adapted Child.

These interactions are known as *life scripts* and recur without interruption (Berne, 1964; Gladding, 2005). The Nurturing Parent and Free Child rarely surface because the Critical Parent is dominant and powerful, even though its source of power is rooted in childhood memories of individuals that frequently no longer have any authority in daily living.

"Berne holds that life scripts can be rewritten if people become more conscious of what they are thinking and make concerted efforts to change" (Gladding, 2005, p. 159). Therefore, clinicians can use TA to confront clients' self-destructive patterns of defective behavior and faulty thought patterns and illuminate their origin. They can learn that they have choices and are not simply victims. The words and actions that created and exacerbated the shame-based identity and that have created an interpersonal debt do not have to enslave them. Clients can choose to "relinquish the victim role and the rewards that go with it" (McCullough et al., 2000, p. 147).

Clinicians help clients understand that they have value in spite of their past and find ways to reinforce that message until clients believe it. Healing from the fear of losing yourself and the fear of incompetence comes when clients realize that pleasing others is not important. It is about being their own authentic self and elevating their self-esteem by finding abilities and actions that generate personal pride. Healing is about humanity, autonomy, and competence; it is about being "good enough."

It is extremely important that clinicians use caution and proceed slowly when challenging the games clients are playing to repress the truth (Berne, 1964, Powell, 1998). Remember clients have lived with their damaged interpersonal bridges for so long that their affect-binds have been experientially erased. They keep themselves together through self-deception because the truth is too uncomfortable, according to their boisterous internal scripts. "Choosing evil as evil is a psychological impossibility. . . . Consequently, to deny the truth I cannot admit, and to do the deed I cannot approve, I must necessarily rationalize until the truth is no longer true and the evil becomes good" (Powell, p. 100).

Clients must be committed to the therapeutic process and trust that the therapist will not abandon them as they expose this interpersonal imperfection. Being authentic is the greatest gift clinicians can give their clients because being honest with one's self and engaging in honest communication with clients establishes a role model for them. "The most healing message anyone can give someone with this kind of fear [fear of abandonment] is that they really want to be with them" (Potter-Efron & Potter-Efron, 1999, p. 9). We are not their judge. As we remove their masks, we remove their defenses and leave them naked. "If the psychological pieces come unglued, who will pick them up and put poor Humpty Dumpty Human Being together again?" (Powell, 1998, p. 101).

We must not attempt to do the work for them. That is their job. We must empower clients to find their own unique journey through this tangled web. We must empower their Adult ego state to become an advocate for their Adapted Child and empower their own internal Nurturing Parent to comfort them and affirm their personal worth. We must offer empathy, draw appropriate boundaries, and, most important, we must be steadfast in our integrity to make the journey with them as they empower their Adult to mediate between the Parent and the Child to become healthy people and find internal balance.

Instructions

This activity can be introduced once clinicians have determined that trust in the therapeutic relationship has been established and group members are committed to actively work on their faulty life scripts. It is helpful to use it sooner, rather than later, because it can empower group members to begin disputing their fault-finding Critical Parent ego state. A brief introduction to the concept of shame-based identity and an introduction to Transactional Analysis are both necessary and helpful because group members can begin to identify their negative internal dialogues and begin to recognize specific ego states related to their scripts.

This activity can be done with one representative group member who responds to the group leader's questions or the group as a whole can respond. One new crisp dollar bill is needed. Hold up the dollar bill and ask the individual client or group members the following questions:

- What it this?
- What might be something that you could buy with it? (Clients usually say something like soda or candy.)
- How do you know it has worth? (They have been taught, government says so, bought an item with a dollar before)

Talk about the crispness of the dollar, which makes it easier to use in automated vending machines. Crumple the dollar bill up into a tight ball. Throw it on the floor and stomp it down with the heel of your shoe. While doing that, talk about taking it outside and stomping it into the ground. This would add dirt to the wrinkles. Talk about perhaps putting it in the washing machine, writing on it, and other actions that would make it "used."

Pick the dollar up and spread it out. Repeat the same questions again. After the client has responded, point out the limitations of the dollar bill now (for example, probably would not work very well in an automated vending machine with all its wrinkles). Ask the following questions:

- What has changed about the dollar?
- Have any of these actions changed the value of the dollar?
- If the government says this is worth 100 pennies and can be exchanged for anything of value worth 100 pennies or less, then certainly we do not have the power or the authority to say that it has lost its value simply because certain circumstances have happened to the bill. If we can say that about the dollar bill, then how could this be applied to you and the circumstances that you have survived in your past?

It is important that group members understand that there are *limitations* based on what has happened to the dollar bill, but it does not change the *value* of the dollar. What has happened in the group members' past does not change their personal value either.

The group leader can either ask each person to provide their own dollar or provide a dollar for each group member; however, each group member needs to have a wrinkled dollar bill to take home with them. Instruct them to put the dollar in a safe place where it will be seen every day at least once a day. When they see it, ask them to verbally say to themselves, "I am valuable." Initially, clients report providing this personal affirmation is difficult and do not feel comfortable doing this exercise. However, as they continue to do it, their internal script begins to change until they realize that they do have worth regardless of past circumstances.

Variation

Clinicians may use a dollar bill with ink stains or that has clear indications that it is worn. Compare and contrast this dollar bill with the crisp bill as to which one has more value. Although each possess different properties (e.g., one stands up and the other does not, one "feels" cleaner than the other), there is no difference in value; one is just more used than the other.

A dollar coin may also be introduced for comparison to the crisp dollar bill. It is important to point out the similarities (they are both worth a dollar) and the differences. The coin can not be crumpled up or torn, will never change its original shape, and probably would not be damaged if washed. However, there are some limitations based on physical characteristics. The coin is rigid, it cannot be used in an automated vending machine, people do not like to carry it in their pockets, and it is about the size of a quarter so it might be confused for value. These limitations are about inconvenience not about value. One of the distinct advantages of the coin over the dollar is its durability.

Brief Vignette

Jane was initially uncomfortable with the idea of being involved with a support group for clients with an abusive childhood, but after being assured that it would be a closed group and all the members had been victims of childhood abuse, she agreed to participate in the thirteen week group experience. During the third week of group, I was comfortable that everyone trusted the group process and each other, as indicated by the details and emotions shared during the meeting.

Jane volunteered to share some painful parts of her childhood story during the processing of the assigned written homework. Jane shared that her mother had physically abused her from an early age, and she indicated multiple scars on her arms and face to substantiate these claims. Although he was gone for extended periods of time, for approximately ten years her father sexually abused her when he was home. However, she indicated that he eventually divorced her mother and disappeared when Jane was sixteen.

Jane was a highly educated, successful young woman in her mid-thirties who described herself as a "successful workaholic" without any real friends. She admitted she spent an excessive amount of time on work because she feared failure. "The money is nice, but it is not about material gain. I am so afraid that someone will decide I do not belong in upper-level management and fire me. Besides, I wouldn't know what to do with free time anyway." She recognized that her success was evidence of her value to her company, but she was unable to silence the internal negative messages that frequently reminded her she was worthless. These descriptors identify shame-based identity in the form of workaholism (L'Abate et al., 1992).

When I introduced and processed the dollar bill activity (per the instructions), she cried when I said "You are valuable! It doesn't matter what happened to you in your childhood. You have worth!" She said, "No one ever told me I was valuable before." Several other group members also cried and said this was a powerful realization for them as well.

I gave each of the group members a wrinkled, worn dollar bill, asked them to put it some place where they would see it every day and repeat, "I am valuable" whenever they saw it. Each week, I asked about their dollars and if they were giving themselves daily affirmations. Most group members initially reported that it was very uncomfortable and they felt dumb, but they all did it. As the weeks went by, their reactions changed and insights were gained.

The first week or two Jane admitted that she was doing it simply because it was homework. However, about four weeks after she started, Jane reported, "Over the weekend, something sort of snapped for me and I experienced a huge 'ah-ha' moment! I have been allowing other people to make me feel inferior to them. What happened to me as a child was painful and tragic, but I survived it! I am no longer that person, and I refuse to let others keep me in that box!" Jane started drawing boundaries with people at work. Sometimes it worked and sometimes it did not. She struggled with drawing boundaries because it was new behavior, but for the first time, she admitted it was worth the struggle. This was a similar significant turning point for many of the group members as well.

The purpose of this affirmation activity was to empower Jane's Adult to silence the negative, very verbal Critical Parent that was inside her head and break the faulty childhood script with the Adapted Child. As a child, Jane had learned that she was a "hateful child" from her mother and that she was a "wanton child" from her father. As the Adult became stronger, it also empowered the Nurturing Parent to repair the damaged Adapted Child. The Nurturing Parent also granted the Free Child permission to engage in fun activities without feeling guilty.

Jane continued on for a second thirteen weeks of group and was able to find balance between her ego states. As her Adult gained strength, Jane learned to utilize TA terminology to rewrite the negative scripts. It was during the final session of this second group experience that Jane realized she had completely lost her nervous giggle, was very comfortable with appropriate eye contact, and had developed what she called "a kick butt attitude."

As a terminating summary to end group, I asked, "What has been helpful?" Jane indicated that she had a new understanding of how her past impacted her current life ("identified by the wrinkles in the crumpled dollar bill," she said). She still tended to be distrustful of people in the beginning; however, as she interacted with them, she was learning to establish healthy boundaries. "I am learning to trust my instincts and open myself up to appropriate friendships. I can play without feeling guilty. Who knows—maybe I'll have a million of these one dollar bills one day. After all, I feel like a million dollar woman now!"

Suggestions for Follow-Up

Clients can continue to use the dollar bill on a daily basis to empower their Adult to challenge the negative scripting between the Critical Parent and Adapted Child. The counselor could also bring into the group a crisp dollar bill, a worn dollar that is heavily stained and faded, and a dollar coin into future sessions and ask clients to identify which fits best at the moment.

Contraindications

This activity can be accompanied by other interventions (such as guided imagery, relaxation techniques, and self-esteem building activities) and caution needs to be used that it is not introduced too early into the therapeutic relationship. Group members may leave therapy and discount the technique or fail to comprehend the full potential of the dollar. Trust and confidence in the clinician must be established first to be sure that group members will actually use the activity.

The clinician needs to understand the concept of shame-based identity and the basics of Transactional Analysis. Although this technique may be utilized with clients of all ages, they must have the cognitive ability to process and apply this activity. Extreme caution needs to be used to not discount the client's past history and its impact on present behavior as you untangle the web of confusion and lies.

Readings and Resources for the Professional

Claude-Pierre, P. (1997). *The secret language of eating disorders: The revolutionary new approach to understanding and curing anorexia and bulimia.* New York: Times Books.
Ferrara, F. F. (2002). *Childhood sexual abuse: Developmental effects across the lifespan.* Pacific Grove, CA: Brooks/Cole.

Bibliotherapy Sources for the Client

Bradshaw, J. (1995). *Family secrets: The path to self-acceptance and reunion.* New York: Bantam Books.
Middleton-Moz, J. (1990). *Masters of disguise: Shame & guilt.* Deerfield Beach, FL: Health Communications.

Simon, S. B., & Simon, S. (1990). *Forgiveness: How to make peace with your past and get on with your life.* New York: Warner Books.

Smalley, G., & Trent, J. (1990). *The blessing.* New York: Pocket Books.

Weitzman, S. (2000). *"Not to people like us": Hidden abuse in upscale marriages.* New York: Basic Books.

References

Berne, E. (1964). *Games people play: The basic handbook of transactional analysis.* New York: Ballantine Books.

Bowlby, J. (1969). *Attachment and loss* (Vol. 1), *Attachment.* New York: Basic Books.

Bradshaw, J. (1988). *Healing the shame that binds you.* Deerfield, FL: Health Communications.

Brothers, J. (2005, February 27). Shame may not be so bad after all. *Parade*, 4-6.

Cassidy, J., & Shaver, P. R. (Eds.). (1999). *Handbook of attachment: Theory, research, and clinical applications.* New York: Guilford Press.

Gladding, S. T. (2005). *Counseling theories: Essential concepts and applications.* Upper Saddle River, NJ: Pearson Education.

Karen, R. (1994). *Becoming attached: First relationships and how they shape our capacity to love.* Oxford, UK: Oxford University Press.

Kaufman, G. (1992). *Shame: The power of caring* (3rd ed.). Rochester, VT: Schenkman Books.

L'Abate, L., Farrar, J. E., & Serritella, D. A. (Eds.). (1992). *Handbook of differential treatments for addictions.* Needham Heights: MA: Allyn and Bacon.

McCullough, M. E., Pargament, K. I., & Thoresen, C. E. (2000). *Forgiveness: Theory, research, and practice.* New York: Guilford.

Potter-Efron, P. S., & Potter-Efron, R. T. (1999). *The secret message of shame: Pathways to hope and healing.* Oakland, CA: New Harbinger.

Potter-Efron, R. T., & Potter-Efron, P. S. (1989). *Letting go of shame: Understanding how shame affects your life.* Center City, MN: Hazelden Educational Materials.

Powell, J. (1998). *Why am I afraid to tell you who I am?* Allen, TX: Thomas More Publishing.

Tangney, J. P., & Dearing R. L. (2002). *Shame and guilt.* New York: Guilford.

Wilson, S. D. (1990). *Released from shame: Recovery for adult children of dysfunctional families.* Downers Grove, IL: InterVarsity Press.

14

Building a Bridge: An Experiential Group for Adult Survivors of Sexual Abuse

Pat L. Sims
W. Jeff Hinton
Mary Ann Adams
Charles K. West

I count him lost, who is lost to shame

Plautus

Type of Contribution: Activities

Objective

The goal of these activities is to facilitate the reduction of the guilt, shame, isolation, and stigmatization felt by adult female survivors of childhood sexual abuse. Resolution of shame and guilt in the early sessions of group therapy is the foundation that allows the participants to utilize the remaining sessions for goal setting and skill building.

Rationale for Use

The impact of sexual abuse on women is well documented (Browne & Finkelhor, 1986; Briere & Runtz, 1988). Long-term psychological consequences of sexual abuse include depression, anxiety, sexual dysfunction, relational dysfunction, guilt, distrust, anger, self-destructive behaviors, phobias, substance abuse, poor body image, low self-esteem, sleep disturbances, self-mutilation, aggression, and revictimization (Alexander & Lupfer, 1987; Briere & Runtz, 1988; Browne & Finkelhor, 1986; Jackson, Calhoun, Amick, Maddever, & Habif, 1990). Time alone does not appear to ease the impact that childhood sexual abuse has on the lives of women. Therefore, without intervention, the aftereffects of abuse can continue to interfere with a woman's emotional, physical, spiritual, and relational functioning throughout her life.

Shame as a consequence of sexual abuse is a common theme found throughout the literature (Fiering, Taska, & Lewis, 1998). Many of the behavioral and psychological symptoms experienced by adult survivors are related to internalized feelings of shame. Kaufman (1985) postulates a developmental theory of shame that suggests shame originates within the context of interpersonal relationships. According to Kaufman (1985), the emotional bond that develops between two people through trust, care, and respect is known as an "interpersonal bridge." When this interpersonal bridge is damaged and one member of the relationship feels betrayed by the other, shame occurs (Ridley, 1993). The feeling of shame is an internal process that results in feelings of self-doubt, inferiority, inadequacy, and alienation. Shame is the experience of being bad or wrong. Kaufman (1996) also suggests that we believe others can see our inadequacies and know that we are bad and that leads to feeling transparent. Abuse victims go to great lengths to hide or cover these feelings of shame in an attempt to reduce transparency. He refers to the inner experience of shame as a sickness within the self, a sickness of the soul (Kaufman, 1996).

It is easy to see how children are especially susceptible to the development of a shame-based identity due to their stage of development. According to Piaget and Inhelder (1958), children are very egocentric, believing they are the center of the universe and that everything revolves around them. Young children, who are frequently told by adults that it is their fault when bad things happen to them, believe that they have somehow caused the sexual abuse. Because sexually abused children are often told that the abuse is their fault, the toxic shame that they internalize keeps them silent. The abuse experience remains largely undisclosed throughout their life until the aftereffects of the trauma interfere with their functioning and they seek help (Zupancic & Kreidler, 1998).

Once sexual abuse issues have been identified and sufficiently explored during individual therapy, most clinicians move their clients toward group therapy as the treatment of choice (Blake-White & Kline, 1985; Tsai & Wagner, 1978). Turner (1993) suggests that the primary reason why group treatment is so effective in helping sexual abuse survivors is that the participants are allowed and encouraged to break their silence and talk about what has happened to them. Most women receive individual therapy prior to entering a survivor group, and as valuable as that process is, it does not significantly impact the feelings of shame and feelings of being different from everyone else. It is group treatment that provides a safe place for sexual abuse victims to explore and resolve feelings of guilt and shame thus reducing the sense of isolation and the feelings of being different (Berliner & MacQuivey, 1996; Gagliano, 1987; Knittle & Tuana, 1980).

Instructions

Group Format

The format followed by the authors is a closed, time-limited, focused sexual abuse resolution group based on the model developed by Goodman and Nowak-Scibelli (1985). The group lasts twelve sessions and is broken into three broad phases focusing on (a) the past, with an emphasis on the participant's experiences as a child (Phase One); (b) the present, focusing on current functioning (Phase Two); and (c) the future, emphasizing goal setting and skill building (Phase Three). Due to the limited number of sessions and the necessity for safety, each group is restricted to no more than six participants. The purpose of this chapter is to share activities that are utilized in Phase One when the primary focus is on the women's experiences of shame and isolation.

Building a Bridge

Restoring the interpersonal bridge is the first principle in the treatment of toxic shame (Kaufman, 1985). Developing a therapeutic alliance between the group facilitators and the participants and among the participants is foundational to this intervention. Group facilitators must be emotionally engaged and be perceived as caring, supportive, and trustworthy in order to provide an atmosphere safe enough for disclosure. Safety is further created by establishing ground rules for the group regarding format and structure and around issues of confidentiality.

The first session is devoted to introductions and getting to know one another as well as for the establishment of group rules. In order to set the stage for the next few sessions of working with the child within, each participant is asked to sit on the floor and is given paper and crayons. They are asked to draw a picture of a safe place that includes a bridge. The bridge is the conduit for getting to the safe place. On the bridge, they write words or draw pictures of the things they need to help them to cross the bridge into safety. The goal of this activity is to help provide some containment for the women as they tell their story. The bridge is also a metaphor for restoring the interpersonal bridge that has been damaged as a result of a violation of a prohibited boundary.

Telling the Story

The next three sessions are devoted to each participant telling her story and the impact it had on her childhood. Clients are encouraged to tell only as much as they are comfortable sharing. It is important that they are in control of the process and are able to set boundaries around what they feel comfortable disclosing. They begin by talking about the picture of the bridge they drew and what they need from the group in order to tell their story. This enables the women to identify and give voice to their needs, which have typically been suppressed. Women with a shame-based identity do not feel entitled to their needs so this activity in itself begins to empower them.

The process of having the women tell their story early in the group formation builds cohesion among the group members. As each adult survivor breaks the secret shame by making traumatic, stigmatizing events known to others within the group, the other group members are able to provide validation and acknowledgement of the feelings of shame (Ridley, 1993). The telling of her story and the subsequent validation from group members frees the woman from the control the trauma has had on her life. This also has the effect of building interpersonal bridges between the participants and the group facilitators as trust, caring, and empathy are experienced and internalized.

The Child Within

Adult survivors frequently feel guilty and responsible for their own abuse and, as a result, are angry with themselves for not stopping the abuse or saying no. They consistently remember their prior abuse from an adult perspective and give adult abilities to the child they once were. In order to recognize a child's vulnerability and to put the responsibility where it belongs, the participants are given two assignments: (1) Go to a playground and watch the children play and interact with one another and take the opportunity to swing or play themselves and (2) Bring a picture of themselves at the age the abuse first took place to group. During the group session, the women are asked to talk about their experiences at the playground. Most women are astonished to see how truly young and vulnerable the children are. Each participant is then asked to show the picture of herself as a child and talk about her childhood at that time, remembering not only the abuse but other activities and events from her childhood.

This activity serves two purposes: (a) recognition of a child's vulnerability and innocence and the culpability of the adult for the abuse and (b) recognition that not everything that went on during that time was damaging to them. This activity begins the process of holding the adult accountable for the abuse by recognizing the powerlessness of a child. It also enables each woman to have a more balanced remembrance of her childhood. Too often, they perceive their entire childhood negatively due to the sexual abuse. The ability to remember positive events in their childhood helps put the abuse into the context of other life events and reduces the sense of damage.

I Can Take Care of You: A Guided Imagery

Building on the previous work done with the exercises of Building a Bridge and The Child Within, participants are encourage to nurture the child within and, as adults, to protect the child with the resources and power that comes from being an adult. Frequently, the adult survivor disowns the part of herself that needed to be loved and nurtured as a child but was instead sexually abused (Ridley, 1993).

The goals of the imagery are (1) to develop an image of a safe place that can facilitate the development of self-soothing behaviors and (2) to develop a sense of competence as an adult who is able to care for the child part of oneself without all of one's behaviors and emotions being controlled by embedded childhood reactivity. This guided imagery activity is used in session where the participants are taught to relax through deep breathing and then given directives with enough silence (ten to twenty seconds) after each statement to give the participant time to process. This activity is adapted from the Creation of an Inner Sanctuary activity (Esplen & Garfinkel, 1998), a commonly used imagery intervention found in the literature for the creation of a safe place. Participants are given the following directives by the facilitator:

> Make yourself comfortable. . . . Close your eyes and allow your body to feel loose and comfortable. . . . Take a deep breath . . . slowly . . . a deep breath. . . . Concentrate on your breathing as you count silently to yourself. . . . Inhale, In . . . one . . . two . . . three. . . . Out . . . one . . . two . . . three . . . [repeat several times]. . . . Feel yourself relax as you breathe. . . . Breathe out slowly. . . . Concentrate on your breathing . . . slowly and deeply . . . breathing deeply. . . . As you breathe out, notice that you begin to feel more and more relaxed. Tension is draining from your body. Let the painful feelings go . . . go from your body . . . they will go . . . and soon you will feel more in control . . . and more at ease. Continue breathing slowly. Breathe in . . . and out . . . breathing slowly.
>
> Imagine yourself in some beautiful natural environment. . . . It can be any comforting place that appeals to you . . . in a meadow . . . on a mountain . . . in a forest . . . or beside a lake or an ocean. . . . Feel the environment around you . . . see the beauty of it . . . the quiet and pleasant rhythmic sounds of the environment. . . . Feel the warmth on your skin . . . the breeze feels so warm and gentle. Notice the smells in this environment. . . . This is your special place . . . notice the feelings and impressions that you begin to experience. . . . Now, continue exploring your surroundings . . . and do anything that you would like to do to make it your special place and comfortable for you. . . . If you would like to build some type of shelter or house . . . begin to imagine its structure . . . or perhaps you would like to surround the whole area with a golden light of protection and safety. Create and arrange things that are there for your convenience . . . and enjoyment . . . in order to establish it as your special place. . . . Every time that you return you will feel these warm feelings . . . these feelings of safety . . . and increased understanding . . . and peace.
>
> You are feeling safe and secure . . . you are sitting in a place that is safe and protected. . . . As you relax you notice a little girl in the distance. . . . As you observe her, notice how she looks, how she sits. . . . You decide to go and talk to her. . . . Ask her to tell you about herself . . . what she feels. . . . Ask her what she needs from you. . . . Reach out to her. . . . Let her know you are there for her. . . . Ask her if there is anything else she needs from you. . . . Let her know you will be there for her when she needs you. . . . Notice how she looks now. . . .
>
> It is almost time to say good-bye. . . . When you are ready, tell her good-bye. . . . Tell her you will see her again later. . . . Notice how you feel. . . . Breathe in . . . and out . . . in . . . and out. . . . And when you are ready to leave . . . just count backward slowly from five . . . to . . . one . . . and you can leave. . . . Notice how relaxed you feel. . . . The tension that you felt before has left and you feel more in control . . . and more calm . . . and you feel more positive . . . and trustworthy . . . that you can be in touch with your inner self . . . and feelings. . . . You feel much more relaxed. . . . As you breathe in . . . and out . . . as you slowly open your eyes. . . .

After the guided imagery, the women take turns processing their experience with the guided imagery and what feelings and images surfaced for them.

Goodie Sheets (All Sessions)

Each participant, as well as each of the group leaders, has a goodie sheet, which is a piece of construction paper with her name on it. All of the sheets are placed in the middle of the floor at the end of the session. Each participant takes someone else's goodie sheet and writes something positive about that person. She then returns it to the floor and picks up another one until all goodie sheets have been written on. After everyone is through, each participant gets to read her own goodie sheet and see what others wrote about her. This is done after each session and as the weeks progress, the comments move from rather superficial comments after the first session to deep expressions of affirmation by the last session. After the very last session, each participant takes her goodie sheet home with her. This activity builds self-esteem and a healthier view of oneself. The process of affirmation and validation by others also facilitates the process of repairing the interpersonal bridge and reducing feelings of shame and transparency. This activity is, by far, reported to be the most favored by all group members.

Suggestions for Follow-Up

Group therapy that provides a caring, supportive environment for each adult survivor of sexual abuse to give voice to her story of trauma enables her to put an end to the toxic shame that has inhibited her emotional, psychological, relational, and spiritual growth. The success of the early sessions in moving the women from a shame-based identity to one of empowerment lays the foundation for success in the middle and late stages of group therapy where the focus moves to skill building and goal setting. Remaining sessions should include content about appropriate boundaries, intimacy, and sexuality. The development of assertiveness skills, anger management abilities, and healthy coping strategies are also important and can be practiced within the group sessions. When a woman has been freed of the shame that binds her, she is liberated to try new things and to grow in ways previously unimagined.

Contraindications

Careful screening of clients is important for the development of a successful group. All participants must have the recommendation of their individual therapist prior to being accepted into the group. Significant work around the development of ego resources and personal stability must have been accomplished prior to entering the group (Courtois, 1999). Sufficient work in developing grounding and containment skills, self-care, self-soothing skills, and mood regulation should be done in individual therapy before moving to the group process. Participants must not be in crisis and must continue in individual therapy in order to maintain additional support during the group process.

This activity would not be recommended for clients with dissociative identity disorder (DID) as it can be very disruptive to the group process if a client with DID shifts into an altered state or personality, particularly a child state. For a short term, time-limited group, it may be more than the group can manage, which calls for the exclusion of those clients or at least a careful evaluation of this risk factor. The activities themselves would not be harmful to clients with DID (in fact, they are utilized quite often with them); however, the activities may not be best suited to a group setting that includes clients with DID. This group work is based on experiences with adult female clients, and it is not known if it would be as successful with male survivors of sexual abuse.

Readings and Resources for the Professional

Courtois, C. (1988). *Healing the incest wound: Adult survivors in therapy.* New York: W.W. Norton & Co.

Meekums, B. (2000). *Creative group therapy for women survivors of sexual abuse: Speaking the unspeakable.* London: Jessica Kingsley Publishers, LTD.

Bibliotherapy Sources for the Client

Bass, E., & Davis, L. (1994). *The courage to heal: A guide for women survivors of child sexual abuse* (3rd ed.). New York: Harper & Row.

Gil, E. (1983). *Outgrowing the pain: A book for and about adults abused as children.* New York: Dell.

References

Alexander, P. C., & Lupfer, S. L. (1987). Family characteristics and long-term consequences associated with sexual abuse. *Archives of Sexual Behavior, 16,* 235-245.

Berliner, L., & MacQuivey, K. (1996). A therapy group for female adolescent victims of sexual abuse. In M. Rosenbaum (Ed.), *Handbook of short-term therapy groups* (pp. 101-116). Northvale, NJ: Jason Aronson.

Blake-White, J., & Kline, C. M. (1985). Treating the dissociative process in adult victims of childhood incest. *Social Casework, 66,* 394-402.

Briere, J., & Runtz, M. (1988). Symptomatology associated with childhood sexual victimization in a nonclinical adult sample. *Child Abuse & Neglect, 12,* 51-59.

Browne, A., & Finkelhor, D. (1986). Impact of child sexual abuse: A review of the research. *Psychological Bulletin, 99*(1), 66-77.

Courtois, C. (1999). *Recollections of sexual abuse: Treatment principles and guidelines.* New York: W. W. Norton & Co.

Esplen, M. J., & Garfinkel, P. E. (1998). Guided imagery treatment to promote self-soothing in bulimia nervosa: A theoretical rationale. *Journal of Psychotherapy Practice and Research, 7,* 102-118.

Fiering, C., Taska, L., & Lewis, M. (1998). The role of shame and attribution style in children's and adolescents' adaptation to sexual abuse. *Child Maltreatment, 3,* 129-142.

Gagliano, C. K. (1987). Group treatment for sexually abused girls. *Social Casework: The Journal of Contemporary Social Work, 68,* 102-108.

Goodman, B., & Nowak-Scibelli, D. (1985). Group treatment for women incestuously abused as children. *International Journal of Group Psychotherapy, 35,* 531-544.

Jackson, J. L., Calhoun, K. S., Amick, A. E., Maddever, H. M., & Habif, V. L. (1990). Young adult women who report childhood intrafamilial sexual abuse: Subsequent adjustment. *Archives of Sexual Behavior, 19,* 211-221.

Kaufman, G. (1985). *Shame: The power of caring.* Cambridge, MA: Schenkman.

Kaufman, G. (1996). *The psychology of shame* (2nd ed.). New York: Springer.

Knittle, B. J., & Tuana, S. J. (1980). Group therapy as primary treatment for adolescent victims of intrafamilial sexual abuse. *Clinical Social Work Journal, 8,* 236-242.

Piaget, J., & Inhelder, B. (1958). *The growth of logical thinking from childhood to adolescence.* New York: Basic Books.

Ridley, P. (1993). Kaufman's theory of shame and identify in treating childhood sexual abuse in adults. *Journal of Psychosocial Nursing, 31,* 13-17.

Tsai, M., & Wagner, N. N. (1978). Therapy groups for women sexually molested as children. *Archives of Sexual Behavior, 7,* 417-427.

Turner, S. (1993). Talking about sexual abuse: The value of short-term groups for women survivors. *Journal of Group Psychotherapy, 46,* 110-121.

Zupancic, M. K., & Kreidler, M. C. (1998). Shame and the fear of feeling. *Perspectives in Psychiatric Care, 34,* 29-34.

15

Web of Entanglements

Markie L. C. Blumer

Type of Contribution: Activity/Homework

Objective

There are three main goals in the Web of Entanglements activity. One is to assist the therapist and client in clearly defining the immediate problems and goals in therapy. In other words, it can be employed as a problem-identifying device or as a clarifying tool. The second is to help visually show how a client's problems are interconnected. By doing this, clients see that by changing one problem, they have the opportunity to effect change in other areas. Finally, by seeing problems shared in a group setting, it can help clients recognize how many issues they have in common. This can help group members form relationships with one another, help them to bond over their problems, and create empathy among group members.

This activity was originally designed for women who have substance and alcohol abuse problems. However, it can apply to many different populations, including individuals, couples, and families.

Rationale for Use

According to the 2001 National Survey on Drug Use and Health, approximately 7.2 million adult women report illicit drug use and 65 million report using alcohol in any given month, with 31 million engaging in binge drinking and 8.6 million in heavy drinking (Substance Abuse and Mental Health Services Administration [SAMHSA], 2002). Among pregnant women, approximately 3.3 percent report using illicit drugs and use of alcohol is reported by 9.1 percent of women in any given month period (SAMHSA, 2003b).

Male and female substance abusers differ in many ways in relation to use, with the problems stemming from drug use, drugs of choice, relapse patterns, and preferences for treatment as just some of the ways in which they differ (McCollum, 2003; Finkelstein, Kennedy, Thomas, & Kerns, 1997). Problems with drinking and driving, public intoxication, burglary, fighting, and workplace incidents are typically associated with male drug abuse, whereas typical problems for females are related to their own mental and physical health and the well-being of their children. In terms of drugs of choice, men typically prefer the polydrug use of alcohol and marijuana, while women are more likely than men to engage in the daily use of cocaine.

Traditionally, alcohol and substance abuse treatment has been based on a male clientele. Techniques in treatment have historically focused on the use of confrontational methods, rather than methods of nurturance. It has been noted that women respond better to the later (Wallis-Hill, 1999). Issues of most concern to female substance abusers, such as health needs, loss, trauma, domestic violence, shame, guilt, sexuality, pregnancy, and parenting, have been overlooked by traditional male-based treatment modalities (McCollum, 2003; Finkelstein et al., 1997).

Given the myriad of differences between male and female substance abusers, it seems a necessity that agencies provide safe places for women, in particular, to talk about the specific concerns they face during treatment (McCollum, 2003). One way to help facilitate this is through the use of women's groups. Despite this need, according to the National Survey of Substance Abuse Treatment Services (SAMHSA, 2003a), only 35 percent of treatment facilities offer specific groups for women and only a 14 percent offer groups for pregnant or postpartum women. It is important to keep in mind that, although a woman's web of relationships can be part of the basis of her substance abuse issues, relationships with others, including group members, can also be a huge source of strength in her recovery (Wallis-Hill, 1999).

From this perspective, it follows that women with substance abuse issues can truly benefit from women-only support groups that can provide a way for the members to form healthy relationships with other women. The process of working with female clients in the group setting has been shown to be extremely successful in counteracting the experience of individualization that many women experience in relation to their problems and in fostering a sense of empowerment through connectivity with other women (Avis, 1991). Key to helping women recover is to focus on encouraging a woman to examine her relationships with herself and others and providing information about issues specific to women, such as women's health needs, loss, trauma, domestic violence, shame, guilt, sexual abuse, pregnancy, and parenting. It is important that a leader listen to a woman's fears and begin to empower her by clarifying what she is and is not responsible for in relation to herself and her web of relationships (Avis). A group leader can model this behavior early on in the group process so that the group members can see this and learn to do it with each other and themselves.

Theoretical Approaches

The primary theoretical focus for this activity is systemic with a feminist lens. In systemic thinking, people are mutually influenced by and an influence on the people they exist with, including family, friends, and larger systems. There is really no way to separate someone from the system in which they live, as people exist within multiple levels of systems—family, societal, individual—all of which operate simultaneously (Minuchin, 1974). A person can have a problem at one level of a system and this can influence other systems. Along the same vein, intervention in one system can create change in other systems as each system is interconnected.

This web of interconnectedness seems even more evident when we look at it from a gendered perspective. Women seem to be more vulnerable to substance abuse problems when they exist in a web of unhealthy relationships and thus can develop "relationships" with a substance to help them cope with the negative impact of relationships or the disconnection they experience from positive relationships (Byington, 1997). Women can easily find themselves in potentially harmful relationships as they experience positions of negation, over responsibility, and being ignored by those with whom they are in meaningful relationships, which can be seen as a larger symptom of the dominant patriarchal system in which we all exist. From these kinds of positions and larger messages from society and loved ones, most women come into therapy believing that they are to blame for their own problems (Avis, 1991).

It is important for a therapist operating from a feminist approach to focus on empowerment, which can start with understanding more about the social context that shape women's lives and behaviors including political, economic, biological and social constraints (Avis, 1991). Typically, women seem to thrive when they are well connected in positive relationships with others, which can lead to self-care and self-empathy (Byington, 1997).

Therapeutic Approaches

It is to be expected that early on in group therapy, participants are often tentative and vague about the group process and what they hope to gain through it. In relation to this, often times they are only able to state in broad terms what they want to focus on in terms of goals (Corey & Corey, 2002). This activity then can be helpful in giving a client a chance to share all of their problems and give them a way to clearly identify the most pressing problem in their lives. It is of the utmost importance that the therapist helps the client clearly define the problem and determine how it affects the person and her or his place in the social system, for without a clear definition of the problem, a solution cannot be worked toward quickly (Fisch, Weakland, & Segal, 1982). It is also the group leader's responsibility to help translate the vague ideas and problems that group member presents with into clear, prioritized, and workable goals (Corey & Corey).

A typical way that a therapist can help a client to focus on the main presenting problem is to ask specific questions and "get curious" in regard to one main presenting problem of a client (Fisch et al., 1982). However, sometimes this approach is not as effective as one would hope. The Web of Entanglements activity is an alternative to just asking questions to clarify the presenting problem, as it provides the client with an opportunity to talk about all their problems in a more structured way. This activity has the advantage of being able to help the therapist get a clear definition of the problem, while also giving the client an opportunity to share many of their problems.

An important part of the group process, particularly in the initial stages of the group, is to establish group cohesion among the participants (Corey & Corey, 2002). A cohesive group is one where the members feel a sense of togetherness that creates an incentive for the members to share and leads to feelings of relatedness. However, often in the early stages of a group, members do not reveal much about themselves other than their public selves; it is not until group members share more about their pain and take risks that the group starts to develop a sense of cohesiveness. One of the essential components of an effective group is empathy and cohesiveness, and it is part of the group leader's responsibility to help develop greater empathy within the group members.

One way for a group leader to build group cohesion in the initial stages is to have the members share meaningful parts of themselves and develop individual and group goals. Through the process of sharing meaningful parts of themselves with each other, there is a greater potential for the people to practice empathy with each other (Corey & Corey, 2002). The Web of Entanglements activity can be a way to help members share these meaningful parts of themselves. By seeing that they share similar pains and experiences, cohesion and positive relationships can take place relatively quickly between members. The cohesiveness, coupled with having an opportunity to visually see the world through the other person's eyes, can lead to genuine empathy between group members.

Instructions

For this activity, the therapist will need to first gather the materials to make the Web of Entanglements. This includes a package of 3×5 or 4×6 index cards, skeins of yarn of various colors, writing utensils, scissors, and clear tape. After the initial introductory and icebreaker sessions, this activity can be assigned in the second or third group session as homework and then discussed in the third or fourth group sessions. It is often better to use this activity early on in the group or individual setting to most efficiently and effectively assist with problem identification and the fostering of group cohesion and empathy.

The therapist asks group members at the end of a group session to think over the course of the week about the multitude of problems and issues they are experiencing and with whom they are experiencing them. He or she then gives out between five and ten index cards per person and a writing utensil to take home. The therapist asks members to write on one side of the card the institution or person they are having a problem with. Institutions are defined as any individual person or group of people in a personal or professional context. This can include social services, schools, jobs, churches, legal system, treatment, extended family, spouse, children, cat, dog, and so forth. For as many institutions or people that the client is having a problem with, the client should write a single card for each so there are as many cards as institutions. On the backside of each of the problem cards, the clients should write the main problem they are experiencing in relation to this particular institution or person. After they have completed this task at home, the therapist instructs them to hold onto their cards and bring them to the next session in preparation for the completion of the activity.

At the start of the next group, group members get out their problem cards that they have prepared. The therapist gives each client a different color skein of yarn and a pair of scissors. The therapist explains to them that they are now going to construct their Web of Entanglements and gives the following instructions:

> Imagine you are in the center of your problems and that your problems are surrounding you like an imaginary web, where each circle of the web represents an institution and the problem that is associated with it. To make your web, you will need to cut out various lengths of yarn. The start of each piece of yarn will be at the center of the web where you are standing. At the end of the cut piece will be each problem card. You are to cut different lengths to each piece of yarn. Use the shortest piece of yarn to place the problem of greatest importance closest to you in your Web of Problems or Entanglements. Use the longest piece of yarn to place the problem that is of least importance furthest away from you in your Web of Entanglements.

After completion, the group members then take turns sharing their Web of Entanglements with the group.

Clients need to feel safe, supported, and encouraged in order to share openly. To help foster a sense of safety, it can be important to briefly reassure the clients of confidentiality within the group. It is essential that the therapist offer support and encouraging feedback throughout the process of sharing the group activity. When efforts are made to share, it can be reinforcing for the therapist to comment on the courage that this takes and to recognize and acknowledge the person for doing so. It can also be helpful to comment on how hard it is to share about ourselves, to go first, and to talk about feelings, since we do not often have a chance to share this much about ourselves.

It can be effective for the therapist to remind the clients of the goal of the activity and the process, which is to share with one another about themselves and their problems, with the ultimate goal of reducing some of the problems in their lives. It is extremely important, especially in a women's group, not to use a coercive or confrontational approach to get members to share. An example of this might be informing the clients that they *have* to share or share certain things and in certain ways, rather than letting them know that they can chose to share, when to share, and how much to share.

As the clients share their webs, it is important that the therapist model for the group the commonalities shared between group members with regard to their problems. Questions can include the following:

- Who do you think shares this problem with you?
- How do you think they handle this problem? How is this different from the way you handle your problem? How is it the same?

This kind of connectivity helps foster the sense of group cohesion and empathy among members.

From a systemically, brief, and strategic perspective, it can also be important for the group leader to ask questions such as the following:

- Why a problem is of more or less importance?
- How are the problems interconnected?
- What would happen to this problem if another problem was solved?
- Who else might this be a problem for both inside and outside of your web? Who might it not be a problem for either inside or outside the web?
- Who might be helpful in "devouring" the problem?

From a feminist approach, here are some questions that could be helpful:

- Which of these problems do you feel most responsible for and which ones not?
- If you weren't responsible for it or solely responsible, who would be responsible?
- What part does being a woman play in the problems? What part does society?
- How might this problem be experienced differently by a man? Would it even be a problem for a man?

In relation to substance abuse, these questions could be helpful:

- How have these problems or this problem influenced your substance use or gotten you to drink or use drugs?
- What would happen to these other problems in the web if substance abuse dissolved from your life?

While each client describes their web and answers questions posed, the therapist should be noting, mentally or on paper, what the clients report. It is important for the therapist to note themes that emerge in the form of similarities or commonalities among group members and their problems. It is also key for the therapist to note the individual differences or exceptions to the themes. When all of the clients have completed, or in the process of completing, the sharing of their webs, the therapist can use a dry erase board or chalkboard to write down the themes. From here, the therapist and the clients may have a clearer picture of the problems of greatest importance and a place to start in their Webs of Entanglements. The process of formulating group goals can also be established. Further, each client has now had the opportunity to fully share the multitude of problems they are currently experiencing. From identification of the individual exceptions to group themes, individual goals can be established as well.

Like any group process or activity, tension can emerge between group members as a result of this activity. Sometimes group members can have difficulty understanding differences in how people handle their problems and accepting these differences. Certain members may want to provide advice to members about how to get out of a situation that is congruent with how they themselves would do so. While advice is often provided with good intentions and is well received, sometimes some members can find advice from others uncomfortable, presumptuous, and unhelpful. If this happens, it can be helpful as a group leader to take time during the activity to point out that while there are similarities in each Web of Entanglements, there are also individual differences. Further, the therapist should remind members to keep in mind that everyone handles their own relationships and lives differently.

Variations

Individuals, Couples, and Families. The activity can be used in working with individuals, couples, and/or families. With an individual, it could be done in much the same as previously described, with more of a focus on promoting joining between the therapist and client. In the context of individual work, it could also be viewed as more of an assessment tool and/or a way to symbolically outline goals for treatment.

The activity could be adapted to work with a couple as either a separate assignment for each member of the dyad or as a joint assignment for the couple to work on together to come up with a clear, joint problem definition. From a feminist perspective, if used with a couple, it could also be a way of creating a conversation about gender differences and power differentials.

The activity could also be used with a family. It could be assigned to each family member separately or as a collective family assignment. Carrying out this activity within the context of the family can symbolically represent and help family members become conscious of how interconnected their issues are. This can help take the blame for a problem off of one person and place it within the framework of the family system.

Web of Resources. The activity can also be used in the context of pointing out the resources in the client's life rather than her or his problems or the ways the problems are entangled. In this case it would be considered a Web of Resources. This variation may be more akin to therapeutic approaches like solution-focused, and it can still foster a sense of group cohesion and empathy from the perspective of bonding over similarities in resources rather than bonding over issues and problems.

Brief Vignette

This activity was used in the context of a women's substance abuse group in an agency setting. This group typically consisted of six women and took place one time per week for approximately an hour and a half per meeting. The Web of Entanglements was presented to the group as described previously. The activity was assigned in the fourth group session, and it was the main focus of discussion in the group for the next two to three sessions. This activity was primarily used because the leader was experiencing difficulty in getting the group members to talk openly with one another about their issues related to substance abuse and other areas of their lives. Comments made early in the group process by members were that it was difficult to share freely because they feared they could not trust the other group members. From the group leader's point of view, this was a common occurrence for group members early in the group process, particularly those with a presenting problem of substance abuse, since they have often repeatedly experienced violations of trust.

One woman in the group was Laura, who had been in recovery for over twenty-five years from a heroin addiction but had experienced a relapse in the last year by using the prescription drug oxycontin. Laura was middle aged, married, and had a teenage daughter. She was one of the older participants in the group. She was a seemingly open woman, had reported very positive experiences with women's groups, and was a natural leader in the group process. Laura volunteered to describe her web first.

The institution/person she named as being closest to her in her web was her daughter. She reported that the problem she saw between herself and her daughter was her failure to maintain sobriety, therefore disappointing her daughter and not maintaining her image of being a strong female role model for her. As the group members shared their webs, this seemed to be the most recurring—that of disappointing family members in general, whether a child, a spouse, a parent, or a sibling—followed by feelings of failing in the expectant role as a woman. Questions focused on who shared this problem in the group and feminist-oriented questions seemed to have the most impact on the members when this theme emerged.

Laura also identified a man on the outer part of her web as being a problem for her in the past but not so much in the present. She reported that this man had contributed to her use of heroin when she was much younger. She shared that this man had raped her and she had originally felt guilty and ashamed after this experience. She reported that this person had been a virtual stranger and that it had be one of the most painful experiences in her life. She stated that the last time she went through a treatment program, she had had an opportunity to process the rape through women's groups, and that this had been more helpful in her recovery than almost any other aspect of treatment. She encouraged other group members to share similar experiences, if they had experienced them, because she believed it to be helpful for recovery. This became the second most common theme in the group—one of being abused sexually by a stranger, acquaintance, friend, boyfriend, or family member (It has been documented that the number of women in treatment who report sexual or physical abuse is two to three times more than women in the general public [McCollum, 2003]). Questions on who shared this problem and how group members coped seemed to have the effect of building group cohesion, fostering empathy among members, and tapping into feelings of empowerment for group members. The discussion focusing on substance abuse seemed to reveal that sexual abuse and the feelings associated with this act led the women to use more and more frequently to mask their pain. Again, that women use alcohol and drugs to manage their symptoms associated with these kinds of traumas is consistent with the literature (McCollum).

Once Laura and other group members started sharing their webs with each other, it was remarkable to see the difference in open dialogue flowing among the members. The activity seemed to hold their attention and enabled them to start talking more freely. The reaction to the activity was a positive one, with group members commenting that they felt they had learned more about each other and that they had similar stories and problems. In this respect, the fostering of cohesion became evident.

The third group member to share her Web of Entanglements was a younger woman, Mary, who was living with a male partner and her youngest son. Mary had recently lost her older son in an accidental event. She had been using prescription oxycontin illegally for approximately three years and had been sober for a six-month period. She shared the two themes previously mentioned and also introduced a problem that had not been discussed through the group activity previously. She placed her partner as closest to her in her web and reported that he was physically, verbally, and emotionally abusing her. While no other group member reported this as a current problem in their Web of Entanglements, all of the group members reported that some form of these abuses had been a problem for them historically. Again, the literature supports that many substance-abusing women report involvement in abusive relationships with male partners (McCollum, 2003). Brief questions like, "Who else is this a problem for, either inside or outside the web?" and "Who might be helpful in devouring this problem?" seemed helpful in assisting a woman in working through this problem in their web. (As the group leader, I also did a thorough assessment of violence in the relationship between this client and her partner, as well as possible abuse toward the child.)

Based on the themes revealed, some of the goals for the group that were developed were improving group member self-esteem, provision of information on handling guilt and shame as potential relapse triggers, learning how to recognize realistic expectations of oneself as a woman, techniques for taking care of oneself and not just other people, psychoeducational material on working through different forms of abuse, and the processing of feelings, thoughts, and behaviors around each of these areas.

Overall, the group members seemed to not only talk more and in a more open manner, they also seemed to begin to express more empathy for one another. This became particularly clear in the later sessions using the Web of Entanglements. By the last overt discussion of the web, the group members started commenting on similarities between people and their problems, with empathic feelings associated with their statements. It was also evident in future sessions that the activity assisted in opening the empathy pathways between people where they had previously seemed closed. Group members also reported that they felt like their voices had been heard by having an opportunity to fully disclose and share all of their problems. From the leader's point of view, this was invaluable to hear, see, and experience, as women do not often have an opportunity to feel empowered by having their voices heard.

Suggestions for Follow-Up

The Web of Entanglements can be revisited several times during the group process. It can be helpful for the group leader to remind group members of how they are connected through webs of relationships with one another and others in their lives. This can refocus the group on cohesiveness and empathy at times when these feelings are needed. As a problem- and goal-identifying tool, the therapist can use the web to remind clients of the problem they are working on currently and how it is impacting the other related problems and people from their web. Finally, it can be used to bring closure to the group by having clients recap what their web was like when entering the group and how it has changed since that time. Clients can also be encouraged to reflect on the part they, as well as other group members, had in these changes.

Contraindications

Use caution before applying any activity in the therapeutic setting. As most members of the mental health professional community know and understand, there is no one-size-fits-all therapeutic approach that is effective for all clients all of the time. With this in mind, it is important when using this activity in the therapeutic setting that it be used in conjunction with other interventions from the model the therapist uses.

This particular activity can get people to see their problem as being part of a web related to other people and agencies. In conjunction with this, it can be invaluable for the therapist to be sure that the clients also recognize that they have a part in their web of relationships. This can be particularly true in the case of abuse, especially if the client is in the role of abuser, where it is important that the person not shift responsibility for their actions to others. Remember to let the client know about the therapist's role in the system as a mandatory reporter of abuse as well.

It is also important to note that this particular activity is based primarily on experiences with groups of female substance abusers only and not other populations. In the author's experience, it is not known if this activity would be helpful or appropriate with men or mixed gender populations.

Readings and Resources for the Professional

Cook, D. (1991). Shame, attachment, and addictions: Implications for family therapists. *Contemporary Family Therapy: An International Journal, 13,* 405-420.

Flores, P. (1988). *Group psychotherapy with addicted populations.* Binghamton, NY: The Haworth Press.

Roberts, L. J., & McCrady. B. S. (2003). *Alcohol problems in intimate relationships—identification and intervention: A guide for marriage and family therapists.* Rockville, MD: National Institute on Alcohol Abuse and Alcoholism.

Wolin, S., & Wolin, S. (1993). *The resilient self: How survivors of troubled families rise above adversity.* New York: Villard Books.

Bibliotherapy Sources for the Client

Basco, M. R. (1999). *Never good enough: Freeing yourself from the chains of perfectionism.* New York: Free Press/Simon & Schuster.

Canfield, J., Hansen, M. V., Ackerman, R., Peluso, T., Seidler, G., & Vegso, P. (2004). *Chicken soup for the recovering soul: Your personal, portable support group with stories of healing, hope, love and resilience.* Deerfield Beach, FL: Health Communication, Inc.

Lerner, H. G. (1985). *The dance of anger: A woman's guide to changing the patterns of intimate relationships.* New York: HarperCollins.

Rich, A. (1986). *Of woman born: Motherhood as experience and institution.* New York: W. W. Norton & Co.

Williams, M. D. (2002). *A new beginning—recovery workbook: Reproducible exercises to help overcome addictive behaviors.* Wellness Reproductions & Publications, LLC.

References

Avis, J. M. (1991). Power politics in therapy with women. In T. J. Goodrich (Ed.), *Women and power: Perspectives for family therapy* (pp. 183-200). New York: W. W. Norton & Co.

Byington, D. B. (1997). Applying relational theory to addiction treatment. In S. L. A. Straussner & E. Zelvin (Eds.), *Gender and addictions: Men and women in treatment* (pp. 31-46). Northvale, NJ: Jason Aronson, Inc.

Corey, M. S., & Corey, G. (2002). *Groups: Process and Practice* (6th ed.). Pacific Grove, CA: Brooks/Cole, Thomson Learning.

Finkelstein, N., Kennedy, C., Thomas, K., & Kerns, M. (1997, March). *Gender-specific substance abuse treatment.* Washington, DC: Center for Substance Abuse Prevention.

Fisch, R., Weakland, J. H., & Segal, L. (1982). *The tactics of change: Doing therapy briefly.* San Francisco: CA: Jossey-Bass Publications.

McCollum, E. E. (2003). Women and substance abuse. *Family Therapy, 2*(6), 24-27.

Minuchin, S. (1974). *Families and family therapy.* Cambridge, MA: Harvard University Press.

Substance Abuse and Mental Health Services Administration (2002). *Results from the 2001 National Household Survey on Drug Abuse: Volume I. Summary of national findings* (NHSDA Series H-17, DHHS Publication No. SMA 02-3758). Rockville, MD: U.S. Department of Health and Human Services, Office of Applied Studies.

Substance Abuse and Mental Health Services Administration. (2003a). *National survey of substance abuse treatment services* (N-SSATS). Arlington, VA: U.S. Department of Health and Human Services, Office of Applied Studies.

Substance Abuse and Mental Health Services Administration. (2003b). *Results from the 2002 National Survey on Drug Use and Health: National findings.* Rockville, MD: U.S. Department of Health and Human Services, Office of Applied Studies.

Wallis-Hill, C. (1999). Women who abuse substances may benefit from a different approach to treatment [Electronic version]. *Children's Services Practice Notes: For North Carolina's Child Welfare Social Workers, 4,* 4.

16

Adult Children of Alcoholics/Children of Alcoholics: Family Description

Shari M. Sias
Glenn W. Lambie

Type of Contribution: Activity

Objective

The objective of the Family Description activity is to provide children of alcoholics (COA) and adult children of alcoholics (ACOA) an opportunity to become better acquainted with each other through sharing family experiences. Also, this activity encourages the use of empathic listening, which can decrease feelings of isolation among group members and increase group cohesiveness.

Rationale for Use

The National Association for Children of Alcoholics (NACoA) (2000) reported that in the United States in the 1990s, 28 million people were children or adult children of alcoholics. Parents/caregivers who abuse alcohol (a) often fail to provide a nurturing environment for their children; (b) many are ineffective in meeting their children's academic, emotional, physical, and social needs; and (c) in some cases, the children become caretakers for the parents/caregivers (Lambie & Sias, 2005).

The family dynamics and communication patterns of families in which COA are raised are often dysfunctional. Emotional communication in families with alcoholism is often more critical, conflictual, and avoidant in nature (Gabarino & Strange, 1993; NACoA, 1998; Segrin & Menees, 1996). These families tend to be closed systems, family members are discouraged from establishing relationships outside of the immediate family, and the "family secret" of alcohol abuse is hidden from others in the community (Edwards, 2003; Lambie & Sias, 2005; White & Savage, 2003).

All family members, including children, are affected by the parental/caregiver alcohol abuse; the family system leads the children to make unhealthy interpersonal and intrapsychic accommodations, which often adversely influence their psychosocial development (White, 2005). In addition, addiction is a multigenerational issue, in which this biopsychosocial disorder often is passed from one generation to the next. Brook et al. (2003) found COA to be four times more likely than non-COA to develop alcohol abuse or dependence.

Children of alcoholics often show negative psychosocial effects, including (a) poor impulse control, (b) acting out behavior in school, (c) poor academic functioning, (d) low self-esteem, and (e) a lack of sense of control in their lives (Lambie & Sias, 2005). Clinical and research findings further suggest that as these children grow into adulthood, they are at risk for a variety of mental health issues including low self-esteem, relational problems, difficulty managing anger, and perfectionism (Bosworth & Burke, 2001), anxiety disorders (Knowles & Schroeder, 1990; NACoA, 1998; Reich, Earls, Frankel, & Shayka, 1993), conduct disorders (NACoA, 1998; Reich et al.), less secure attachment (Jaeger, Hahn & Weinraub, 2000), and higher levels of psychological distress (Kashubeck, 1994). Thus, parent/caregiver alcohol abuse has potential long-term social, psychological, cognitive, and behavioral consequences for all family members.

Research suggests that COA and ACOA are in need of specialized therapeutic interventions (Robinson & Rhoden, 1998). Interventions designed to decrease clients' feelings of isolation and increase self-understanding have been found most effective. Therefore, a therapeutic approach facilitating the group processes of universality (that is, sense of commonality and belonging) and family reenactment (systemic understanding) is likely to be most effective.

Group therapy has been found effective for COA (Arman, 2000; Sciarra, 2004). Group work can increase self-esteem, build trust, reduce feelings of isolation and increase coping skills (Corey, 2004). In addition, therapy groups provide a safe forum for COA to learn to identify and express feelings, to safely cope with family problems, to learn about alcohol abuse and its effects on the family, and to learn how to have fun (Lambie & Sias, 2005; Substance Abuse and Mental Health Services Administration [SAMHSA], 2003).

Many ACOAs struggle with taking care of themselves emotionally and spend a great deal of time taking care of others (Abbott, 1991). Thus, in addition to supporting ACOA's sense of connection to others and systemic understanding, taking responsibility for one's self and letting friends and loved ones do the same is another appropriate therapeutic goal.

Group therapy has been identified as an appropriate and, in some cases, the preferred method of treatment for ACOA (Cermak, 1991). In a survey of forty-five colleges and universities, Bosworth and Burke (2001) found that the most frequent campus counseling services offered to collegiate ACOA were individual therapy, ACOA groups (twelve-step), and counseling groups. When asked to rank the sixteen most critical counseling services, ACOA support groups and group counseling were ranked third and fourth, respectively. Cermak and Brown (1982) also found group therapy to be an effective modality for treating ACOA.

Family Description is a structured group therapy activity that is effective in reducing feelings of isolation, achieving group cohesiveness, and identifying issues that may need to be addressed during the counseling process.

Instructions

At the beginning of the group therapy session, each member is asked to write a description of his or her family. The instructions may be left open-ended or the group therapist can provide prompting questions, such as the following:

- What adjectives would you use to describe your family of origin?
- Who had the closest relationships growing up?
- Are you most like your mother or father? Why?
- What were some of your family's traditions?
- Looking back, what would you like to change about your family of origin?

After the group members have completed the writing task, each member is asked to share his or her family description. In order for each individual to have the group's full attention, one person at a time sits in the center of the group and shares his or her family description. Group members are instructed to listen and give the person speaking their total attention, without talking or interrupting.

This activity can be very effective. Individuals rarely have the total attention of others and often do not feel heard. Having the undivided attention of the group is a new and powerful experience. In addition, the group provides a safe place for personal exploration and sharing. As group members share, common themes often emerge, including (a) ways of coping with a family member's substance abuse, (b) feelings of embarrassment and/or shame about the addicted individual's behavior when under the influence of substances, and (c) wishing their family life was more predictable (e.g., less hectic and chaotic). Any of these themes can be further explored in group therapy sessions. Because individual group members determine the depth of disclosure, the Family Description activity can be used during the early or later stages of group development.

The Family Description activity can be adapted for COA by having group members draw pictures of their family rather than writing a description. The group facilitator will need to provide colored markers, crayons, and drawing paper. Also, an appropriate space is needed to allow for the children to comfortably draw (such as a large table or floor space). The instructions given are, "Draw a picture of your family." If asked for further explanation, simply add "Just draw a picture of your family anyway that you would like." The instructions are left open-ended, allowing for the personal expression of each child. After the drawings are completed, the group members take turns presenting and discussing their drawings. The therapist can encourage the sharing of pictures by asking questions such as the following:

- Tell me about your picture.
- Tell me a story about your picture.
- Tell me who is in your picture.

Common themes often emerge in the children's drawings. Some possible themes include emotion expression such as feelings of fear or sadness, the desire to spend time with the addicted parent/caregiver, and the need to take care of others.

Brief Vignette

The following vignette, of a newly formed family support group, illustrates the use of the Family Description activity in group therapy for adult children of alcoholics. The group was made up of eight ACOA, five women and three men, ranging in ages from twenty-one to thirty-two. They were referred by the individual therapists of their family member, who was seeking primary substance abuse treatment. Prior to joining the group, each member was seen individually for a prescreening and group orientation interview by one of the two group leaders. The goals of the interview were to (a) assess each prospective member's current level of functioning; (b) assess the member's appropriateness for the therapy group; and (c) clarify the nature, purpose, structure, expectations, and rules of the group. The group met for two sessions prior to participating in the Family Description activity. The first meeting was introductory and the second was an education session about substance use, misuse, abuse, dependence, and addiction.

The Family Description session began with a brief check-in from each of the group members, followed by an explanation of the group activity, including the fact that written descriptions would not be collected by group leaders and each member would decide how much information to share with the group. The group activity began with the following statement from one of the leaders:

Today's activity will help each of you get to know one another better. What I would like for you to do is take a few minutes and write down a description of your family of origin. What was it like growing up in your family? What adjectives would you use to describe your family? What were some of your family traditions?

Group members were given approximately ten minutes to write their description. After all members were finished writing, they took turns sharing family descriptions. The members were encouraged to give their undivided attention to the person speaking.

All of the group members but one discussed the impact of substance abuse on their family. Some discussed (a) their fear of bringing friends home due to parental substance abuse, (b) difficulties experienced during the holidays (such as increased alcohol use and family violence), (c) broken promises, and (d) the differences experienced during periods of sobriety. After the members shared their family descriptions, the group discussed similarities and differences among the descriptions. Several group members expressed a feeling of relief that others had been through similar experiences. Others said that this exercise was difficult for them because they had never discussed what occurred in their families before. At this point in the group, the leaders began to normalize some of the feelings of relief as well as feelings of discomfort at discussing the "family secret" of alcoholism or drug addiction. The discussion then focused on addiction and its effects on the family and closed with a summary of the shared experiences and feelings found among the group members.

Suggestions for Follow-Up

The Family Description activity can be the first step in helping group members become acquainted and establish trust, build empathic listening skills, and begin to identify issues that require further exploration. Some issues or concerns, such as emotional expression in families with alcoholism, may be best approached within a psychoeducational group format. Additional support from twelve-step groups, such as Al-Anon, may also prove beneficial.

Contraindications

Prescreening of prospective group members is always necessary prior to initiating group therapy. In addition, therapy groups and their goals should match clients' needs, abilities, and functioning. The Family Description activity is not designed for clients who are experiencing an acute crisis (for example, those who have suicidal/homicidal ideations, untreated clinical depression or post-traumatic stress disorder) or are currently using mind-altering substances. If a client is in active addiction, a group that focuses on the needs of individuals using alcohol and other drugs may be more appropriate. Clients grappling with other issues, such as physical or sexual abuse, may require individual therapy rather than group therapy.

Reading Resources for the Professional

Brown, S., & Lewis, V. (1999). *The alcoholic family in recovery: A developmental model*. New York: Guilford Press.

Edwards, E. (1998). *Treating chemically dependent families: A practical systems approach professionals*. Center City, MN: Hazelden.

Edwards, E. (2003). *Working with families: Guidelines and techniques* (16th ed.). Durham, NC: Foundation Place Publishing.

Kinney, J. (2003). *Loosening the grip: A handbook of alcohol information*. New York: McGraw-Hill.

Bibliotherapy Sources for the Client

Abbott, J. (1991). *Talk, trust, and feel.* New York: Hazeldan Foundation/Ballantine Books.

Bettie, M. (1987). *Codependent no more: How to stop controlling others and caring for yourself.* New York: Harper/Hazelden.

Black, C. (1982). *It will never happen to me.* Denver, CO: MAC Printing and Publishing.

Ehrler, B. (2000). *Learning to be you—it's an inside job: Recovery and healing for the loved ones of the substance-addicted.* Murray, UT: Just Be Publishing, Inc.

Seixas, J. S., & Youcha, G. (1985). *Children of alcoholism: A survivor's manual.* New York: Crown Publishers, Inc.

Wegscheider-Cruse, S. (1987). *Choice-making for co-dependents, adult children and spirituality speakers.* Deerfield, FL: Health Communications, Inc.

Woititz, J. G. (1983). *Adult children of alcoholics.* Hollywood, FL: Health Communications, Inc.

References

Abbott, J. (1991). *Talk, trust, and feel.* New York: Hazeldan Foundation/Ballantine Books.

Arman, H. F. (2000). A small group model for working with elementary school children of alcoholics. *Professional School Counseling, 3*(4), 290-294.

Bosworth, K., & Burke, R. (2001). Collegiate children of alcoholics: Presenting problems and campus services. *Journal of Alcohol and Drug Education, 40*(1), 15-25.

Brook, D. W., Brook, J. S., Rubenstone, E., Zhang, C., Singer, M., & Duke, M. R. (2003). Alcohol use in adolescents whose father abuse drugs. *Journal of Addictive Disease, 2*(1), 11-43.

Cermak, T. (1991). *Evaluating and treating adult children of alcoholics, volume two: Treatment.* Minneapolis, MN: Johnson Institute Professional Series.

Cermak, T. L., & Brown, S. (1982). Interactional group therapy with adult children of alcoholics. *International Journal of Group Psychotherapy, 32*(3), 375-389.

Corey, G. (2004). *Theory and practice of group counseling* (6th ed.). Belmont, CA: Books Cole.

Edwards, E. (2003). *Working with families: Guidelines and techniques* (16th ed.). Durham, NC: Foundation Place Publishing.

Gabarino, C., & Strange, C. (1993). College adjustment and family environments of students reporting parental alcohol problems. *Journal of College Student Development, 34,* 261-266.

Jaeger, E., Hahn, N. B., & Weinraub, M. (2000). Attachment in adult daughters of alcoholic fathers. *Addiction, 95*(2), 267-276.

Kashubeck, S. (1994). Adult children of alcoholics and psychological distress. *Journal of Counseling and Development, 72,* 538-543.

Knowles, E. E., & Schroeder, D. A. (1990). Personality characteristics of sons of alcohol abusers. *Journal of Studies on Alcohol, 51,* 142-147.

Lambie, G. W., & Sias, S. M. (2005). Children of alcoholics: Implications for professional school counseling. *Professional School Counseling, 8*(3), 266-273.

National Association for Children of Alcoholics. (1998). *Children of alcoholics: Important facts.* Retrieved January 27, 2005, from http://www.nacoa.net/impfacts.htm.

National Association for Children of Alcoholics. (2000). *Children of addicted parents: Important facts.* Retrieved January 27, 2005, from http://www.nacoa.net/pdfs/addicted.pdf.

Reich, W., Earls, F., Frankel, O., & Shayka, J. J. (1993). Psychopathology in children of alcoholics. *Journal of the American Academy of Child and Adolescent Psychiatry, 32,* 995-1002.

Robinson, B. E., & Rhoden, J. L. (1998). *Working with children of alcoholics: The practitioner's handbook* (2nd ed.). Thousand Oaks, CA: SAGE Publications, Inc.

Sciarra, D. T. (2004). *School counseling: Foundations and contemporary issues.* Pacific Grove, CA: Brooks/Cole Thomson Learning.

Segrin, C., & Menees, M. M. (1996). The impact of coping style and family communication on the social skills of children of alcoholics. *Journal of Studies on Alcohol, 46,* 137-146.

Substance Abuse and Mental Health Services Administration. (2003). *Children's program kit: Supportive education for children of addicted parents* [DHHS Pub. No. (SMA) 03-3825]. Rockville, MD: Author.

White, W. L. (2005). Fire in the family: Historical perspectives on the intergenerational effects of addiction. *Counselor: The Magazine for Addiction Professionals, 2*(6), 20-25.

White, W., & Savage, R. (2003). *All in the family: Addiction, recovery, advocacy* [online]. Retrieved January 27, 2005, from http://www.bhrm.org/advocacy/recovadvocacy.htm.

17

Holding the Weight of Grief at Arm's Length: Tasks for Resolving Grief

Susan A. Adams

Type of Contribution: Activity

Objective

The goal of this activity is for clients to recognize that they control their grief and that they must empower themselves to acknowledge and express their sorrow in a unique way that is beneficial to them. Often, clients attempt to push away grief, but this frequently serves to intensify a painful loss rather than reduce it. Through symbolic representation, they become aware that carrying their grief at arm's length, over an extended period of time, keeps them stuck in their grief. This prevents them from embracing the reality that the influence and memory of the deceased will never truly go away.

Rationale for Use

Death is a taboo subject for many individuals. This unexpected stressor breaks an attached bond, throws life out of balance, and often creates confusion about one's direction and purpose in life. Often the grief associated with death is quietly ignored, sometimes for years, until something happens to bring all that unexpressed emotion and unresolved grief to the forefront (Adams, 2001). "Loss experiences are buried in a conspiracy of silence. With rare exceptions, nobody wants to talk about loss" (Deits, 1992, p. 2).

Many find themselves ill equipped to process the strong flood of emotions associated with loss. Western society sends a subtle, albeit silent, message that mourning should be brief. Our society dictates a three-day mourning process, as evidenced by the standard funeral leave policy, and this leave is frequently limited only to one's spouse, child, or parents. However, these policies do not take into account significant relationships that cannot be dictated by blood or marriage ceremonies. When we open ourselves up to form relationships, we open ourselves to pain. "The greater the potential for loss, the more intense those reactions and the more varied" (Worden, 2002, p. 8).

It is through Bowlby's (1980, 1973, 1969) work on attachment that we understand that human beings strive to form strong emotional bonds with others for the purpose of safety and security. When those bonds are broken through death, very specific reactions are generated, along with the most intense pain an individual is capable of experiencing (Crenshaw, 1996). Freeman (2005) said, "[Bowlby] believed that the suppression of grief inhibits a natural sequence of painful emotional reactions that, unless allowed to progress naturally, can lead to psychological and physical illness" (p. 45).

The Group Therapist's Notebook
© 2007 by The Haworth Press, Inc. All rights reserved.
doi:10.1300/5576_17

When death is sudden, there are a number of complicating issues. "The loss cuts across experiences in the relationship and tends to highlight what was happening at the time of death, often causing these last-minute situations to be out of proportion with the rest of the relationship and predisposing the bereaved to problems associated with unrealistic recollections and guilt" (Freeman, 2005, p. 99). The bereaved may search for years to find resolution to the emotional dissonance created by the loss as they search for new meaning to reestablish a sense of balance.

Using Transactional Analysis (TA) in grief work can provide insight that allows a resolution to mourning to occur. According to Berne (1964), each individual is composed of three primary ego states: Child, Parent, and Adult. The Child ego state is the first to develop and is subdivided into two forms: the Adapted Child and the Natural (Free) Child. The Adapted Child's compliant behavior is learned as a youngster from its interaction with the Parent ego state. The Free Child is the spontaneous, fun-loving child that impulsively reacts to life. The Parent is composed of two influences known as the Nurturing Parent, who comforts and praises the child, and the Critical Parent, who finds fault and prevents people from feeling good about themselves. The Adult is not subdivided, functions without emotion, and is not related to chronological age. This ego state tests reality, thinks objectively, and gathers data, all without emotion. The task of the Adult is to mediate between the Parent and the Child. All three ego states have value when maintained in a healthy balance. However, when something happens to disturb that balance, it is necessary for analysis and reorganization of the personality.

According to TA, everyone determines how he or she interacts with others (defined as transactions) according to a life script, developed by the age of five (Gladding, 2005). Dysfunction occurs when these life scripts trigger crossed transactions (inappropriate ego state is activated) or ulterior transactions (two ego states operating simultaneously but disguising each other).

Pearson and Stubbs (1999) suggested that an individual's historical record of death experiences help create a pattern of beliefs, values, rituals, and acceptable responses. These are the templates for attitudes and perceptions that govern future reactions, because it is from this depth of knowledge and experience that the bereaved draw from to make meaning out of their personal dissonance. When these templates are based on a childhood experience of grieving, they frequently are faulty and need to be rewritten to facilitate appropriate grief work.

"Berne holds that life scripts can be rewritten if people become more conscious of what they are thinking and make concerted efforts to change" (Gladding, 2005, p. 159). One of the grief tasks suggested by Worden (2002) is to "emotionally relocate the deceased and move on with life" (p. 35). An end to active grieving is not about removing the person from one's life, but about finding an appropriate place for the deceased in their emotional life. "When the bereaved find a method to express their grief, their heart will become 'unstopped,' and they can move through their pain" (Adams, 2001, p. 28).

Therefore, clinicians can use the easily understood terminology of TA plus the goal-directed, contractual nature of the theory to raise the clients' awareness of internal scripts so that change can occur. This empowers them to identify their own unique way through the grief process. This theoretical approach supports the empowerment of the individual; therefore, it appeals to many cultures and diverse world populations (Gladding, 2005).

Instructions

As the clinician works with grieving clients, it is important for him or her to "listen between the lines" and look for grief clues, such as cracks in the voice, eyes tearing up, changes in facial expression, discomfort with certain topics, and strong emotions that appear disproportionate or inappropriate. Therapeutic techniques are used to help clients identify that they are in control of their grief and have a choice about how and when it needs to be expressed. These techniques facilitate expression of thoughts and feelings that have been avoided, discounted, or ignored by others.

This technique can be used with males or females from adolescents to adults. The female pronoun was selected because the vignette that follows is about a female client.

Use a clear, plastic drinking glass that is about 16 to 20 ounces in size. Fill the glass a little over three-quarters full. The fact that it is not full will indicate that clients have dealt with some of the grief work. Bring the glass into the therapy room before the clients arrive.

When you introduce the technique to the group members, hand one client in the group the glass and ask her to hold it with her arm fully extended, as if trying to get the glass as far away from her body as possible. Ask the client and other group members to tell you how heavy they think the glass is. The actual weight is not important; you want them to understand that the glass is really not heavy at all.

As the client continues to hold the glass at arm's length, reflect on something that has been shared in the session. This is a time filler but does not have to be unproductive time. The purpose is to have the client hold the glass in this position for a minute or two in order to realize that the glass gets heavier as she holds it in this position. While the client maintains this position, ask the following questions:

- If you hold the glass like this for five minutes, how heavy will it feel?
- How heavy will it feel if you held it for an hour? For a day? For a week?

It is important that the clients understand that the weight of the glass does not change; however, the longer it is held in this position, the heavier it feels. In fact, if was held like this for any extended period of time, it certainly would become painful and could become crippling. The time spent processing the increasing weight will depend on the group members and the individual client holding the glass. After they begin to understand that the weight of the glass and water do not change, but the burden becomes heavier the longer it is held fully extended, ask the group the following questions:

- If you must keep the glass, what could you do to make it more manageable and give your arm a brief rest? (For example, bend her elbow, rest her arm on her leg, switch hands, set the glass down on the floor for a brief period or drink some of the water.) The concept here is that each individual client controls what happens to the glass of water.
- Ask the client to drink a sip of the water and ask, "How did drinking some of the water help your fatigue as you hold the glass?"
- How do the glass and the water relate to your grief?

Clients can easily link the growing weight of the water with the weight of their grief. However, it is difficult for them to understand that they have choices related to their grief. Sometimes they have held onto their grief for so long that it has become a fixed part of their being. Sometimes they have learned to overlook it or push it away from conscious thought, or they think they have successfully ignored it.

The awareness that results from this technique provides multiple opportunities for the clients to understand that they are in control of their grief, just as they are in control of the glass of water. Once they comprehend that they are in control, they can then begin to explore options of expressing their grief.

Variation

This technique can also be successfully utilized with couple and family groups. Provide enough glasses of water for everyone to have their own. Clear, plastic water bottles of various shapes can be used also. Each person can select his or her own water container, which illustrates that each person has a different perspective on grief. They also deal with grief differently and can make different choices about handling their grief. This can help group members understand that everyone does not necessarily deal with their grief the same way or within the same timeframe.

This can illustrate that we carry our grief differently, and each of us can choose to put it down, to experience our grief (drink some of the water), or to leave it alone— depending on a variety of issues.

Brief Vignette

Pat entered the parental loss group to deal with her father's death, which had occurred fifty years before. Her youngest daughter had recently left home and Pat reported that she felt overwhelmed by a sense of loss. This loss had caused many old memories related to her father's death to resurface, which surprised her. Pat thought these had been buried long ago but found that she was struggling with anger and guilt, two common emotions that surface when dealing with conflicted grief (Crenshaw, 1996; Freeman, 2005).

She was the youngest of four children and reported that her family had been close until her father died on her eighth birthday. Her family left home early that morning to spend the day with her grandmother. Pat forgot the new doll that she had bought with her grandmother's money and asked her dad to go back and get it, which he did. The family started out again, but about six blocks from the house, a truck carrying large sheets of plate glass ran a stop sign and struck their car at the driver's door. The glass shattered and a piece of it came through the open window, decapitating her father. Pat was sitting directly behind him and was splattered with her father's blood.

During the confusion following the wreck, the family did not realize that Pat had suffered a slight concussion until her uncle was putting her to bed late that evening. All day, her repeated complaints of a headache were ignored as the family attempted to make funeral plans and cope with this difficult situation. Throughout the day, Pat was told to go lie down, and none of the children were included in the "adult discussions" about what had happened.

For fifty years, Pat's Adapted Child ego state believed that she caused her father's death. Of course, her current Adult ego state cognitively realized that this was a child's magical thinking, but the Critical Parent in Pat's head repeatedly played the accusatory internal scripts ("It's your fault Father is dead!", "Our family was poor because of you!", "Everyone is mad at you and kept sending you to your room so you would be out of the way!"). However, her Adult ego state had previously not been empowered to negotiate the conflicting scripts and silence of the Critical Parent because Pat did not possess the maturity or life experience to create that meaning.

Pat had carried this burden for five decades and, like other members of the group, did not understand how to let it go. By using the glass of water, Pat and other group members were able to understand that they were making a choice to carry the full glass around at arm's length, and it had gotten heavier as time passed, just like their guilt burden. They recognized that they had a choice to find productive ways to express their grief and release the guilt they felt related to their individual parent's death. In Pat's case, she broke down when her Adaptive Child ego state was finally given permission to grieve and release the guilt she has carried for "causing the accident." She sobbed much as a child would, and her language reverted to childish terminology (for example, she referred to her father as "Daddy" even though she previously used the label "Father" when she talked about him). She realized that she could hold it or put it on the floor for a little while to give her arm a rest. It was her choice. Other group members were able to link this insight to their own parental grief experiences.

Pat also recognized that her grief had prevented her from being fully committed to intimate relationships with her family of origin because she resented the fact that no one had listened to her when she complained about her head hurting. She realized that the anger and guilt had separated her from her mother and her siblings.

Other group members were able to identify ways that they used their grief as a shield to separate them from other family members for a variety of subtle reasons. After discussing the options they had, the group members acknowledged that this was an enlightening concept for them, and they were able to use other cognitive techniques to give voice to their grief (Adams, 2001; Cavaiola & Colford, 2006).

Over the next seven group sessions, Pat talked about the accident and expressed her unresolved grief that had been buried for years. Through the use of additional creative techniques, she released the guilt associated with the responsible she felt for her father's death. This process strengthened the Adult ego state to effectively negotiate and rewrite the internal accusatory scripts between the Critical Parent and the Adapted Child ego states. Pat realized that she could make choices about how and when to grieve in the future and she no longer needed anyone's approval to meet her own needs in this area.

At the end of our therapy, several of the group members identified the water glass technique as the "ah-ha" moment for them because they were finally able to understand that they had choices about "carrying around" their deep sorrow. It was this activity that helped them understand the Adapted Child's inadequacy to completely process and resolve the burden of guilt and anger they experienced because of their parental loss.

Suggestions for Follow-Up

This technique could be utilized in subsequent sessions to empower clients to "drink" part of the grief in a variety of ways (for example, talk about the deceased, talk about changes and/or fears since the death, focus on the legacy that the deceased left, etc.). Clients are empowered to process the grief in pieces as they become problematic or step away from it when they decide not to deal with their grief. This technique can also help clients realize that they can separate themselves from the grief without losing the person they loved. As a result of this awareness, the client is free to celebrate that the person's influence will always remain with them because the deceased is part of their memory. Each group member could be given a glass or asked to bring an empty bottle of some kind to an early group session. This technique could be initially demonstrated with all group members or each member could be included after the demonstration with one group member.

Contraindications

Even though this is a cognitive activity, clients must be able to link this analogy to their life experiences related to their grief. The technique might not be appropriate for clients who have experienced a recent loss because the technique may appear to discount the grief for some clients. It also might not be beneficial to clients with reduced cognitive ability because they might lack the ability to draw abstract conclusions from this cognitive technique.

Readings and Resources for the Professional

Brabant, S. (1996). *Mending the torn fabric: For those who grieve and those who want to help them.* Amityville, NY: Baywood.
Caplan, S., & Gordon, L. (1995). *Grief's courageous journey: A workbook.* Oakland, CA: New Harbinger.
Fitzgerald, H. (1994). *The mourning handbook.* New York: Fireside.
Grollman, E. A. (Ed.) (1995). *Bereaved children and teens: A support guide for parents and professionals.* Boston: Beacon.
Sanders, C. M. (1999). *Grief the mourning after: Dealing with adult bereavement* (2nd ed). New York: Wiley.
Shapiro, E. R. (1994). *Grief as a family process: A developmental approach to clinical practice.* New York: Guilford.

Bibliotherapy Sources for the Client

Albom, M. (1997). *Tuesdays with Morrie: An old man, a young man, and life's greatest lesson.* New York: Doubleday.
Davidson, J. D., & Doka, K. J. (Eds.). (1999). *Living with grief: At work, at school, at worship.* Levittown, PA: Brunner/Mazel.
Dower, L. (2001). *I will remember you: A guidebook through grief for teens.* New York: Scholastic.
Gilbert, R. (1999). *Finding your way after your parent dies: Hope for grieving adults.* Notre Dame, IN: Ave Maria Press.
Golden, T. R. (2000). *Swallowed by a snake: The gift of the masculine side of healing.* (2nd ed.). Gaithersburg, MD: Golden Healing.
O'Conner, J. (1997). *Heaven's not a crying place: Teaching your child about funerals, death, and the life beyond.* Grand Rapids, MI: Fleming H. Revell.
Smith, H. I. (1999). *A Decembered grief: Living with loss while others are celebrating.* Kansas City, MO: Beacon Hill.
Staudacher, C. (1991). *Men & grief: A guide for men surviving the death of a loved one.* Oakland, CA: New Harbinger.
Trozzi, M., & Massimini, K. (1999). *Talking with children about loss: Words, strategies, and wisdom to help children cope with death, divorce, and other difficult times.* New York: Perigee.
Zonnebelt-Smeenge, S. J., & De Vries, R. C. (2001). *Getting to the other side of grief: Overcoming the loss of a spouse.* Grand Rapids, MI: Baker.

References

Adams, S. A. (2001). *Teaching the mourning song.* Denton, TX: Author.
Berne, E. (1964). *Games people play: The psychology of human relationships.* New York: Ballantine Books.
Bowlby, J. (1969). *Attachment and loss* (Vol. 1), *Attachment.* New York: Basic Books.
Bowlby, J. (1973). *Attachment and loss* (Vol. 2), *Separation: Anxiety and anger.* New York: Basic Books.
Bowlby, J. (1980). *Attachment and loss* (Vol. 3), *Loss.* New York: Basic Books.
Cavaiola, A. A., & Colford, J. E. (2006). *A practical guide to crisis intervention.* Boston: Lahaska.

Crenshaw, D. A. (1996). *Bereavement: Counseling the grieving through the life cycle.* New York: Crossroad.

Deits, B. (1992). *Life after loss: A personal guide dealing with death, divorce, job change and relocation.* Tucson, AZ: Fisher Books.

Freeman, S. J. (2005). *Grief & loss: Understanding the journey.* Belmont, CA: Thompson Brooks/Cole.

Gladding, S. T. (2005). *Counseling theories: Essential concepts and applications.* Upper Saddle River, NJ: Pearson Education.

Pearson, C., & Stubbs, M. L. (1999). *Parting company—Understanding the loss of a loved one: The caregiver's journey.* Seattle, WA: Seal Press

Worden, J. W. (2002). *Grief counseling and grief therapy: A handbook for the mental health practitioner* (3rd ed.). New York: Springer.

18

Grief and Loss:
Healing Through Group Therapy

Jane Roberts

Type of Contribution: Activities/Handouts

Objective

The goal of grief counseling and group activity is to guide the individual through four main tasks that are generally seen as essential to resolving grief following any loss (Worden, 2002). Although still within the realm of normal adaptive behavior, grief represents a marked change in one's state of mental and physical health in that the individual may experience a depressed mood, a heightened sense of anxiety, or other variations in normative functioning. The activities outlined here pertain to four essential tasks of grieving:

- Accepting the reality of the loss
- Dealing with deep thoughts and feelings about the loss
- Adjusting to living without the lost one
- Saying good-bye and reinvesting in life

ACCEPTING THE REALITY OF THE LOSS

Rationale for Use

To fully understand loss, we must first understand the concept of psychological attachment, the condition that makes loss possible. A theoretical viewpoint that informs the use of an intense discussion and opportunity to ventilate feelings surrounding bereavement is known as attachment theory, developed by British psychologist John Bowlby (1977). Bowlby proposes the theory that attachment arises from such basic needs as safety and security. The formation of attachment occurs early in life and is considered normative behavior basic to survival. In the study of attachment, Bowlby concluded that any separation or loss (of a desired person, object, event, or situation) results in automatic, instinctive, cognitive, and behavioral adaptation.

We think of this constellation of changes in thinking or behaving as grief or mourning, two terms used interchangeably here. Evidence exists that most humans react to separation or loss with some degree of grief. This is a psychosocial theory and explanation of the grieving process, even though grieving people typically exhibit physiological or biological symptoms as well, such as an upset stomach or hyperactivity and pressured feelings due to anxiety. Thus, for many reasons, the process of grieving can be likened to a state of healing. The following exercise facilitates the healing mechanism.

Instructions

It can be reassuring to a group member that others experience the same or similar social, emotional, and cognitive grief reactions following the loss of a loved one. This is, of course, one reason to use a group venue to address grief and the ways in which to deal with the resultant thoughts and feelings. The group exercise most likely to be helpful in dealing with the reality of the loss is simple discussion, sharing of individual experiences, and an initial opportunity to express thoughts and feelings. This conversation can consist simply of telling the events of the loss: whether the lost one experienced a long and debilitating illness, whether the loss was sudden and unexpected, initial reactions such as shock or denial, and the like. The bereaved person may wish to talk about the event itself, if he or she was present at the time of the death. If the group member was not present at the death of the loved one, then a description of the feelings brought about by having been away at the time of the death may be cathartic. Each group member may then compare thoughts and feelings such as sadness, guilt, remorse, and regrets that have arisen since the event.

For this group activity, the therapist will first need to develop a structured outline for group discussion, and to assemble paper and pens or pencils for group written reflections. A prepared handout or worksheet should include the items listed below, as well as room for the group member to write reflections, although 5 × 7 inch lined note cards can also be used (see Handout 18.1). The topics for discussion should include (but are not limited to) the following:

- Obsessive thoughts about the deceased
- Disbelief, denial, derealization, or sense of dreaming
- Confusion
- Sense of presence of the deceased
- Visual or auditory hallucinations

When the therapist has distributed the handouts or lined cards to group members, they are instructed to write their experiences that coincide with each of the listed topics. The therapist then encourages group members to share as many reflections with the group as they feel comfortable in sharing. It can be very reassuring to a client that others have experienced the same seemingly "disturbing" or "abnormal" reactions, which are actually quite typical reactions and not at all unusual in the presence of grief. Although this exercise in identifying and acknowledging psychosocial reactions to grief and loss is simple and basic, the consequent discussion and opening up of feelings surrounding the loss is often remarkable and can set the tone for open, uninhibited sharing of thoughts and feelings during subsequent group sessions. It can also lead to a discussion of the value of group therapy and of the support and understanding of others who have endured similar losses, facilitating continuing group attendance and solidarity among group members.

Suggestions for Follow-Up

For follow-up, the therapist may wish to have group members take their note cards or handouts home and reflect on the similarity of the revelations with other group members', as well as the normalizing effect of discovering others' similar experiences and reactions to the grieving process.

DEALING WITH DEEP THOUGHTS
AND FEELINGS SURROUNDING THE LOSS

Rationale for Use

Although all members of a group will not have had exactly the same experiences and reactions to a loss, there will be many similarities, and there are specific emotions that are often inadvertently repressed or more consciously suppressed. Anger may be one particularly elusive feeling. Anger is not always easily dealt with and can be frightening to family members or friends of the bereaved. However, expressed in the therapeutic environment, anger can be more readily managed. If not targeted appropriately toward the grief situation, anger can be displaced onto medical personnel, family members, the clergy, or others. If not discharged, it can also be turned inward or "retroflected," then experienced as depression or suicidal inclination.

This group exercise can elicit thoughts and feelings of anger or frustration that might otherwise remain unexpressed, but which are permissible and can be competently handled within the safe environment of the group and therapist. The experienced grief counselor will always address anger, depressed mood, or suicidal ideation in some manner, if only to broach the subject to group members who perhaps are not forthcoming with those feelings.

Instructions

Because anger is not always best addressed directly, or because directly addressing the topic does not always elicit candid discussion, the therapist can utilize the following exercise to identify and deal with such strong emotions. The therapist distributes two self-stick notes (a size large enough to write legibly in 2 to 3 inch block letters is most feasible) to all group members. Group members are then instructed to write on one sticky note "what I miss about [the lost person]". On the other sticky note, the group member writes "what I don't miss." Each group member then attaches the notes to a shirt collar or lapel (one on each shoulder, for example), and mingles with other group members to read one another's notes.

Generally, participants have no difficulty writing "what I miss" and easily note some shared activity such as "cuddling on the sofa." However, the second question often elicits a moment of stunned silence, then sometimes a chuckle or laughter when writing "dirty socks on the floor" or "arguments about money." Participants typically do not expect the second question and will often appreciate the moment of comic relief while studying and sympathizing with others' notations. The ensuing discussion will likely turn serious, of course, and can allow expression of the repressed anger surrounding missed opportunities, such as aging together or quiet cuddling, while acknowledgment of things not missed can put at least some aspects of the loss into a different perspective. In addition, this exercise often has the effect of implicitly conveying that grief and loss group work is not exclusively serious and soul-wrenching.

Suggestions for Follow-Up

Following this exercise, the therapist might ask for reflections upon changes in feelings or new awareness of feelings and the deeper emotions that have occurred during the intervening time between group sessions. Giving the group members time to reflect between sessions is often an effective method of eliciting additional thoughts and feelings.

ADJUSTING TO LIVING WITHOUT THE LOST ONE: TASK LIST

Rationale for Use

Many bereaved people are astounded to learn the components and normal manifestations of grief reactions (Muller & Thompson, 2003). During adjustment to the loss, typical grief reactions can include somatic or physical distress, preoccupation with images of the deceased, guilt (including survivor guilt), anger or hostility, irritability, lethargy, or anergia (Parkes & Weiss, 1983; Shuchter & Zisook, 1987). In addition, extreme sadness or anxiety can occur, as well as fatigue or numbness, feelings of helplessness, and yearning for the lost one. Perhaps more unexpected, many people feel a sense of relief or emancipation, especially if a lengthy or consuming illness required a good deal of caregiving and "caregiver burden." Grief can feel overwhelming, yet it is a universally experienced phenomenon. This exercise can help the group members observe, comment on, and support one another in their efforts to "get on with" tasks and decision making without the input of the lost one.

Instructions

The therapist briefly explains the issue of adjustment and elicits ideas and empathy for the concept of needing to maintain (or, in some cases, to initiate) independence with daily activities. The therapist distributes sheets of paper and asks group members to write at least ten daily or weekly tasks, specifying those tasks for which the deceased routinely took charge. Group members will often list such things as bill paying, minor household repairs, cooking, or taking out the trash. Instead of initiating discussion about each member's own tasks listed, however, the therapist has each group member pass the list to the person on his or her right. Each group member then reviews his or her neighbor's list and identifies the tasks he or she is already doing, if any. Generally, people, even in their bereavement, have already begun to carry out the normal activities of daily life, even if they had considered themselves unable to do them (Worden, 2002). This exercise serves to show how many of those small daily adjustments have already been made or are in the process of being made. It can also show the similarity of tasks that one might find overwhelming, and this is the rationale for having each individual review the lists of other group members. This task can also demonstrate that tasks considered incrementally are much more easily handled than are a multitude of tasks considered in aggregate, which makes these tasks seem much less overwhelming and insurmountable.

Variation

The therapist instructs group members to do the same exercise, substituting decision-making tasks that must be executed, especially noting decisions often considered to be within the purview of the deceased or decisions that formerly would have been made jointly.

Suggestions for Follow-Up

Follow-up to this exercise may involve a subsequent group session, in which the therapist asks group members to report and reflect on additional tasks or decisions that were made during the intervening week. Discussion can then surround group members' reactions to having done more or less than expected at this juncture in the bereavement process, and a plan can be made for increasing the level of daily tasks or decision making to be completed during the next week.

SAYING GOOD-BYE AND REINVESTING IN LIFE: LIFE REVIEW SCRAPBOOK

Rationale for Use

Bereaved individuals eventually must reexamine what life holds in store and must move on in the absence of the loved one who was lost. Some individuals obviously do so more easily than others, and some have more social and emotional support or experience with grief from prior losses. Because saying good-bye to the lost one is a recognized grief process need, group exercises for saying good-bye to the lost individual abound in the literature. Group therapists often have the bereaved individual write a letter, plant a tree to commemorate the loss, and the like. These memorial activities are very effective and have the added impact of providing a remembrance when the bereaved repeatedly encounters a living memorial such as a growing plant.

A related activity suited to groups is offered here, again with the intent that group members can support, advise, and learn from one another, thus enhancing and expanding the opportunities for growth and continued development following any loss. Because concrete, tangible materials and objects can sometimes serve to facilitate closure in the face of loss, this activity can be useful in that manner and can serve as a transitional object between the event of the loss and the continuation of one's necessary daily activities. This intervention offers group members hands-on physical activity, as well as a memento to take home and permanently display or show to family and friends. For an end-stage group, this activity can also serve to help group members review and reminisce about life generally and to reflect upon their group therapy experience.

Instructions

This activity requires some preparation, explanation, and gathering of materials at the session prior to the activity session or informative handouts can be distributed at the session prior to the current meeting. The group members are instructed to bring in mementos, such as letters, award certificates or documentation of other honors, photos depicting family life or life with the deceased, simple needlework, or similar objects pertaining to life with the deceased. Color or black and white copies of these items are also acceptable. The therapist explains that each group member will be putting together a scrapbook with these mementos.

The therapist assembles simple, notebook style three-ring binders or more elaborate scrapbooking materials, as well as plastic sleeves outfitted for three-ring binder application. A small label maker or other hand-held printing device can be used to label photos and other memorabilia that will be entered into the scrapbooks. A sample scrapbook prepared by the therapist (with careful consideration of confidentiality and self-disclosure, if applicable) is a helpful example.

The therapist divides the group into pairs or small groups of not more than three individuals. The therapist describes the development and content of a life review "lifeline" and distributes a printed example and template (see Handout 18.2). Explaining that events and processes that are considered to be positive in one's life are placed above the line, and events that are considered negative or painful go below the line, the therapist encourages members to create their own lifeline. The Life Review Lifeline becomes the first page of the scrapbook and is slipped into the first plastic sleeve.

The therapist then allows time for group members to review one another's mementos and briefly describe the meaning of each. After examining mementos in the small group setting, members place their objects in the plastic sleeves and assemble a scrapbook with each sleeved object constituting one page of the scrapbook. Group members then type or write a brief description of the object, such as FAMILY AT LAKE MANATEE: SUMMER, 1999. After rejoining the larger group, each member briefly relates a description and the meaning of the objects, including the reason for the choice of that particular memento for the scrapbook and for permanent remembrance.

The client is reminded that objects can be added or changed as deemed suitable when the scrapbook is taken home. Group discussion can include recounting memories, plans for scrapbook object inclusion in the future, and ideas for other memorial endeavors. The therapist can elicit conversation about closure, the utility of support by peers, and the overall experience of grief and loss.

Suggestions for Follow-Up

When group members reconvene following this exercise, they may wish to share their scrapbooks and to note whether they have added material or mementos during the intervening days or weeks since the prior group session. Group members may be more ready at this later time to share the emotions and memories surrounding the scrapbook entries. The therapist might also ask whether group members have shown the scrapbooks to family or friends, thus initiating conversations about mutual reminiscences regarding the deceased.

Contraindications

For several subsets of the population of bereaved individuals, there may be contraindications for any of the exercises described here. Cognitively impaired individuals, for example, may not be able to fully participate or understand the significance of these interventions. Those with dementia or other thought disorders would not be appropriate candidates for group grief work, in consideration of their own abilities and of the continuity of group processes. Similarly, bereaved persons who exhibit symptoms of clinical depression would be better served by a referral for in-depth, insight-oriented individual treatment. Even seemingly basic or simple group activities may elicit in such clients overwhelming psychological or socio-emotional material more appropriate to individual therapy.

Readings and Resources for the Professional

Black, D., & Urbanowicz, M. A. (1987). Family intervention with bereaved children. *Journal of Child Psychology and Psychiatry and Allied Disciplines, 28,* 467-476.

Brown, J. T., & Stoudemire, G. A. (1983). Normal and pathological grief. *Journal of the American Medical Association, 250,* 378-382.

Dush, D. M. (1988). Balance and boundaries in grief counseling: An intervention framework for volunteer training. *Hospice Journal, 4,* 79-93.

Kane, R. L. The role of hospice in reducing the impact of bereavement. *Journal of Chronic Disease, 39,* 735-742.

Lehman, D. R., Ellard, J. H., & Wortman, C. B. (1986). Social support for the bereaved: Recipients' and providers' perspectives on what is helpful. *Journal of Consulting and Clinical Psychology, 54,* 438-446.

Shutz, W. (1967). *Joy: Expanding human awareness.* New York: Grove.

Yalom, I. D., & Vinogradov, S. (1988). Bereavement groups: Techniques and themes. *International Journal of Group Psychotherapy, 38,* 419-446.

Bibliotherapy Sources for the Client

Burns, D. (1980). *Feeling good: The new mood therapy.* New York: Signet.

Epstein, M. (1998). *Going to pieces without falling apart.* New York: Broadway Books.

Grief Share: http://www.griefshare.org/ A clearinghouse of grief groups and online resources.

Westberg, G. E. (1971). *Good grief: A constructive approach to the problem of loss*. Philadelphia: Fortress Press. (Also available in large print.)

White, M. (1999). *Dolor acerbo y dulce esperanza*. (Harsh grief, gentle hope). Spanish language. Los Angeles: Vida Publishers.

Web sites of many hospice organizations list practical as well as professional resources.

References

Bowlby, J. (1977). The making and breaking of affectional bonds. *British Journal of Psychiatry, 130,* 201-210.

Muller, E. D., & Thompson, C. L. (2003). The experience of grief after bereavement: A phenomenological study with implications for mental health counseling. *Journal of Mental Health Counseling, 25*(3), 183-204.

Parkes, C. M., & Weiss, R. S. (1983). *Recovery from bereavement*. New York: Basic Books.

Shuchter, S., & Zisook, S. (1987). The therapeutic tasks of grief. In S. Zisook (Ed.), *Biopsychosocial aspects of bereavement*. Washington, DC: American Psychiatric Assocation.

Worden, J. W. (2002). *Grief counseling and grief therapy*. New York: Springer Publishing Co.

HANDOUT 18.1. REFLECTIONS WORKSHEET

Using the following grid, complete any sections that reflect your personal experiences following a significant loss. For example, if you have experienced obsessive thoughts about your loved one, you might enter "cannot sleep due to overwhelming thoughts" in column 2. Then under column 3, you might note "wish to be able to relax and go to sleep" or "wish to learn to think about other things before going to sleep."

Process Related to the Loss	My Experience	My Thoughts/Feelings Related to the Experience
Obsessive Thoughts		
Disbelief		
Denial		
Confusion/Disorientation		
Visual or Auditory Experiences		
Other		

Roberts, J. (2007). Grief and loss: Healing through group therapy. In D. R. Viers (Ed.), *The group therapist's notebook: Homework, handouts, and activities for use in psychotherapy* (pp. 127-135). Binghamton, NY: The Haworth Press.

HANDOUT 18.2. LIFELINE: SAMPLE

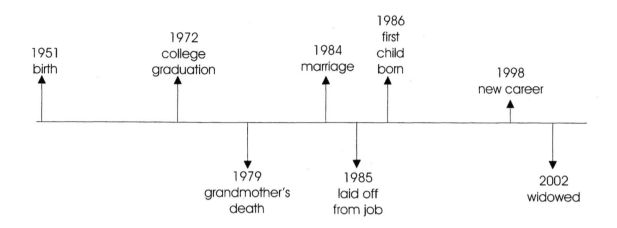

Roberts. J. (2007). Grief and loss: Healing through group therapy. In D. R. Viers (Ed.), *The group therapist's notebook: Homework, handouts, and activities for use in psychotherapy* (pp. 127-135). Binghamton, NY: The Haworth Press.

SECTION IV:
INTERVENTIONS FOR ADOLESCENT
AND COLLEGE-AGE GROUPS

19

The How-To Book:
A Model-Driven Process
for Group Work with Adolescents

Dave Bryant

Type of Contribution: Handout

Objective

The objective of the How-To Book is to introduce the concept of purposeful change as a possibility for the participant and to provide a model-driven vehicle for the desired, voluntarily self-identified change. The questions in the How-To Book (Handout 19.1) are very straightforward and designed to

- stimulate and focus the process of the group,
- provide a sense of self-evaluation as the participant chooses to, or chooses not to, progress through the Stages of Change, and
- teach the process as a universally applicable system for behavioral change.

Rationale for Use

This process leans heavily on two major, well-established theoretical conceptualizations: Stages of Change, developed as part of the Transtheoretical Model (Prochaska & Norcross, 1994), and Rational Emotive Therapy (RET), as developed by Albert Ellis (Ellis & Grieger, 1986). The first theoretical base is the Stages of Change. Utilization of this model as an intervention for youth has been documented by Moody and Lupton-Smith (1999). The stages seem to work both as a way to understand how purposeful behavioral change can occur and as a way to self-monitor progress in the group. The stages are as follows:

- Precontemplation (Stage One): Not even thinking about change
- Contemplation (Stage Two): Thinking about change
- Preparation (Stage Three): Getting ready to change, making a plan
- Action (Stage Four): Working your plan, putting your plan into action
- Maintenance (Stage Five): Keep on working your plan

The definitions as presented seem unsophisticated but, in this concise, vernacular form, can easily be remembered by the participant. The stages are introduced to the participants during the first few weeks of the group through brief explanation, followed by liberal use of examples and role-plays. The participants use the back of the last page of their How-To Book to list and define each stage, which serves as a ready reference. The stages are referred to frequently by the facilitator and are integrated into the How-To Book.

The second theoretical base is Rational Emotive Therapy, known to be a highly effective form of cognitive-behavioral therapy that is utilized in both individual and group formats (Ellis & Grieger, 1986). The basic tenant of RET is that thinking creates emotion—that is, our reactions to events, people, and situations are in our control and are determined by the views/perceptions we have about events that occur. Essentially, we react to our thinking about an event, person, or situation; our reactions and feelings are not caused by the event, person, or situation. This is a very foreign concept, especially to children and adolescents who are struggling with psychosocial milestones and often blame others for their shortcomings rather than looking at themselves (Erikson, 1968).

The change process involving RET is as follows:

A = Activating Event: This can be a person or situation to which we react.
B = Belief: This is the belief or thinking that we apply that determines our feelings about and reactions to the activating event.
C = Emotional Consequence: This is the feeling that is a result of our belief or our thinking.
D = Define and Debate: This is the change process that involves challenging the belief(s) or thinking that determines the feelings and reactions.
E = The New Effect: This is our new-found ability and willingness to semiautomatically use this system of thinking to determine how we feel.

Ellis and Grieger (1986) state that humans are born with the capacity to think irrationally and the therapy or corrective process is one of challenging irrational thinking, leading to healthier, more rational living.

Although the spirit of RET is present throughout the how-to process, the RET model is literally taught at the Preparation stage. It is a very effective way of helping the participant deal with the question in the How-To Book "What's standing in the way?" which presents the participant with the opportunity to confront the irrationality of blaming others for their difficulties.

Instructions

The How-To Book is a nine-page workbook that was developed as a psychoeducational tool for group intervention with adolescents between the ages of twelve and seventeen. It consists of a series of questions, and presents the group participant with the opportunity for behavioral change and a method to facilitate the desired change with support and assistance from a creative and energetic group process. Each page consists of a single question, an indication of the stage that question addresses, and as much room for the several answers/thoughts/musings/loose associations/artistic expressions/doodles to each question that inevitably occurs as part of the discussion and feedback process. Prior to starting the group, the facilitator should make copies of the workbook for each member and some extras as necessary. It is helpful to copy each page of the workbook in a different color for easy reference.

Referrals for this group typically come from school counselors, principals, and teachers. Prescreening is an important aspect of forming the group. Once referral has been made, the facilitator meets with the potential participant, describing in detail the intent and purpose of the group and the methods used (the How-To Book, the use of group initiatives, role-playing and supportive discussion and feedback, the Stage of Change framework, and the strategic use of Rational Emotive Therapy). The facilitator then asks if the participant is interested in participating in the group and gives the participant the group protocol (Exhibit 19.1). The participant is not required to commit to change of any kind, only to indicate an interest in participating.

The structure of the group consists of two separate but closely related segments: the group initiative and the working segment of the group.

The Group Initiative

The use of highly interactive, noncompetitive group initiatives is known to develop group cohesion and to establish and maintain individual and collective trust in a group setting (Rohnke, 1984). In applying this principle to the how-to process, the initiative is explained in the context of trust building and the necessity for trust among group members due to the personal nature of the information involved in completing the How-To Book. The same initiative is used to begin, and sometimes end, each session. The constant presence (once a week, every week) of the same

EXHIBIT 19.1.
PROTOCOL: THE HOW-TO GROUP

I. Population served
   A. Youth between the ages of twelve and fourteen or fourteen and seventeen that are experiencing difficulties with any of the following: substance abuse, anger management, motivation, difficulty in relationships (home/school, peer/adult), and/or generalized defiance.
II. Referral Process
   A. Referral to the group can be generated by the school counselor, teacher, or school principal
III. Format
   A. Frequency: One time per week for either one half hour or one hour
   B. Each group is divided into two distinct segments
      1. A warm-up initiative
      2. Working in the How-To Book
IV. Goals, Purpose, Intent
   A. To experience how to trust, to trust, and to be trusted by other group members
   B. To gain a working, functional knowledge of the process of personal change
      1. Self-determining whether change is desired
      2. Identifying the risks and benefits associated with change
      3. Self-identifying areas of personal change
   C. Learn a stepwise approach to personal change that can be generalized to any area of a participant's life
   D. Learn how to accept and tolerate assistance from others as part of the process of personal change
V. Philosophical Base
   A. Stages of Change, from the Transtheoretical Model (Prochaska & Norcross, 1994)
   B. Rational Emotive Therapy (Ellis & Grieger, 1986)
VI. Group Facilitator Associated with Community Services, the facilitator is a licensed mental health counselor.

initiative provides the group and individual members with (a) in vivo information regarding the group's ability and willingness to function cooperatively and (b) an experiential indicator of the degree of trust that exists between the group members at that specific point in time. It also provides the members with immediate feedback regarding the group's readiness to approach the task of working in the how-to process. There are some groups that initially have extreme difficulty functioning in a cooperative manner. The group initiative is often utilized to address this difficulty.

The initiative that is used is called a group juggle, which involves tossing objects among participants. The initiative begins with one object and increases gradually as the juggle continues. The number of objects rarely exceeds the number of participants. The following instructions are given verbatim at the beginning of every group:

1. "You can throw this object to anyone in the room."
2. "Use the person's name whom you are throwing it to."
3. "Throw it in such a way as he or she can catch it."

It is important to note that the objects used are of a noncompetitive nature. Balls, of any sort, stuffed animals, or other soft objects are selected with fun, uniqueness, noncompetitiveness, and safety in mind.

The Working Segment of the Group

Instructions for this segment of the group are deceptively simple. Each participant has an opportunity to participate or to work in each session. The work of the participant is guided by the How-To Book, included as Handout 19.1 at the end of this chapter. The instructions are "Take it from the top," meaning start at the beginning. The working participant then begins reading and answering each question. If the participant's answer to the first question ("Do you want to make any changes in your life?") is no, then the participant is in the Precontemplative stage. The facilitator offers a short, supportive (not persuasive) comment to the Precontemplative participant about the difficulty of personal change and moves to the next participant without judgment or hesitation.

If the answer is yes, the participant begins addressing the change desired and moves to the other questions in the workbook, writing down his or her thoughts about each question. These thoughts may cover the entire page and may appear in seemingly nonrelated forms (such as scribbling, logos, phrases, loosely connected ideas, cartoon characters, and so forth), but with coaching and question asking from the nonworking participants, these expressions will culminate in clear and operational answers to each question. The facilitator carefully and enthusiastically explains that the questions seem simple but, in effect, are extremely difficult; for if the participant could answer the questions immediately and without struggle, there would be no need for them to be in the group.

The role of the other group members at this point is to follow the working member in their How-To Books but not record their own answers. The facilitator teaches and coaches the nonworking participants to ask helpful and clarifying questions of the working member. This coaching often takes the form of literally whispering questions to ask in the nonworking member's ear. Done enthusiastically and boldly by the facilitator, this can be a very humorous subprocess.

Each time a member chooses to work, the same process is utilized, that is, "Take it from the top." Member frustration with having to repeat the questions and their responses many times dissipates when the facilitator explains that they are not only involved in changing but also in learning how to change; a process that can be generalized and used for a lifetime.

Brief Vignette

A thirteen-year-old middle-school student was referred to the group by his teacher, through the school counselor, for "having a bad attitude" and being disrespectful and generally disruptive through his overt defiance toward the teacher during class. The child was screened and was given the opportunity to join the group. He did so, stating that, ". . . my attitude gets me in trouble."

A new group was beginning, and others in the group knew him as a long-term friend and classmate and were familiar with his "attitude."

Contemplation Stage

Because of his familiarity with the other group members, he integrated into the group easily. He quickly became involved in the how-to process and self-identified, "I want to change my attitude at school with teachers." Having immediately declared his intent to change his behavior, he placed himself solidly in the Contemplation stage, skipping the Precontemplation stage.

Preparation Stage

After ten to twelve sessions of clarifying, recording his answers in the How-To Book, role-playing, being angry with other group members for "asking the same questions over and over and over" ("but what is it that you want to change?"), and eventually stating what he wished to change, he began developing a plan to change. Through the questioning and clarifying process, the member gradually began to define exactly what he wished to change from the very general attitude to, "I want to stop talking back to Ms. _____ when she asks me to do something, like to be quiet or to do my work, even if I think she's wrong and being a b—h." The other group members had full knowledge of his attitude and had often witnessed it (and had been entertained by it) on many occasions through the years. They also recognized his need to change and were supportive of his efforts.

When addressing the question "What's standing in the way?", RET was introduced to assist the participant at looking at himself in terms of his beliefs versus external causes for his reactions to the teacher. Beliefs that were driving his feelings and reactions included toe following: "I must control this situation," "I must look good in front of my friends," and the core belief, "I must not let women tell me what to do."

When addressing the question "Who can help me?", he responded with the usual answers: my friends and the group. While in the process of answering this question, the facilitator coached him to think about going to the identified teacher for assistance and incorporating her into his change process. This was met with uproarious laughter from the participant and other group members. Through explanation and role-plays demonstrating how this idea might work, the participant and other group members began to actively consider the idea viable.

Action Stage

Asking the teacher for help was not an easy concept for the participant, having previously leaned heavily on defiance as the core element in his relationship with the teacher. After several role-plays, involving other group members with the participant playing himself and then the teacher, and several more weeks of facilitator coaching and member feedback in regard to the viability of the idea, he began to see that the teacher could be a valuable resource in his attempts to change his attitude.

He developed a plan that involved approaching the teacher and explaining that he was involved in a process to help him change his attitude. He would also make clear that he was "tired of getting in trouble" and needed her assistance. He explained to the teacher that he was going to control his defiance in her classroom and toward her. His plan further called for him to ask the teacher for feedback on whether his plan was working and for him to periodically re-approach the teacher for a, how-am-I-doing? discussion.

The participant followed through with this plan. He had much success with the plan, and his teacher was very responsive toward his initiative to change.

Maintenance Stage

He was able to control his attitude toward the teacher by using deep breathing, utilizing behavioral strategies such as counting to ten, recalling the role-plays, remembering that his reactions and feeling were driven by his beliefs, and thinking about the consequences of his behavior prior to acting. As he reported his progress to the group, he regularly received feedback from the group members (some of whom were in the class with the participant) and received much praise for his ability and willingness to initiate his plan.

This synopsis of this participant's desire to change, and his decision to follow through with change as presented here sounds very simple and clear cut. His change process was anything but smooth, however, punctuated by refusal to work because of what he perceived as group members asking the same questions over and over, absences from the group when his work became to intense for him, anxiety about following through with his plan, and overcoming the beliefs that were driving his defiance. He was able to overcome these personal obstacles and, with the help of the group and the facilitator, he approached the teacher and enlisted her as a resource in his change process.

Suggestions for Follow-Up

As this workbook is meant to take the client from the beginning stages of the group to the end, there is no formal follow-up. Once the client reaches the maintenance stage in his or her problem-resolution procedure, it is prudent for the facilitator to continually check in with participants and provide feedback regarding their progress. If the client identifies a new area of desired change, the client can start to work on this problem in a new workbook. Members rarely want the group to end and, as a way to stay involved in the process, have suggested a "meeting every once in a while to see how we are doing." One group suggested that they "stay on to help the new ones" (a new group was being formed).

Although this activity was designed for youth between the ages of twelve and seventeen, recent experience has shown that, with some creative simplification, the process is also applicable and effective with fourth and fifth graders. Males and females can be involved in both co-educational and single-gender formats.

Contraindications

Groups are not for everyone. There are children who find it difficult to function in groups of this nature. This could be for a variety of reasons, including extreme defiance as manifested by a tendency to disrupt or to be violent, suspiciousness as manifested by fear, or children who may be experiencing extreme emotional disturbances.

Mild to moderate developmental delays are not a factor, providing the child can comprehend the process. The screening process is a very important element in forming a group and can help children, with these and other precluding challenges, in finding more appropriate interventions.

Readings and Resources for the Professional

Ellis, A., & Grieger, R. M. (Eds.). (1986). *Handbook of rational-emotive therapy* (Vol. 2). New York: Springer

Prochaska, J., & Norcross, J. (1994). *Systems of psychotherapy: A transtheoretical analysis* (3rd ed.). Brooks/Cole, Pacific Grove, CA

Bibliotherapy Sources for the Client

Covey, S. (1998). *The seven habits of highly effective teens.* New York: Fireside.

Fox, A. (2000). *Can you relate? Real world advice for teens on guys, girls, growing up, and getting along.* Minneapolis, MN: Free Spirit Publishing.

McGraw, J. (2000). *Life strategies for teens.* New York: Fireside.

References

Ellis, A., & Grieger, R. M. (Eds.). (1986). *Handbook of rational-emotive therapy* (Vol. 2). New York: Springer

Erikson, E. H. (1968). *Youth and crisis.* New York: W. W. Norton & Co.

Moody, E., & Lupton-Smith, H. (1999). Interventions with juvenile offenders: Strategies to prevent acting out behavior. *Journal of Addictions and Offender Counseling, 20*(1), 2-20.

Prochaska, J., & Norcross, J. (1994). *Systems of psychotherapy: A transtheoretical analysis* (3rd ed.). Brooks/Cole, Pacific Grove, CA.

Rohnke, K. (1984). *Silver bullets: A guide to initiative activities.* Hamilton, MA: Project Adventure, Inc.

HANDOUT 19.1.

PRECONTEMPLATION STAGE

DO I WANT TO MAKE ANY CHANGES IN MY LIFE?

Page 1

Bryant, D. (2007). The how-to book: A model-driven process for group work with adolescents. In D. R. Viers (Ed.), *The group therapist's notebook: Homework, handouts, and activities for use in psychotherapy* (pp. 139-154). Binghamton, NY: The Haworth Press.

CONTEMPLATION STAGE

WHAT DO I WANT TO CHANGE?

Page 2

Bryant, D. (2007). The how-to book: A model-driven process for group work with adolescents. In D. R. Viers (Ed.), *The group therapist's notebook: Homework, handouts, and activities for use in psychotherapy* (pp. 139-154). Binghamton, NY: The Haworth Press.

CONTEMPLATION STAGE

IS IT POSSIBLE TO CHANGE IT?

Page 3

Bryant, D. (2007). The how-to book: A model-driven process for group work with adolescents. In D. R. Viers (Ed.), *The group therapist's notebook: Homework, handouts, and activities for use in psychotherapy* (pp. 139-154). Binghamton, NY: The Haworth Press.

PREPARATION STAGE

WHAT'S STANDING IN THE WAY?

Page 4

Bryant, D. (2007). The how-to book: A model-driven process for group work with adolescents. In D. R. Viers (Ed.), *The group therapist's notebook: Homework, handouts, and activities for use in psychotherapy* (pp. 139-154). Binghamton, NY: The Haworth Press.

PREPARATION STAGE

HOW CAN I CHANGE IT?

Bryant, D. (2007). The how-to book: A model-driven process for group work with adolescents. In D. R. Viers (Ed.), *The group therapist's notebook: Homework, handouts, and activities for use in psychotherapy* (pp. 139-154). Binghamton, NY: The Haworth Press.

PREPARATION STAGE

DO I NEED ANY HELP?

WILL I LET ANYONE HELP ME?

WHO CAN HELP ME?

Page 6

Bryant, D. (2007). The how-to book: A model-driven process for group work with adolescents. In D. R. Viers (Ed.), *The group therapist's notebook: Homework, handouts, and activities for use in psychotherapy* (pp. 139-154). Binghamton, NY: The Haworth Press.

ACTION STAGE

What NOW? I've been talking about change, NOW what do I DO about it?

Bryant, D. (2007). The how-to book: A model-driven process for group work with adolescents. In D. R. Viers (Ed.), *The group therapist's notebook: Homework, handouts, and activities for use in psychotherapy* (pp. 139-154). Binghamton, NY: The Haworth Press.

MAINTENANCE STAGE

DID IT GO LIKE I THOUGHT IT WOULD?

SHOULD I TRY IT AGAIN?

WHAT WOULD I DO DIFFERENTLY?

Bryant, D. (2007). The how-to book: A model-driven process for group work with adolescents. In D. R. Viers (Ed.), *The group therapist's notebook: Homework, handouts, and activities for use in psychotherapy* (pp. 139-154). Binghamton, NY: The Haworth Press.

MAINTENANCE STAGE

HOW CAN I KEEP UP THE GOOD WORK?

Bryant, D. (2007). The how-to book: A model-driven process for group work with adolescents. In D. R. Viers (Ed.), *The group therapist's notebook: Homework, handouts, and activities for use in psychotherapy* (pp. 139-154). Binghamton, NY: The Haworth Press.

20

How to Be Different and Still Belong

Brigid Noonan

Type of Contribution: Activities/Handouts

Objective

This activity can be utilized with adolescent clients struggling with issues of independence and belonging. The focus of the group is to assist clients in recognizing that independence and a sense of belonging can coexist constructively and in a positive manner.

Rationale for Use

This activity is used for adolescent clients concerned with how to assert themselves independently, yet still feel optimistic about themselves as family, peer group, and community members. Adolescents will learn that, although hard to maneuver, they can become more independent without abandoning their roles at home, school, work, and within the community. In doing so, clients begin to take responsibility for their thoughts, feelings, and actions and learn healthy ways to both engage and disengage in positive and adaptive relationships.

It is important for clients to learn these skills, because with them, they are more readily able to understand and appreciate the significance of developing physically, cognitively, and socially. Erickson (1963) noted that adolescents look to determine what is distinct and unique about themselves (Identity versus Identity-Confusion Stage). Discovering both strengths and limitations, adolescents search out roles that will serve them best in their future personal, sexual, career, political, religious, and other roles. This search of roles leads adolescents to try out different parts or choices to determine if there is a fit with how they view themselves and their capabilities. This process helps the adolescent begin to understand their identity by reducing the roles and making choices about different aspects of the self.

Erickson (1963) further posited that adolescents who struggle in discovering these roles and choices, in finding a suitable identity, might struggle in different ways. For example, socially the adolescent may adopt unacceptable roles, such as difficulty in forming and maintaining close personal relationships that can follow them throughout life. In essence, the core sense of self (identify) does not organize. Those that are successful in developing a sense of self learn that their uniqueness is a strength in their psychosocial development

Instructions

It is critical that the therapist have experience working with adolescents. In addition, the therapist needs to structure separate age-specific groups, split by the ages of twelve to fifteen and sixteen to eighteen. The group should not exceed eight members, the group is time limited (eight sessions), and each session is 90 minutes in length. A comfortable setting is suggested, and if possible, the location should be adjacent to the outdoors. Group members should be interviewed by the therapist in order to rule out any serious psychopathology. So that issues of group norms, rules and confidentiality are not breached, each member should sign the Agreement Plan (Handout 20.1).

The following materials are needed for the sessions: journals (the therapist can bring one for each group member, however, members may want to go out and get their own), paper, pens, Magic Markers, white T-shirts, T-shirt making materials (glue, glitter pens, etc.), CD player or tape player, and soft squeeze balls.

First Session

The first session is crucial in terms of setting the norms and rules of the group. At intake, the client is requested to complete, as homework, an explanation, in any form they wish, as to why they would like to be in the group. Examples include a poem, a rap song, or simply a few written lines describing their reasoning. The therapist opens the group by asking members to share their explanations. After each member has shared, the therapist asks the members what they observed and heard. How each member has chosen to share their explanation is important to note, as art, music, and drama therapy will be utilized during the remaining sessions. The therapist will also share what he or she saw and heard in the explanations given.

Toward the end of the session, the therapist introduces a journal and asks that for the remainder of the sessions each member begin the journaling process of his or her reactions to the group. The therapist should stress that it is not mandatory, but suggested that members' journal so they can record any changes they may experience. The therapist will then introduce the Wrap-Up Response List (Handout 20.2) that members will complete during each session. The Wrap-Up Response List gives each member an opportunity to touch on feelings experienced during the group. It is optional whether members share these feelings with the group and facilitator. Members will keep their lists until the termination session.

Subsequent Sessions

Depending on the information shared in the first session, the therapist can utilize a multitude of topics and experiential activities. These activities can support group members in helping recognize that asserting their independence does not necessarily compromise relationships with others. Tools learned in these sessions can include how to effectively communicate, creating a connection between body and mind, learning that juggling is not just an act, and the importance of processing feelings.

Effective communication and resolving conflicts (1 to 2 sessions). This activity teaches adolescents to use "I-statements" by incorporating acting and drawing skills. The purpose of this activity is three-fold. The first is to teach I-statements, the second is learning to listen and read nonverbal cues in order to understand I-statements, and the third is for members to learn how to get their needs met without rocking the boat. Learning about how to use I-statements appropriately and successfully can assist the adolescent in developing what Marcia (1980) called identity achievement status.

Prior to the session, the therapist should create scenarios for the group to play the game. Examples include the following:

- Asking for a later curfew
- Fight with Mom/Dad/Caregiver/Sibling/Friend and you are at fault
- Fight with Mom/Dad/Caregiver/Sibling/Friend and he or she is at fault

- Receiving a bad grade and how to explain
- Asking someone for a date
- Telling someone no
- How to compromise
- Meeting expectations

The therapist should also set up the meeting space with the materials used for playing the game, such as writing tablets, a dry erase board and markers, or other writing utensils. A chalkboard and chalk can also be used.

The therapist gives an example of an I-statement by asking for a volunteer from the group. Picking an innocuous scenario (for example, when a friend talks behind your back) the therapist walks the group through how to appropriately and effectively use I-statements. The therapist will use one of the following formats: "When I heard that you were talking behind my back I felt _____. I'm wondering why you did this?" or "I felt _____ when I heard you talking behind my back. I thought we were friends; what's happened?" The therapist makes sure the group understands I-statements prior to breaking the group into teams.

The group will be split into two equal teams. Using a scenario, each team will come up with appropriate I-statements in reaction to the scenario. Similar to the game of Pictionary or charades, team members will need to use their acting and drawing skills to come up with an I-statement. If there is a particular scenario that a group member would like to work on, the member(s) can ask the therapist to act out this scenario. The therapist will be the timekeeper so that each member of the group has an opportunity to act on a scenario. Each team attempts to guess the statements being drawn or acted.

After members are split into groups, the activity begins, remembering that each member gets a chance to act or draw. Thirty minutes prior to the end of the group session, the therapist will ask members to reflect on the experience and have each member fill out the Wrap-Up Response List. After filling out the list, members are asked to share one (or more) aspect of themselves that they learned while role-playing this activity.

How do you take care of you? (1 or 2 sessions). In this activity, group members interview each other to understand the importance of physical and emotional well-being. Each group member interviews another member for a few minutes and then the members switch, with the interviewee then acting as the interviewer. Examples of questions include, but are not limited to, the following:

- How do you take care of yourself physically?
- What kinds of activities are you involved in?
- How often do you engage in these activities? By yourself? With someone? Do you engage in team sports?
- Do you notice any changes in how you feel when you do/do not engage in physical activities?
- What kinds of changes do you notice?
- How do you see the connection between physical activity/well-being and emotional well-being?
- Before this interview, had you given any thought to the two?

Each person takes a few minutes and writes down what their interview partner has told them.

After writing it down and getting confirmation, the therapist collects the responses and writes down each response on a tablet or chalkboard, taking care not to match any responses with a particular group member. The therapist then leads a discussion on the way group members take care of themselves, incorporating the themes learned in the interviews. The therapist can also provide psychoeducation on the importance of maintaining emotional well-being through activities and exercise. During the final 30 minutes of group, member will have the opportunity to talk about the experience (Wrap-Up Response List and journaling).

A juggling act. The therapist will put together a compilation of songs from different musical genres, such as rock and roll, hip-hop, country and western, rhythm and blues, classical, jazz, techno, Latin, Caribbean, and African. Group members are asked to respond to the music played in relationship to themselves, their family, friends, and any community involvement. Having a clear understanding of the makeup of the group members (history, structure and culture), the therapist can provide a successful experience in an effort to build on the group members' identity (McFadden, 1999).

After playing the compilation, the therapist can ask the following questions:

- What kinds of feelings (if any) does the music bring to mind when played?
- Particularly for older adolescents who might be working within the community, how do the group members balance their busy lives?
- How do they view the relationships they have formed with people?
- Do they see both the similarities and differences or do they only see one or the other?

The therapist will throw out the squeeze balls when playing the music and encourage members to keep the balls in the air. This helps to illustrate to the group members that although there are many balls in the air, group members, using the tools learned (such as I-statements), can effectively manage their busy lives.

During the final 30 minutes of the group session, members will have the opportunity to talk about the experience (Wrap-Up Response List and journaling). This session slowly introduces termination. Ask members to bring their journals with them for the last two sessions.

Celebrate your success! (1 to 2 sessions). The last two sessions will focus on termination. Utilizing a space for group members to spread out (outside, weather permitting and as long as confidentiality can be ensured), the focus of the last two groups will be on the themes touched on during the previous sessions. The termination groups will assist members in recognizing the importance of taking care of the self physically, emotionally, and cognitively but not focusing all of their attention on themselves. Although sometimes difficult to maneuver, focusing attention on family, work, and friends can add a richness and fullness to the adolescents' life that they may not have realized. The previous group activities may possibly encourage the group members to look outside the self or, as Erickson (1963) theorized, develop a positive identity.

The therapist will ask members if they are willing to share what they have written in their journals and will lead a discussion on the themes that emerge from the Wrap-Up Response List and journals. The therapist will then ask group members how they would like to celebrate the end of the group. Giving suggestions such as making a CD, making T-shirts, or writing a group poem, members will have the opportunity to create a safe experience of their own making. The important issue is that the group members create the experience, not the therapist.

Suggestions for Follow-Up

Before beginning each session, the therapist conducts a "go-round" to check-in with clients about the time between sessions. Depending on what has transpired between groups, this will help the therapist to determine what happens within the group. The sessions mentioned above are guidelines when working with these groups of individuals.

Contraindications

Some clients may not be comfortable with the experiential nature of these activities. The therapist needs to use his or her clinical judgment to decide whether or not to continue any activity, particularly if group members articulate that they are uncomfortable. When challenged, some group members may withdraw and/or terminate early. It is imperative that the therapist recognize ambivalent behaviors as such and help the client work through his or her feelings before early termination. Methods of encouraging participation before early termination include stopping the experiential activity and inviting members to process their feelings about the activity. If there are members who are somewhat reluctant, the therapist can ask open-ended questions that may elicit responses to indicate what feelings come up during the activity. As with any issue of resistance, it is important to discuss the issue with the group.

Readings and Resources for the Professional

Carrell, S. (2000). *Group exercises for adolescents: A manual for therapists*. Thousand Oaks, CA: Sage Publications.

Clendenon-Wallen, J. (1991). The use of music therapy to influence the self-confidence and self-esteem of adolescents who are sexually abused. *Music Therapy Perspectives, 9,* 73-81.

Corey, M. & Corey, G. (2001). *Groups: Process and practice* (6th ed.). Belmont, CA: Wadsworth Publications.

Hitchner, K., & Tifft-Hitchner, A. (1996). *Counseling today's secondary students: Practical strategies, techniques & materials for the school counselor.* Upper Saddle River, NJ: Prentice Hall.

Hobday, A., & Ollier, K. (1999). *Creative therapy with children & adolescents: A British psychological society book.* Atascadero, CA: Impact Publishers.

Ivey, A. E., Pedersen, P. B., & Ivey, M. S. (2001). *Intentional group counseling.* Belmont, CA: Wadsworth/Thomson Learning.

Jongsma, A. E., Peterson, L. M., & McInnis, W. P. (1999). *Brief adolescent therapy homework planner.* New York: John Wiley & Sons, Inc.

Jongsma, A. E., Peterson, L. M., & McInnis, W. P. (2000). *The adolescent psychotherapy treatment planner* (2nd ed.). New York: John Wiley & Sons, Inc.

Levy-Warren, M. (1996). *The adolescent journey: Development, identity formation, and psychotherapy.* New York: Jason Aronson, Inc.

Malekof, A. (1999). *Group work with adolescents: Principles and practice.* New York: The Guilford Press.

Pledge, D. (2004). *Counseling adolescents and children: Developing your clinical style.* Belmont, CA: Wadsworth/Thomson Learning.

Bibliotherapy Sources for the Client

Glasser, W. (2002). *For parents and teenagers: Dissolving the barrier between you and your teen.* New York: HarperCollins Publishers, Inc.

Nikkah, J. (2000). *Our boys speak: Adolescent boys write about their inner lives.* New York: St. Martin's Press.

Shandler, S. (1999). *Ophelia speaks: Adolescent girls write about their search for self.* New York: Perennial Currents.

References

Erickson, E. H. (1963). *Childhood & society*. New York: W. W. Norton & Co.

Marcia, J. (1980). Identity in adolescence. In J. Adelson (Ed.), *Handbook of adolescent psychology*. New York: John Wiley & Sons, Inc.

McFadden, J. (Ed.) (1999). *Transcultural counseling*. (2nd ed.). Alexandria, VA: American Counseling Association.

HANDOUT 20.1. AGREEMENT PLAN FOR GROUP PARTICIPATION

- I agree that I will attend each session of group. I am excused from group with notification one time only as the group will meet eight times.

- I agree to stay in group until the group meets each goal identified. If I choose to leave group before the group ends, I will complete the following before leaving

    —Meet individually with the therapist;
    —Discuss with the group feelings of leaving; and
    —Attend at least three more sessions of group after telling the group of my departure so that we can discuss my leaving and come to closure about terminating group.

- Relationships with my group members will be nonsexual only. If there are any interactions with group members, they will not be kept secret from the group and will be shared with the group.

- I will, to the best of my ability, listen, honestly share, and respect each member of the group.

- Everything that is said in within the group stays within the group! Confidentiality will not be broken. I will not share group members' names with anyone outside of group. I can share the topic of what goes on; however, no names can ever be shared.

I, _____, agree to accept all of the above.

Signature: _____

Date: _____

Noonan, B. (2007). How to be different and still belong. In D. R. Viers (Ed.), *The group therapist's notebook: Homework, handouts, and activities for use in psychotherapy* (pp. 155-162). Binghamton, NY: The Haworth Press.

HANDOUT 20.2.
WRAP-UP RESPONSE LIST:
HOW I FELT IN GROUP

These are just suggestions. If you have other feelings, write them down!

Group # _____

_____ Comfortable

_____ Uncomfortable

_____ Relieved

_____ Not Interested

_____ Safe

_____ Loved

_____ Warm

_____ Disconnected

_____ Enlightened (lightbulb went on)

_____ Stupid

_____ Frustrated

_____ Angry

_____ Sad

_____ Calm

_____ Stressed

_____ Worry-free

_____ Anxious

_____ Crabby

_____ Heard

_____ Seen

_____ Challenged

_____ Jealous

_____ Creative

_____ Productive

_____ Cheerful

_____ Interested

_____ Helpful

_____ Mad

_____ Glad

_____ Preoccupied

_____ Hopeful

_____ Thankful

Other feelings: _____

_____

_____

_____

Noonan, B. (2007). How to be different and still belong. In D. R. Viers (Ed.), *The group therapist's notebook: Homework, handouts, and activities for use in psychotherapy* (pp. 155-162). Binghamton, NY: The Haworth Press.

21

Acting Out:
Dramatic Life-Skills Activities

Trey Fitch
Jennifer Marshall

Type of Contribution: Activities

Objective

The purpose of the activities is to develop communication skills and debate negativistic thinking to develop a more healthy self-image. These activities were adapted from a healthy body image group (O'Dea & Abraham, 2002) but apply well to any self-concept related topics.

Rationale for Use

The increased self-reflection that surfaces in early adolescence often leads to increased self-consciousness (Meece, 2002). Sadker and Sadker (1994) linked this self-consciousness to decreases in self-esteem as children become adolescents, although those losses are often short-lived. These losses are especially noted in adolescent females (Vernon & Clemente, 2005).

O'Dea (2004) researched effective treatment methods for one aspect of self-concept, body image issues and found self-esteem and coping skills activities to be helpful when working with adolescent females. She found communication training, relaxation training, and cognitive interventions improved body satisfaction and self-concept. When students communicated better, they fostered healthier relationships with their family and friends. Further, cognitive interventions encourage teens to identify pessimistic and self-defeating thoughts and replace them with more reasonable and adaptive perspectives. The belief "I am unpopular at school" is replaced with a more realistic notion that "some people like me and some do not, and that is okay."

The authors have expanded on O'Dea's (2004) techniques for adolescents who desire more activity and less talk in counseling. Using drama activities allows adolescents to practice new skills in a safe environment (Goldstein, 1988) and to develop awareness using experiential methods. Role-playing and dramatic activities allow adolescents to go beyond just talking about the issues by integrating behavior, thought, and emotion within a dramatic context. These activities are used to enhance the counseling process by making it more participatory and active.

Instructions

The group leader chooses one activity for each one hour session. It is helpful to limit all groups to four to eight members to encourage sharing and participation. If the group is new or still in the norming stage, Drama Activities 3 and 4 are preferred because they require less personal disclosure. Otherwise, the group leader can go through the activities sequentially. Sometimes a particular concern arises that matches well with one of the activities, in which case it would be appropriate to skip ahead to that activity.

- Drama Activity 1: It's in your head
- Drama Activity 2: Negative thought debate
- Drama Activity 3: Media message debate
- Drama Activity 4: Communication skills to develop self esteem

Drama Activity 1: It's in Your Head

This activity uses drama skits to show how someone struggles with stress. The purpose of this activity is to act out the thoughts (internal) and social pressures (external) that relate to a specific conflict.

Begin by asking each member to write down and/or discuss a specific example of when they had a conflict with someone and did not know how to react. For example, you need to confront someone who is spreading rumors or your parents want you to do one thing and your friends want you to do something else. Discuss several of the examples that are verbalized and then ask for a volunteer to let the group act out his or her story. In the unlikely case that nobody volunteers, spend time making group rules on participation and create a fair system for selection of participants (such as drawing straws or rotating around the group).

The steps for this activity are as follows:

1. One of the group members volunteers to identify and describe a stressful situation.
2. The group members create a cast, which consists of members acting out the following voices:
   a. Director: group leader or member who guides the characters to act out the scenario
   b. Lead: group member with the stressful situation
   c. Protagonist: group member who represents the inner voice that is supportive
   d. Antagonist: group member who represents the inner voice that is critical
   e. Family voice: group member who voices what the family advises to do
   f. Friend(s) voice(s): group member who relates what friends are telling the lead to do
   g. Problem-solver voice: group member who attempts to voice creative solutions to the problem(s)
   h. Can also add culture voice or others: group member or members who voice common messages from media and societal influences
3. Discuss a loose script, including what each person will do and say in the drama activity. All members participate in writing the scripts using the volunteer's example as the foundation. The group leader will facilitate by asking members to verbalize the positive and negative thoughts related to the problem, the point of view of family members, reactions from friends, and some possible solutions. Multiple solutions can be played out if more than one surfaces.
4. Act out a conversation between different cast members, using the script, with each member acting out their assigned voice. The director will have to facilitate the first attempt by encouraging members and suggesting dialogue. The group leader should expect to coach the members frequently during the first few examples.
5. After the activity, discuss how the situation was resolved by having the participants list the steps leading to the solution. Ask them to specify what messages were especially helpful and have them discuss how it felt being in that particular role.

Drama Activity 2: Negative Thought Debate

This activity involves five individuals, including the main participant who will have his or her negative thoughts debated. This activity applies cognitive therapy by having group members identify negative thoughts, debate the validity of these thoughts, and create more healthy alternatives. The purpose of the debate is to test and alter beliefs that are harmful or self-defeating.

Begin the activity by explaining how we all have realistic and unrealistic perceptions about ourselves and how negative perceptions can lead to depression and poor functioning at school and with friends and family. The leader asks for volunteers or follows preestablished rules of participation, if they exist. The leader can also ask everyone to participate in turn. These questions are then asked to set up the debate.

- How would you describe yourself?
- How would others describe you?
- How has the media impacted your self-concept?
- How realistic are self-criticisms when you think about your self-esteem?

The leader should write out a summary of each response and use them to form the debate.

Have a participant choose a thought or concern that negatively impacts her or his self-concept and self-esteem. Ask the participants to act out an inner dialogue situation using fellow group members in the following roles:

- A person who represents debating thoughts
- A person representing negative thoughts (with caution)
- A person representing media or family messages
- A person representing positive thoughts

The group then starts a short debate, with each person acting out her or his assigned role utilizing the information gathered during with the prediscussion questions listed previously. After the debate, the leader asks the main participant to respond to what she or he heard during the debate and identify what message was the most helpful. The leader can elicit feedback from the main participant and chart helpful and unhelpful arguments on a chalkboard. Each argument is written on the board and he or she rates it on a scale from one to ten, one being unhelpful and ten being helpful. The participant is then encouraged to use self-talk and journaling during the following week to support the helpful messages. Other participants can also have their thoughts debated as time allows.

Drama Activity 3: Media Messages Debate

This activity is the same as the previous debate activity but is focused on helping adolescents fight the effects of media images in regard to their self-concept. Bring in recent magazines that are popular with adolescents. Discuss the images shown in advertisements and in entertainment sections, being careful not to glamorize stars with eating issues. Compare the images to typical sizes and dimensions of people to highlight the distortions. Ask how these images impact their own expectations and if they feel pressure to look like the images.

Discuss media literacy with the group. Focus on the points that model's bodies are unrealistic and do not fit the norm and that magazine editors and photographers digitally shape and enhance pictures. Find pictures of entertainers and models who have been photographed without the benefit of makeup and photographic enhancements. Several actresses have come out with public pictures showing a more natural look. These pictures can help punctuate the concept that adolescents are often surrounded by unrealistic messages and ideals that are impossible to measure up to.

Have students choose a list of positive, reaffirming self-statements (such as, "Models do not look like that in real life" and "I want friends and boyfriends who don't judge me by my looks") they can use when feeling stressed or negative. Sometimes a list of quotes can be useful in this exercise. Two quotes that can be used are "Beauty is not in the face; beauty is a light in the heart," from Kahlil Gibran, and "The best and most beautiful things in the world cannot be seen or even touched—they must be felt with the heart," from Helen Keller.

The group can then act out a drama scene where members' role-play debate between media messages and reality. Use the guidelines for Drama Activity 3: Negative Thought Debate.

Drama Activity 4: Communication Skills to Develop Self-Esteem

The leader should outline basic communication skills to distinguish different styles, including passive, aggressive, and assertive communications. Explain that passive communication is when you refrain from speaking what you really think, but when you do do speak, you do so in a way that limits the message, such as looking away from the other person or speaking too softly. Aggressive communication is explained as communication techniques meant to dominate or control others. With aggressive communication, threatening nonverbal behavior, such as finger pointing or invading the other's personal space, is often used. Arguments are exaggerated and personal attacks are used. Assertive communication is when you speak honestly, even if in conflict, but you do so in a way that respects others. Examples of assertive communication include maintaining eye contact, clear and direct speaking, listening and showing an understanding of the other's arguments, and refraining from personal attacks. Give the group the following example. The passive person looks down and softly explains his or her position and is easily persuaded by the opposing arguments. The assertive person looks at the opponent, speaks clearly, shows an understanding of both sides of the issue, and makes an argument while respecting the opponent. The aggressive person yells, calls the opponent an idiot, and shakes a finger at the opponent.

Discuss some consequences of the previous styles of communication. The leader can also link how one's communication style influences self-image (for example, how passive communication styles often decrease self-concept). The group can then practice assertive communication skills and show examples of negative communication (passive and aggressive) through skits of conflict situations at home, school, and in social areas. Using volunteers from the group, ask members to act out a skit three times, each time using a different style of communication. Explain that members should practice examples discussed previously and list them again (maintaining eye contact, no personal attacks, and so forth). Give them a few minutes in private to discuss the skit.

The rest of the group will watch and identify the style of communication used. After each skit, ask the rest of the group what style was shown and how they recognized the style. Ask them to outline the consequences of the communication style used in the skit. The leader can also ask group members how the different communication styles made the person feel better or worse about themselves.

Situation 1 (use for the model)—Cast: Tina, Julie, Brian, and friends. Tina and Julie both like the same guy, Brian. They are watching him play football and talking about how cute he is. It is after school, and they are throwing the football with other friends. Tina has known Brian longer, but he talks to Julie more often. Show how they can decide who first gets to ask him to homecoming. Show a good (assertive) way and a bad (passive or aggressive) way to do this.

Situation 2—Cast: Joey, Susan, Joey's friends, Susan's friends. Joey and Susan are dating and debating what to do on a Friday night. Susan and her friends would like to go to the movies. Joey and his friends want to hang out downtown. The friends put pressure on them to do what they want. Show how Joey and Susan can come to an agreement. Show the right way and the wrong way to handle the situation.

Situation 3—Cast: Scott, Ron, the bullies, the other students. Ron and his friends (the bullies) try to rule the school. They use intimidation and name-calling to stay in power. They often pick on Scott, who is new to the school. Show how the other students can step in and help Scott without causing a fight. Show a good way and a bad way to achieve this.

Situation 4—Cast: Sister, JoAnne; Brother, Michael; Dad; Mom. The family has two cars, a Lexus and an old, beat-up station wagon. Michael and JoAnne both want the Lexus for prom. Michael says he should get it since he is the guy and *has* to drive. JoAnne says that does not matter and she should get the car. Show a good way and a bad way to solve the situation.

Situation 5—Cast: Diane, Jack, Diane's mother, Jack's mother. Diane and Jack are married to each other. They have a new baby and the change has led to arguments. They are now arguing about who should get up with the baby at night. Jack goes to work earlier than Diane does, but they both work full time. Diane usually gets home later. The scene starts with Diane and her mother talking on the phone about the situation. Then, Jack talks to his mother on the phone about the situation. They both get advice and then talk to each other. Show a good and a bad way to solve this problem.

Situation 6—Cast: Dominic, Boss, three co-workers. Dominic seems to get all the hard projects to do at work. In a meeting, they are giving out new tasks and his co-workers keep pawning off work on him. A big new project is being given to him, and he does not have time to work on it.

Brief Vignette

Cougar High School offered a counseling group for students who were experiencing issues with eating and self-image. Since several members were in the theater club, the leader decided to use drama therapy techniques.

Mrs. Jones, the group leader, explained the It's in Your Head drama activity, and Juanita agreed to present a stressful issue. She just got her volleyball uniform and felt very self-conscious wearing the tight shorts and top. Juanita acted out a role-play with the group members who represented her protagonist/positive self-talk (Sandy complimented me today on my hair), antagonist/negative self-talk (I look fat in this uniform), family messages (you better watch what you eat or you will get fat), and other parts of her thinking that were portrayed by the group members.

At the conclusion, Mrs. Jones processed the activity by asking Juanita what she learned, how she felt during the activity, and what she could do to combat the negative messages in the future. Juanita reported it felt weird having her thoughts out on the table for everyone to see but liked that other group members seemed to have similar concerns. She said she learned that people do not pay as much attention as she assumed, and that is was easy to focus on the negative comments and forget the positive ones. For follow-up, Juanita agreed to journal compliments and any positive statements made toward her during the next week and discuss the journal individually with the group leader.

Suggestions for Follow-Up

In future groups, students can create and direct their own scenarios relating to communication skills, self-concept, and body image issues. Advanced groups and groups with high levels of trust can develop skits and role-plays based on the members' experiences and current issues.

Contraindications

Participation is voluntary but necessary for the group to function properly. Group members must be willing to be active participants in dramatic scenarios representing issues dealing with eating and self-concept. This will need to be addressed in the screening phase. The group composition must include members that feel comfortable with one another. Rules for participation need to be clear early in the process. Failure to participate will eliminate the member from future group sessions. Participation can be encouraged by taking turns, by random drawings, or by volunteering. Finally, group members need to pledge confidentiality and understand that privacy is expected but cannot be guaranteed.

Factors that may exclude members from being in the group include open hostility, a history of violence, severe psychological impairment, and extreme communication anxiety.

Reading and Resources for the Professional

Goldstein, A. (1988). *The Prepare curriculum. Teaching prosocial competencies.* Champaign, IL: Research Press.

Meece, J. L. (2002) *Child and adolescent development for educators* (2nd ed.). New York: McGraw Hill.

O'Dea, J. A. (2004). Evidence for a self-esteem approach in the prevention of body image and eating disorders among children and adolescents. *Eating Disorders, 12*(3), 225-240.

O'Dea, J. A., & Abraham, S. (2002). Eating and exercise disorders in young college men. *Journal of American College Health, 50*(6), 273-279.

Sadker, M. P., & Sadker, D. (1994). *Failing at fairness: How our schools cheat fairness.* New York: Touchstone.

Vernon, A., & Clemente, R. (2005). *Assessment and intervention with children and adolescents* (2nd ed.). Alexandria, VA: American Counseling Association.

Bibliotherapy Source for the Client

Sorensen, M. J. (1998). *Breaking the chain of low self-esteem.* Cincinnati, OH: Wolf Publishing Co.

References

Goldstein, A. (1988). *The Prepare curriculum. Teaching prosocial competencies.* Champaign, IL: Research Press.

Meece, J. L. (2002) *Child and adolescent development for educators* (2nd ed.). New York: McGraw Hill.

O'Dea, J. A. (2004). Evidence for a self-esteem approach in the prevention of body image and eating disorders among children and adolescents. *Eating Disorders, 12*(3), 225-240.

O'Dea, J. A., & Abraham, S. (2002). Eating and exercise disorders in young college men. *Journal of American College Health, 50*(6), 273-279.

Sadker, M. P., & Sadker, D. (1994). *Failing at fairness: How our schools cheat fairness.* New York: Touchstone.

Vernon, A., & Clemente, R. (2005). *Assessment and intervention with children and adolescents* (2nd ed.). Alexandria, VA: American Counseling Association.

22

Using Psychoeducational Groups with Latino(a) High School Students

Edil Torres-Rivera
Loan T. Phan

Type of Contribution: Activities

Objectives

In a psychoeducational model of group work with Latino(a) high school students, the members are expected to

1. Gain a broader perspective and behavioral repertoires through information, discussion, orientation, and understanding their own and others' experiences and development.
2. Have discussions from historical, developmental, social, and familial perspectives.
3. Move from a position of confusion of perceptions, purposes, and processes toward an understanding of causes, etiologies, developmental incidents, alternatives and consequences, and personal and familial experiences related to the topic of discussion.
4. Begin exploring different perceptions, influences, beliefs, and conflicts.
5. Become less emotionally involved with their attitudes and values and develop a cognitive discussion.
6. Be responsible for and participate in discussions, which in turn will augment acceptance, the ability to listen to others' perspectives, self-disclosure of personal and developmental experiences, involvement, and tolerance of others' attitudes, values, and beliefs.

Of specific relevance to each of these group member outcomes is the power of culture and ethnicity in shaping the self in each of their human stories and how important it is for clinicians (group workers) to access these stories (Laird, 1998).

Rationale for Use

The counseling profession has made great strides in its endeavor to counsel minorities from diverse backgrounds. However, much of this progress has been achieved in individual counseling rather than in group counseling (Sue & Sue, 2003; Torres-Rivera, 2004). Furthermore, even less information can be found regarding counseling Latino(a) high school students in group settings (Pedersen & Carey, 2003), and more so in regards to developmental issues, which are specific to ethnic minority high school students. Even though high school counselors can glean some helpful information from the available literature on group work with ethnic minorities (mostly focusing on adults), school counselors may benefit from a group modality that addresses the unique developmental issues with which Latino(a) high school students must contend.

Despite the fact that there is a paucity of literatu. ^ on group work with all ethnic minority students, many school counselors employ groups in order to efficiently serve their overwhelming student-to-counselor ratio (Samide & Stockton, 2002; Schechtman, 2002). When it comes to serving Latino(a) students, many school counselors are trained to assist students to adopt dominant culture values and behaviors by highlighting dysfunctional and destructive behaviors stereotypically associated with Latino(a) students, such as gang activity, high teen pregnancy rate, and drug and alcohol abuse (Bains, 2001). As a consequence, the necessary knowledge and understanding to work effectively with this population remains minimal.

This deficiency needs to be remedied given the rapidly increasing ethnic minority student population. Out of 16,135,061 high school students in the public school system, ethnic minority students accounted for 6,064,869, or 12.5 percent, of the total population in the last census count (U.S. Bureau of the Census, 2000). Furthermore, Latino(a) population in the United States increased from 35.3 million in 2000 to 38.8 million in 2002 (U.S. Bureau of the Census, 2003). Consequently, numerous multicultural counseling experts assert that given the rising population rates of ethnic minorities school counselors need to meet the unique needs of ethnic minority students in the school settings. Given that Latino(a) is the largest ethnic minority population, special attention should be given to this group.

Theoretical Premises of Cultural Differences in Belief Systems

It appears as if counselor trainees are trained by professors and instructors who spend a great deal of time lecturing about the definition of the problem (DeLucia-Waack, 2004). The redundant phrase "you need to conceptualize the problem from the client's perspective" is frequently expressed in supervision sessions. However, it seems as if problems of Latino(a) students are viewed in the same light as those of majority culture–high school students regardless of race, ethnicity, and/or culture. This may be the impression that many counselor trainees receive when reading case notes, vignettes, and case presentations in practicum, fieldwork, and internship courses (DeLucia-Waack, 2001; DeLucia-Waack & Donigian, 2004; Morganett, 1990; Tyson & Pedersen, 2000). This begs the question, "Are we defining the problem from the client's, or in this case the student's, perspective?" The authors assert that school counselors are not defining the problem from the student's perspective nor are they using interventions developed from that position.

In order to work effectively with this population, students' experiences must be used as the building blocks of the counseling relationship. When the official monthly newspaper of the American Counseling Association presented the results of an informal survey given to high school students in 1996, the results indicated that one of the main reason why ethnic minority students did not seek counseling when in need was because they believed that counselors were not "real" (Marino, 1996). In other words, in the view of the ethnic minority students, counselors appeared too perfect, distant, and unable to understand ethnic minority issues. Similar results have been found by other social scientists linked to the counseling profession (Pedersen, 2000; Sue, Ivey, & Pedersen, 1996; Torres-Rivera, Phan, Maddux, Wilbur, & Arredondo, 2006). These findings may require that counselors move beyond traditional roles they are trained to assume.

According to the multicultural counseling and therapy theory (MCT) (Sue et al., 1996), school counselors who work with ethnic minority students must embrace a culture-specific framework. That is, the definition of the problem must come from the student's position, and interventions used must reflect that point of view. Similar to the proposition of MCT is the belief that cultural-identity development is the result of a mixture of experiences (Torres-Rivera,

1996). The variables of gender, language, socioeconomic status, parents' education, religion, and so forth, also have a direct impact on the student's experiences. Attitudes, values, and beliefs are the results of a person's cultural development and, as such, have a direct impact on the individual's feelings and thoughts about his or her particular group of reference, as well as other groups. These feelings and thought processes include the self, how the individual views his or her reference group, how the individual views other minority groups, and how the individual views the dominant culture group. Consequently, it is important that school counselors not only be sensitive to this information but also have a clear understanding of how these experiences will affect the counseling process.

Perhaps one of the most important tenets of MCT is the belief that multicultural counseling is not only about behavioral change, but also about creating liberation, consciousness, and critical thinking for the students. That is, school counselors must help students to be able to create their own reality based on their experiences and value systems that are consistent with their own attitudes, values, and beliefs, which may or may not diverge from dominant culture values (Torres-Rivera, Phan, Garrett, & D'Andrea, 2005).

Roles of the School Counselor Group Worker

The role of the school counselor as a group worker is a complex and challenging one but may be one of the most influential and significant roles in the lives of the students. For this reason, it is important that the school counselor have the understanding, knowledge, desire, commitment, and ability to work with ethnic minority students. A clear understanding of what culture means is a necessary ingredient. Even though a number of people have defined culture in many different ways, this chapter concentrates on Stewart's (1972) five components of culture.

1. Activity—How do people approach activity, decision making, problem solving, and deciding what is important in one's life?
2. Definitions of social relations, role definition (for example, sex roles)—How do people with different statuses relate to each other, and what is the meaning of friendship?
3. Motivations—What is important to accomplish in the culture (job, money, fame, wisdom, etc.)? Is cooperation or competition the main method of motivating people?
4. Perception of the world—What are the predominant beliefs regarding human nature? What is the nature of truth and property? What is time?
5. Perception of self and the individual—How is the self defined? What is the nature of the individual and his/her identity? What is the makeup of the individual? Who is respected and valued?

Counselors must have a clear understanding of how each of these components is defined in each student's culture as well as in his or her own culture. It is important for the school counselor to understand that the definitions used by the institution more than likely represent the dominant culture and not the student's culture, which may be perceived as oppressive and unfair (hooks, 2003; Pedersen, 2000). It is also imperative that counselors know, understand, and accept the legitimacy of "white privilege" because without this recognition, credibility among ethnic minority students is minimal.

Psychoeducational Model of Group Work Latino(a) High School Students

The main objective of the psychoeducational group modality is interpersonal in nature (Torres-Rivera et al., 2004; Wilbur, Roberts-Wilbur, & Betz, 1981). The psychoeducational group concerns itself with exchanges and responses between group members in regard to their attitudinal value–belief systems. The exchanges, responses, and discussions remain at a cognitive level, and the therapist does not attempt to probe the members emotionally or psychologically. Groups within this modality further concern themselves with the broad potentiality of member behaviors that are available in human interactions. The relationship among members is focused on their interaction with social systems and one another. That is, the relationship is concerned with the examination, exploration, modification, or change of members' attitudes, values, and beliefs by means of member interaction, information, and orientation. This should occur by means of informing, orienting, and educating group members as they interact and receive support in the discussion of topics that are of interest and of common concern to the group members. Group consensus is not an objective of the group (Torres-Rivera, 2004).

Based on the authors' experiences in group work with ethnic minority high school students and in particular with Latino(a) students, the cultural dynamics, issues, and discussion topics germane and of common concern to group members include the following: identity, family, relationships, friendship, intimacy, love, sexuality, responsibility, language, decision making, power, rules, surviving, music, heroes (heroines), discrimination, fairness, and studying. As mentioned earlier, Latino(a) students' worldview shapes their attitudes, values, and beliefs. Therefore, while their concerns as students might be similar to those of the dominant culture, the different experiences as Latino(a) students and the different worldviews required to understand that issues need to be seen as cultural issues and discussion topics are in multicultural variance with those of the white, middle-class culture in the United States.

Thus, it is proposed that the use of a psychoeducational group modality, with the previously stated discussion topics, is an appropriate model for this particular group of high school students to examine, explore, modify, or change their attitudes, values, and beliefs concerning and emphasizing their cultural differences and similarities with those of the dominant culture. In addition, this model provides enough flexibility for students to feel comfortable enough to be able to be more open and honest with each other, as well as with the facilitator(s) during the group sessions, because the model promotes personal development in a safe environment.

Instructions

Using the guidelines of the psychoeducational group modality, the following model encompasses themes that are in tune with ethnic minority students. The model consists of eight group sessions of 45 minutes each. Each session has a theme, which allows students to begin a discussion. For example, session one focuses on values clarifications, introductions and concerns regarding the students perception of school administrators and school personnel, followed by session two that focuses on the theme of violence, and so on. While each session has a theme, the purpose of the theme is not to restrict the discussions but rather to stimulate the dynamics of the group.

Session 1: Introductions and Values Clarification

First, group facilitators review the purpose of the group, expectations of the group, and rules of the group. Sample rules include no physical violence, no eating, no name calling, the need for confidentiality, and other rules created by the group members. Give students the opportunity to add or delete rules.

Group leaders need to emphasize and explain the limits of confidentiality and boundaries from within the cultural context of the Latin community in a group setting. Confidentiality in the Latino(a) community is viewed as a familial concept, meaning that the counselor must be able to become family by demonstrating respect for and a knowledge of his or her clients. This is accomplished by avoiding direct communication and at the same time demonstrating *seriedad* (seriousness) and sensitivity.

Introduce yourself as the group leader to the students. Ask the students if they have any questions about you. This is done in order to establish rapport and trust and to increase comfort and safety for students to be able to talk about group issues. Then, all group members are instructed to introduce themselves and share their expectations of the group. Ask students to identify some of the issues or themes they would like to discuss (again, this is done from within the Latin community culture).

Values clarification exercise. This is the actual heart of the program, where group members investigate one another's values and beliefs. Tolerance of beliefs and values is a key principle. Learning to respect other people's boundaries leads to a tolerance of others' beliefs and values.

Discuss the meanings and distinctions of tolerance and acceptance. Ask what is important to the students. Have the students make a list of things that are important to them (such as doing well in school, being with family or friends, etc.), and then rank the items on their list. Students should make their lists on their own and then share with the other group members without passing value judgments. For example, if a student was wearing nice shoes, the facilitator may want to ask, "Why is it important for you to wear nice shoes?"

Notice and help students to explore the contradictions, if any, in their values. Value clarification is about observing whether or not their actions match their words. Are the students being consistent about what they say and what they do? Of particular importance here is to deal with the concept of *respecto* [meaning "respect for authority, family and tradition" (Torres-Rivera, 2004, p. 214)] and morality.

Session 2: Violence

This session could be considered a natural sequence or follow-up of the first session in which value clarifications are examined. In this session, the facilitators are tying the lack of tolerance and/or understanding to violence; violence is an outcome of intolerance and misunderstandings. Violent behavior is examined and the discussion focuses on how this behavior could self-defeating. The goal is not about changing behavior, but rather it is about educating the students through sharing information and engaging in discussions. As a result, students acquire greater understanding and knowledge to make their own choices.

Group leaders can ask questions, such as "How strong and resilient are they in resisting to be violent?" or "What usually happens when they are about to become violent?" Sometimes students need to walk away and sometimes they feel they need to stand up for themselves. Ask the group if anyone has suggestions on how to deal with situations that involve violence. What are some other constructive ways to deal with violence? As in the previous session, here the cultural value of *respecto* must be defined from a Latin perspective.

Session 3: Relationships

The group is instructed to reflect on their relationships with parents, friends, teachers, and others. The goal once again is to help them be congruent with their feelings and their behaviors. Group leaders need to look for congruence and incongruence. What do students do to get people to like them? If they say that they do not do things to get people to like them, then why do they choose to do what they do? What do they do to attract people and why do they want to be cool?

Oftentimes, students say that they do not really care what other people think of them. What would happen if they admitted that they do care? If students decide to share something that is important to them, help them to realize that they make those choices and they need to accept the consequences for their actions. It is important, however, to understand that issues of discrimination and differential treatment of students based on such variables as racism, sexism, classism, and homoprejudice will have an impact on whether or not students can truly make a choice. Group leaders must assess if the consequences a student has to accept, based on his or her choices, are culturally fair. If not, counselors must act as an advocate for a student if there is a situation in which the students are being treated differently because of race, ethnicity, gender, sexual orientation, disability, or socioeconomic status.

Session 4: Assertiveness Training

Students need to understand that they may not always get what they ask for or what they want. They need to assert themselves without using violence. Group leaders need to teach them skills on how to mediate their situations. However, is it imperative that the issue of *respecto* be brought out because, in the Latino culture, being assertive may be confused with violence or being pushy, which are characteristics that are antagonistic with the Latin culture. These particular skills are probably among the most difficult to teach. It is the experience of the authors that the only way to teach these skills is by role modeling, using situations that arise in the group as particular teaching points. The authors recommend pausing the group process to point out particular events, situations, or conflicts and how the particular group leader handled it at that point.

Session 5: Reflection

What's next? Ask the students if this is helpful or not helpful to them? What have the students gained from this group?

Session 6: Considering Alternatives

If students did not engage in their present behaviors, what would their lives look like? Group leaders can assist students in developing a plan of how to deal with the issues discussed in this group, including violence, racism, and other topics. Do they have a process to talk about racism? Do they have someone to whom they can talk? Who are their allies? Could this person be a friend, peer, or teacher? Can they talk to their parents, siblings, counselor, or teacher? Can they write their experiences down in a journal? Introduce students to a positive role model, such as a book hero (Che Guevara, Simón Bolivar, Anacaona, etc.), as they leave the group and go back to life in school. During this process students and facilitators can watch the film *Motorcycle Diaries* (Tenkoff, Nozik, Tenenbaum, & Salles, 2004), following school guidelines for showing movies, to reinforce these points.

Mention to all group members that the group has two remaining sessions. Group members should be thinking about the termination of the group and what each student needs to do to say good-bye to the group. Explain to the group members that each individual says good-bye in his or her own way and encourage each student to think about how she or he would like to leave the group.

Session 7: Review and Check-In

How has the group been helpful? What have they learned from this group so far? How are they using this information in their current life? How are they transferring their learning to their real life? Do students think this group would be helpful to other students? Inform students that next week will be the last group session. Ask the group members to think about how they would like to say good-bye to each group member.

Session 8: Termination

Discuss the meaning of termination to the group. What has each group member taken from this group and, perhaps, from specific group members? What has each group member learned about himself or herself and other group members throughout this entire process? What will each group member do with this new understanding and knowledge?

Each group leader will also say good-bye to each student and share his or her connection and counseling relationship with each group member in the context of this group. By doing this, group leaders acknowledge and solidify the work that each group member has contributed to the group and instill the belief that each student is a member of a community, in this case, the group. Students achieve a sense of responsibility and community when they feel that their choices have an impact on themselves, their families, their school, and the community as a whole.

Suggestions for Follow-Up

Follow-up in this model is done very informally and should be used mainly as means to reinforce the concepts of *familismo* [defined as "a preference for maintaining a close connection to family" (Santiago-Rivera, Arredondo, & Gallardo-Cooper, 2002, p. 42)] and *personalismo* ["valuing and building interpersonal relationships" (Santiago-Rivera et al., p. 44)]. This informal follow-up allows the group facilitators using this model to conduct their own self-assessment for to each group.

The idea is that most interventions apply to all individuals has been repeatedly challenged by family therapists and group workers (McGoldrick, 1998; Phan & Torres-Rivera, 2004). However, the fundamental basis for this challenge has been dismissed when working with ethnic minority students and in particular with Latino(a) students. Experts in schools and multicultural counseling issues appear to indiscriminately adapt linear models and behaviorally based interventions in their work with Latino(a) students. The exclusive adoption of the dominant culture models disregards many issues unique to ethnic minority students, such as racial/cultural identity development.

As group workers, we must continue to increase awareness of our own attitudes, values, and beliefs, as well as for those who suffer oppression in our country (Sue & Sue, 2003). When working with Latinos, or any minority group, it is important to understand our personal biases, stereotypes, and assumptions. Many of these assumptions and biases are based on a universalist focus, which does not address differences in experiences and beliefs or the effects of oppression (McGoldrick, 1998). Such biases, stereotypes, and assumptions may unintentionally lead group workers to misdiagnosis and inequal treatment. There also is a need for more societal awareness about discrimination, in general, and Latino(a) clients, in particular. Most counseling and group work texts devote little or no attention to Latino(a) clients, ignoring their unique issues (Arredondo, 1996; Paniagua, 1994; Pedersen & Carey, 2003). Thus, group workers need to be educated about the issues of their Latino(a) members and applicable group work models.

Contraindications

The most important contraindication or caution in using this model is that clients must not be suffering from a personality disorder. The model has never been used with clients with personality disorders, and it may be that these clients need more extensive intervention than this format would allow. While this model refers to Latino(a) clients, we have used it with Asian students and African-American students but not with Native American students.

Readings and Resources for the Professional

Bacigalupe, G. (2000). El Latino: Transgressing the macho. In M. T. Flores & G. Carey (Eds.), *Family therapy with Hispanics: Toward appreciating diversity* (pp. 29-57). Needham Heights, MA: Allyn and Bacon.

Belitz, J., & Valdez, D. M. (1997). A sociocultural context for understanding gang involvement among Mexican-American male youth. In J. G. Garcia & M. C. Zea (Eds.), *Psychological interventions and research with Latino populations* (pp. 56-72). Needham Heights, MA: Allyn and Bacon.

Comas-Díaz, L. (2001). Hispanics, Latinos, or Americanos: The evolution of identity. *Cultural Diversity and Ethnic Minority Psychology, 7*(2), 115-120.

Duran, E., & Duran, B. (1995). *Native American postcolonial psychology*. Albany, NY: State University of New York Press.

Flores, M. T., & Carey, G. (Eds.) (2000). *Family therapy with Hispanics: Toward appreciating diversity*, Needham Heights, MA: Allyn and Bacon.

Flores-Ortiz, Y. (2000). La mujer Latina: From margin to center. In M. T. Flores & G. Carey (Eds.), *Family therapy with Hispanics: Toward appreciating diversity* (pp. 59-76). Needham Heights, MA: Allyn and Bacon

Friedman, M. J., & Marsella, A. J. (1996). Posttraumatic stress disorder: An overview of the concept. In A. J. Marsella, M. J. Friedman, E. T. Gerrity & R. M. Scurfield (Eds.), *Ethnocultural aspects of posttraumatic stress disorder: Issues, research, and clinical applications* (pp. 11-32). Washington, DC: American Psychological Association.

García, G. J., & Marotta, S. (1997). Characterization of the Latino population. In J. G. García & M. C. Zea (Eds.), *Psychological interventions and research with Latino populations*. Needham Heights, MA: Allyn and Bacon.

García, G. J., & Zea, M. C. (Eds.). (1997). *Psychological interventions and research with Latino populations*. Needham Heights, MA: Allyn and Bacon.

Garcia-Preto, N. (1996). Latino families: An overview. In M. McGoldrick, J. Giordano, & J. K. Pierce (Eds.), *Ethnicity and family therapy* (2nd ed.) (pp. 141-154). New York: The Guilford Press.

Garcia-Preto, N. (1998). Latinas in the United States: Bridging two worlds. In M. McGoldrick (Ed.), *Re-visioning family therapy: Race, culture and gender in clinical practice* (pp. 330-344). New York: The Guilford Press.

Han, A. L., & Vasquez, M. J. T. (2000). Group intervention and treatment with ethnic minorities. In J. F. Aponte & J. Wohl (Eds.), *Psychological interventions and cultural diversity* (2nd ed.) (pp. 110-130). Needham Heights, MA: Allyn and Bacon.

Hassid, D., Colpaert, C-J. (Producers), & Anders, A. (Director). (1994). *Mi vida loca: My crazy life* [Motion picture]. (Available from HBO Video, 1100 Avenue of the Americas, New York, NY 10036).

Hough, R. L., Canino, G. J., Abueg, F. R., & Gusman, F. D. (1996). PTSD and related stress disorders among Hispanics. In A. J. Marsella, M. J. Friedman, E. T. Gerrity, & R. M. Scurfield (Eds.), *Ethnocultural aspects of posttraumatic stress disorder: Issues, research, and clinical applications* (pp. 301-338). Washington, DC: American Psychological Association.

Hugen, B. (2001). Spirituality and religion in social work practice: A conceptual model. In M. Van Hook, B. Hugen, & M. Aguilar (Eds.), *Spirituality within religious traditions in social work practices* (pp. 9-17). Pacific Grove, CA: Brooks/Cole Publishing.

Marino, T. W. (1996, August). The challenging task of making counseling services relevant to more populations: Reaching out to communities and increasing the cultural sensitivity of counselors-in-training seen as crucial. *Counseling Today*, pp. 1, 6.

McGoldrick, M. (Ed.). (1998). *Re-visioning family therapy: Race, culture, and gender in clinical practice.* New York: The Guilford Press

Mergal, M. (1993). Puerto Rican feminism at a crossroad: Challenges at the turn of the century. In E. Meléndez & E. Meléndez (Eds.), *Colonial dilemma: Critical perspectives on contemporary Puerto Rico.* (pp. 131-141). Boston: South End Press.

Mirandé, A. (1997). *Hombres y machos: Masculinity and Latino culture.* Boulder, CO: Westview Press.

Moore, J. (1990). Hispanic/Latino: Imposed label or real identity? *Latino Studies Journal, 2,* 33-47.

Oboler, S. (1995). *Ethnic labels, Latino lives: Identity and the politics of (re)presentation in the United States.* Minneapolis, MN: University of Minnesota Press.

Padilla, A. M. (Ed.). (1995). Hispanic psychology: *Critical issues in theory and research.* Thousand Oaks, CA: Sage Publications, Inc.

París Alicea, D. (2000). *Hechos y derechos: Consideraciones en torno a los hombres y su desarrollo.* Puerto Rico: Ediciones Juissa.

Ramírez, R. L. (1999). *What it means to be a man: Reflection on Puerto Rican masculinity.* (R. E. Casper & P. J. Guarnaccia, Trans.) New Brunswick, NJ: Rutgers University Press. (Original work published 1993.)

Rivera-Batiz, F. L., & Santiago, C. (1994). *Puerto Ricans in the United States: A changing reality.* Washington, DC: The National Puerto Rican Coalition, Inc.

Santiago-Rivera, A. L. (1995). Developing a culturally sensitivity treatment modality for bilingual Spanish-speaking clients: Incorporating language and culture in counseling. *Journal of Counseling and Development, 74,* 12-17.

Santiago-Rivera, A.L., Arredondo, P., & Gallardo-Cooper, M. (2002). *Counseling Latinos and la familia: A practical guide.* Thousands Oaks, CA: Sage.

Shorris, E. (1992). *Latinos: A biography of the people.* New York: Avon Books.

Thomas, A. (Producer), & Nava, G. (Director). (1995). *My family* [Motion picture]. (Available from New Line Video, http://www.newline-shop.com.)

Bibliotherapy Sources for the Client

Bacigalupe, G. (2000). El Latino: Transgressing the macho. In M. T. Flores & G. Carey (Eds.), *Family therapy with Hispanics: Toward appreciating diversity* (pp. 29-57). Needham Heights, MA: Allyn and Bacon.

Belitz, J., & Valdez, D. M. (1997). A sociocultural context for understanding gang involvement among Mexican-American male youth. In J. G. Garcia & M. C. Zea (Eds.), *Psychological interventions and research with Latino populations* (pp. 56-72). Needham Heights, MA: Allyn & Bacon.

Comas-Díaz, L. (2001). Hispanics, Latinos, or Americanos: The evolution of identity. *Cultural Diversity and Ethnic Minority Psychology, 7*(2), 115-120.

Duran, E., & Duran, B. (1995). *Native American postcolonial psychology.* Albany, NY: State University of New York Press.

Flores, M. T., & Carey, G. (Eds.) (2000). *Family therapy with Hispanics: Toward appreciating diversity,* Needham Heights, MA: Allyn & Bacon.

Flores-Ortiz, Y. (2000). La mujer Latina: From margin to center. In M. T. Flores & G. Carey (Eds.), *Family therapy with Hispanics: Toward appreciating diversity* (pp. 5976). Needham Heights, MA: Allyn & Bacon.

Garcia-Preto, N. (1996). Latino families: An overview. In M. McGoldrick, J. Giordano, & J. K. Pierce (Eds.), *Ethnicity and family therapy* (2nd ed.) (pp. 141-154). New York: The Guilford Press.

Garcia-Preto, N. (1998). Latinas in the United States: Bridging two worlds. In M. McGoldrick (Ed.), *Re-visioning family therapy: Race, culture and gender in clinical practice* (pp. 330-344). New York: The Guilford Press.

Hassid, D., Colpaert, C-J. (Producers), & Anders, A. (Director). (1994). *Mi vida loca: My crazy life* [Motion picture]. (Available from HBO Video, 1100 Avenue of the Americas, New York, NY 10036).

Mergal, M. (1993). Puerto Rican feminism at a crossroad: Challenges at the turn of the century. In E. Meléndez & E. Meléndez (Eds.), *Colonial dilemma: Critical perspectives on contemporary Puerto Rico.* (pp. 131-141). Boston: South End Press.

Mirandé, A. (1997). *Hombres y machos: Masculinity and Latino culture.* Boulder, CO: Westview Press.

Moore, J. (1990). Hispanic/Latino: Imposed label or real identity? *Latino Studies Journal, 2,* 33-47.

París Alicea, D. (2000). *Hechos y derechos: Consideraciones en torno a los hombres y su desarrollo.* Puerto Rico: Ediciones Juissa.

Ramírez, R. L. (1999). *What it means to be a man: Reflection on Puerto Rican masculinity.* (R. E. Casper & P. J. Guarnaccia, Trans.). New Brunswick, NJ: Rutgers University Press. (Original work published 1993.)

Rivera-Batiz, F. L., & Santiago, C. (1994). *Puerto Ricans in the United States: A changing reality.* Washington, DC: The National Puerto Rican Coalition, Inc.

Shorris, E. (1992). *Latinos: A biography of the people.* New York: Avon Books.

Tenkoff, K., Nozik, M., Tenenbaum, M. (Producers), & Salles, W. (Director). (2004). *Motorcycles diaries* [Motion picture]. (Available from Focus Features, www.focusfeatures.com.)

Thomas, A. (Producer), & Nava, G. (Director). (1995). *My family* [Motion picture]. (Available from New Line Video, www.newline-shop.com.)

References

Arredondo, P. (1996). MTC theory and Latina(o)-American population. In D. W. Sue, A. E. Ivey, & P. B. Pedersen (Eds.), *A theory of multicultural counseling and therapy* (pp. 217-235). Pacific Grove, CA: Brooks/Cole Publishing Company.

Bains, R. K. (2001). Psychotherapy with young people from ethnic minority backgrounds in different community-based settings. In G. Baruch (Ed.), *Community-based psychotherapy with young people: Evidence and innovation in practice.* (pp. 65-74). New York: Brunner-Routledge.

DeLucia-Waack, J. L. (2001). *Using music in children of divorce groups.* Alexandria, VA: American Counseling Association.

DeLucia-Waack, J. L. (2004). *School counseling student handbook and placement manual.* Buffalo, NY: University at Buffalo, SUNY.

DeLucia-Waack, J. L., & Donigian, J. (2004). *The practice of multicultural group work: Vision and perspectives from the field.* Belmont, CA: Brooks and Cole.

hooks, b. (2003). *Teaching community: A pedagogy of hope.* New York: Routledge.

Laird, J. (1998). Theorizing culture: Narrative ides and practice principles. In M. McGoldrick (Ed.), *Re-visioning family therapy: Race, culture, and gender in clinical practice* (pp. 20-36). New York: The Guildford Press.

Marino, T. W. (1996, August). The challenging task of making counseling services relevant to more populations: Reaching out to communities and increasing the cultural sensitivity of counselors-in-training seen as crucial. *Counseling Today,* pp. 1, 6.

McGoldrick, M. (Ed.). (1998). *Re-visioning family therapy: Race, culture, and gender in clinical practice.* New York: The Guilford Press.

Morganett, R. S. (1990). *Skills for living: Group counseling activities for young adolescents, Vol. 1*. Champaign, IL: Research Press.

Paniagua, F. A. (1994). *Assessing and treating culturally diverse clients: A practical guide*. Thousand Oaks, CA: Sage Publications, Inc.

Pedersen, P. B. (2000). *A handbook for developing multicultural awareness* (3rd ed.). Alexandria, VA: American Counseling Association.

Pedersen, P. B., & Carey, J. C. (2003). *Multicultural counseling in schools: A practical handbook* (2nd ed.). Needham Heights, MA: Allyn & Bacon.

Phan, L. T., & Torres-Rivera, E. (2004). Language as an issue in group counseling and psychotherapy. In J. L. DeLucia-Waack, D. Gerrity, C. Kalodner, & M. Riva (Eds.), *Handbook of group counseling and psychotherapy* (pp. 283-294). Thousand Oaks, CA: Sage.

Samide, L. L., & Stockton, R. (2002). Letting go of grief: Bereavement groups for children in the school setting. *Journal for Specialists in Group Work, 27,* 192-204.

Santiago-Rivera, A. L., Arredondo, P., & Gallardo-Cooper, M. (2002). *Counseling Latinos and la familia: A practical guide*. Thousand Oaks, CA: Sage.

Shechtman, Z. (2002). Child group psychotherapy in the school at the threshold of a new millennium. *Journal of Counseling and Development, 80,* 293-299.

Stewart, E. C. (1972). *American cultural patterns*. La-Grange Park, IL: Intercultural Network.

Sue, D. W., Ivey, A. E., & Pedersen, P. B. (1996). *A theory of multicultural counseling and theory*. Belmont, CA: Brooks and Cole.

Sue, D. W., & Sue, D. (2003). *Counseling the culturally different* (4th ed.). New York: John Wiley & Sons.

Tenkoff, K., Nozik, M., Tenenbaum, M. (Producers), & Salles, W. (Director). (2004). *Motorcycles diaries* [Motion picture]. (Available from Focus Features, www.focusfeatures.com.)

Torres-Rivera, E. (1996). Chaos theory as applied to the formation of minority values and beliefs: A multicultural counseling approach. *dialog: The Connecticut Counseling Association Journal, 27,* 44-56.

Torres-Rivera, E. (2004). Group work with Latinos. In J. L. DeLucia-Waack, D. Gerrity, C. Kalodner, & M. Riva (Eds.), *Handbook of group counseling and psychotherapy* (pp. 213-223). Thousand Oaks, CA: Sage.

Torres-Rivera, E., Phan, L. T., Garrett, M. T., & D'Andrea, M. (2005). Integrating Che Guevara, Don Pedro Albizú Campos, and Paulo Freire in the revolution of counseling: Revisioning social justice when counseling Latino clients. *Radical Psychology Journal*. Retrieved October 13, 2005, from www.radpsynet.org/journal/vol4-1/che.html.

Torres-Rivera, E., Phan, L. T., Maddux, C. D., Wilbur, M. P., & Arredondo, P. (2006). Honesty the necessary ingredient in multicultural counseling: A pilot study of the counseling relationship. *Interamerican Journal of Psychology, 40*(1), 37-45.

Torres-Rivera, E., Wilbur, M., Roberts-Wilbur, J., Phan, P. T., Garrett, M. T., & Betz, R. L. (2004). Supervising and training psychoeducational group leaders. *Journal for Specialists in Group Work, 29,* 377-394.

Tyson, L. E., & Pedersen, P. B. (2000). *Critical incidents in school counseling* (2nd ed.). Alexandria, VA: American Counseling Association.

U.S. Bureau of the Census. (2000). *Population and housing detailed tables*. Retrieved June 30, 2003, from factfinder.census.gov/.

U.S. Bureau of the Census. (2003). *Population and housing detailed tables*. Retrieved February 6, 2007, from www.census.gov/population/www/socdemo/compraceho.html.

Wilbur, M. P., Roberts-Wilbur, J., & Betz, R. L. (1981). Leader and member behavior in three group modalities: A typology. *Journal for Specialists in Group Work, 6,* 224-234.

23

Prompted Feedback to Increase Interpersonal Skill Development

Nancy G. Calley

Type of Contribution: Activity

Objectives

The primary learning objective for this activity is to increase interpersonal skill development through the use of prompted feedback. The activity is designed to assist individuals with under-developed social and interpersonal skills increase their understanding of the impact of their behavior on others. Through prompted feedback, initially elicited from the group leader and subsequently given freely without such solicitation, clients are able to learn from one another the influence that their behaviors have on others. Indirect benefits of the activity include the illumination of therapeutic group factors, such as interpersonal learning, development of social skills, and altruism (Yalom, 1995), each of which may expedite the group process.

Rationale for Use

This activity was originally designed for use with juvenile, male sex offenders as a means to increase social skill and interpersonal skill development. There are two primary reasons why this type of strategy is suggested for this population, one resulting from the interpersonal challenges that are characteristic of juvenile sex offenders, and the second focusing on the utilization of the immediacy inherent in group work that allows for in vivo learning. These two critical factors support the use of exercises that can be accomplished within group therapy that promote increased understanding of interpersonal dynamics. The basis for this rationale rests on the notion that what occurs within the group between individuals likely occurs outside of group as well; therefore, the group process is used to promote experiential learning that will ultimately lead to long-term behavior change.

Juvenile sex offenders are characterized by a pronounced lack of interpersonal and social skills (Kazdin, 1994; Miner, Siekert, & Ackland, 1997). As a result, interpersonal skill development should be one of the key treatment issues for clinicians. Not viewed as a single aspect, but rather a complex array of affect and social skills, the following components have been identified as primary treatment targets for intervention: identification and expression of feeling, development of empathy, and development of prosocial relationship skills (National Adolescent Perpetrator Network, 1993). Thus, treatment strategies designed to increase the affective development of the juvenile sex offender are viewed as critical to the youth's treatment and subsequent long-term success.

Treatment of juvenile sex offenders is not to be entered lightly, and a profound understanding of the various contributing and sustaining factors must be fully understood before embarking on such treatment. It is further necessary that the dimension of affective and interpersonal development is explored from both its origins and its consequences. It is in this vein that the link is established between causal factors and subsequent implications, so that work can begin toward establishing interpersonal growth and, thus, the development of protective factors.

The origins of affective and interpersonal development are largely tied to early development, and families of juvenile sex offenders often are marked by instability and disorganization (Righthand & Welch, 2001). These functional challenges faced by the family often are impacted by a parental history of substance abuse, incarcerations, and psychiatric illness (Kelley, Lewis, & Sigal, 2004), as well as a history of victimization as a child (Vizard, Monck, & Misch, 1995). In addition to the family-related contributing factors, early conditioning of nonnormative sexual environments that consist of such events as pairing of intimacy and aggression and sexualized models of cooperation and objectification have often been found to be linked to juvenile sex offending behaviors (National Adolescent Perpetrator Network, 1993).

To further illuminate the complex etiology of the affective domain related to sexual offending behaviors, Marshall, Hudson, and Hodkinson (1993) and Schram, Milloy, and Rowe (1991) noted that a maladaptive interpersonal style may contribute to the offender's cognitive distortion related to the inability to recognize the effects of one's behaviors on another. It is this lack of empathy stemming from stunted interpersonal development that may continue to place the youth at considerable risk of reoffending, if not addressed.

Finally, Vizard et al. (1995) found that as a possible effect of a lack of empathy, juvenile sex offenders were socially isolated. The very notion of social isolation is in direct opposition to the development of interpersonal and social skills, as without interpersonal interactions such development is prohibited. This concept is of particular concern as sexual offenses, like most criminal acts, are cast in secrecy, and as such, this social isolation could be construed as a sustaining factor in the offending behavior (Calley, 2007). As a result, placement in a therapy group ensures that social isolation can no longer exist for the juvenile sex offender, thus allowing for focused attention to interpersonal development.

Interpersonal skill development is a critical component in the treatment of the juvenile sex offender, and therefore, treatment strategies must be designed to specifically target such development. Group therapy, while not only the preferred modality for the treatment of juvenile sex offenders (Lundrigan, 2001; Perry & Orchard, 1992), also presents opportunities to the clinician and client that are otherwise unavailable in individual work. The social microcosm (Yalom, 1995) created by a therapy group allows individual members to interact within the group in the manner in which they engage in interactions outside of the group. It is this type of in vivo experience that lends itself naturally to a focus on group members' interpersonal development. Interpersonal development can occur through the utilization of specific therapeutic group factors, such as imitation; however, the group leader through the use of the prompted-feedback exercise can specifically facilitate such interpersonal development.

Prompted feedback is an exercise facilitated by the group leader at critical times during therapy to promote the giving and receiving of interpersonal feedback. It is through this prompted exchange that group members are able to spontaneously experience the effect of their behavior on others. This focus on empathy is used to continue to promote growth in the youth toward regaining control of personal behaviors by linking maladaptive behaviors with feelings. By tapping into this part of the youth's emotional terrain, the youth is able to viscerally connect personal behaviors to their subsequent impact on others (Calley, 2007). This strategy is loosely drawn from Yalom's (1995) process commentary technique, in which events occurring within the group are utilized as material for interpersonal learning.

It should be noted that while this activity was originally designed for use with juvenile sex offenders, it may also be used with other populations that experience challenges related to interpersonal skill development.

Instructions

As part of orientation to group, the group facilitator provides an overview of group work, outlining the various strengths and benefits of group therapy as well as the limitations to group work. The supporting rationale and type of strategies that may be employed as part of the therapeutic process are explained to group members. When using this intervention with juvenile sex offenders, the facilitator must evaluate a youth's readiness for such interpersonal development based upon the youth's affective development. Such readiness is often reflected by an adequate range (or increase in the range) of affective awareness, coupled with the youth's ability to demonstrate appropriate expression of feeling at least some of the time. Ensuring that each group member has some degree of affective awareness is essential to the group's overall goal of increasing the interpersonal development of group members.

Interpersonal development is discussed as a primary treatment issue, with the group facilitator emphasizing the unique opportunities created by a therapy group for such interpersonal development (engaging in and negotiating multiple relationships). The group facilitator further sets the stage for group members to focus on "process" elements of group (that is, what is happening between group members during group) by drawing group members attention to the notion that what occurs within the group is often a direct reflection of what occurs outside of the group. The group leader explains that in order to focus on the process elements, group members will continuously examine and provide feedback to each group member, including the group facilitator, regarding his or her perception of the group member's behavior and the impact that such behavior is having on him or her.

Prompted feedback can be used to (1) elicit general feedback from a group member, (2) elicit specific feedback from a group member, and (3) bring behavior occurring outside the group into the group for feedback and for comparison with current behavior. Initially, the group facilitator explains that she or he will provide process feedback to each member specifically related to how he or she is experiencing each member (how the behavior of the group member is perceived by the group facilitator and the impact that the member's behavior has on the group facilitator). The group leader then asks each group member to provide process feedback regarding the behavior of the group facilitator. Through the group facilitator's demonstration of this type of process feedback, she or he is able to model the technique for group members while at the same time creating a climate conducive to such feedback by promoting equality among the group membership (that is, the group facilitator is not above receiving such feedback). As the group continues, the group facilitator asks that group members provide such feedback to one another, pointing out how each member is affected by the behavior of another group member.

To assist group members in this task, the group facilitator may ask group members to provide such feedback to individual group members by using the following sentence stem: "I feel _____ when you _____." Other sentence stems that may be used to assist in providing process feedback include "I feel the most comfortable with _____ because _____," or "I am the most uncomfortable with _____ because _____." The group facilitator emphasizes that it is through this type of feedback that group members will increase personal awareness as to the impact that their behavior has on others. The group facilitator may simply provide such feedback to group members or to the group in general at regular intervals or may request feedback from a particular member or multiple group members randomly (general prompted feedback) during the course of the group.

The group facilitator encourages group members to also provide such feedback to each other at regular intervals. When something specific occurs in the group (change in a group member's affect, powerful disclosure, powerful dialogue), the group facilitator will prompt a group member to provide feedback as to the effect of the event (behavior of another group member) on the group member. To facilitate this type of specific prompted feedback, the group facilitator may ask the group member to use the following sentence stem "Right now, I am feeling _____ as a result of _____ behavior/remarks" or another sentence stem specifically tailored for the event. This type of specific prompted feedback takes advantage of the moment, drawing attention to what is happening for an individual group member based on a specific event in the group. As the group continues to mature, group members become more focused on the process elements, identifying when and how they are affected by another group member's behavior, and no longer need to rely on the group facilitator to prompt such feedback.

In the beginning stage of group work, the exercise is primarily directed by the group facilitator as the facilitator elicits feedback from group members regarding what each experienced during the group. This feedback then becomes connected to individual group members wherein group members learn to associate their personal experience with the behaviors/actions of other group members. As group work continues, the facilitator may use the prompted feedback exercise to promote sharing among group members based upon specific occurrences within the group process. Finally, whereas prompted feedback initially relies on the group facilitator, as the group continues to progress, such feedback becomes freely exchanged among group members. It is in this manner that the group is able to establish a new group norm (integrating process feedback into the group process).

Brief Vignette

The following excerpt is based on a group of nine male juvenile sex offenders in residential treatment that had been working together for four months.

Mark was discussing his loss of program points (earlier in the day) due to throwing a chair against the wall. Mark stated, "Sometimes I just get so pissed off that I want to break something! I know it isn't right, but I can't help myself. Top it off, it seems like every time things get going a little better, I do something to mess it up again." Gerri, the group therapist, responded to Mark, stating, "Mark, when I saw you get up before throwing the chair, I was uncomfortable, knowing that you were going to do something you most likely would regret. It made me not want to continue to spend time with you (use of feedback regarding behavior occurring outside the group in the group). However, right now, you are fully in control. As a result, I feel comfortable with you and want to continue to spend time with you" (comparing impact of previous behavior with impact of current behavior).

Later in the session, Gerri asked Terry to share with the group what he had experienced during the session (eliciting general feedback). Terry stated that after listening to Gerri speak about Mark, he realized that he, too, probably made people uncomfortable because he did things that appeared out of control. Gerri commended Terry for being able to take responsibility for his own behaviors and tentatively observed that perhaps Mark's courage had given Terry the ability to look more critically at his own behavior (altruism as a therapeutic factor). Terry agreed that this was probably true.

Gerri then asked Shaun, another group member, to complete the following sentence stem referring to one of the group member's behavior "You make me feel _____ because _____" (eliciting specific feedback). Shaun immediately stated that "Paul makes me feel like he is not part of the group because he doesn't take any chances in the group. You know, you always just sit back and let everyone else do the work, like you don't care—like you're better than us." Scott jumped in to add "Yeah, man, it makes me think I shouldn't say anything either—like why should I put myself out there if you can't put yourself out there." Gerri interjected that "it seems like your fellow group members don't feel you are committed to the group, as you haven't given them any reason to think that you are committed. What do you think about this, Paul?" Paul countered that "I don't know what you want from me. I'm here, ain't I? You seem to be doing okay without me saying anything." Andrew stated, "But that's just it, man. We're doing the work, and you're just along for the ride. It ain't right—you need to show us that you're in this too." Continuing along the thread that began with Shaun's feedback to Paul, the session concluded with the group discussing member participation and how each member showed their commitment to the group.

The vignette reflects the multitude of ways by which prompted feedback can be used within the group to further illuminate group process. Further, this brief demonstration reflects the manner in which specific group factors, such as altruism and interpersonal learning may be illuminated in the group process.

Suggestions for Follow-Up

Depending on the treatment milieu, the technique may also be used during day to day activities to reinforce the constancy of the effects of one's behaviors on others. Material from daily occurrences may be used to continue to promote empathy, thus continuing to promote an in vivo experience of affective development. As interpersonal skill development is viewed as a continuous process, it is important to check-in with clients to ensure that they are still actively engaged in this type of growth. Finally, when working with juvenile sex offenders, it is imperative to ensure that the individual continues to participate in interpersonal relationships, thus guarding against the social isolation that may contribute to continued offending.

Contraindications

When working with juvenile sex offenders, this type of strategy is best utilized as part of a comprehensive treatment approach focusing on the resolution of the complete constellation of factors supporting the continuation of sexual offending. Specific use of prompted feedback toward the juvenile sex offender's interpersonal development should only begin after much time and energy has previously been committed to affective work and considerable progress in this area has been made.

Readings and Resources for the Professional

Barbaree, H. E., Marshall, W. L., & Hudson, S. M. (1993). *The juvenile sex offender.* New York: Guilford Press.

Bloch, S., & Crouch, E. (1985). *Therapeutic factors in group psychotherapy.* New York: Oxford University Press.

Bohart, A. C., & Tallman, K. (1999). *How clients make therapy work: The process of active self-healing.* Washington, DC: American Psychological Association.

Lundrigan, P. S. (2001). *Treating youth who sexually abuse: An integrated multi-component approach.* Binghamton, NY: The Haworth Press.

Yalom, I. D. (1995). *The theory and practice of group psychotherapy* (4th ed.). New York: Basic Books.

Bibliotherapy Sources for the Client

Bays, L., Freeman-Longo, R., & Hildebran, D. (1999). *How can I stop? Breaking my deviant cycle.* Holyoke, MA: NEARI Press.

Freeman-Longo, R., & Bays, L. (1999). *Who am I and why am I in treatment?* Holyoke, MA: NEARI Press.

Kahn, T. J. (1990). *Pathways: A guided workbook for youth beginning treatment.* Brandon, VT: Safer Society Press.

Watson, D. L., & Tharp, R. G. (1993). *Self-directed behavior: Self-modification for personal adjustment.* Pacific Grove, CA: Brooks/Cole.

References

Calley, N. (2007). Integrating theory and research: The development of a research-based treatment model for juvenile male sex offenders. *Journal of Counseling and Development, 85,* 131-142.

Kazdin, A. E. (1994). Interventions for aggressive and antisocial children. In L. D. Eron, J. H. Gentry, & P. Schlegel (Eds.), *Reason to hope: A psychosocial perspective on violence and youth* (pp. 337-377). Washington, DC: American Psychological Association.

Kelley, S. M., Lewis, K., & Sigal, J. (2004). The impact of risk factors on the treatment of juvenile sex offenders. *Journal of Addictions and Offender Counseling, 24*(2), 67-81.

Lundrigan, P. S. (2001). *Treating youth who sexually abuse: An integrated multi-component approach.* Binghamton, NY: The Haworth Press.

Marshall, W. L., Hudson, S. M., & Hodkinson, S. (1993). The importance of attachment bonds in the development of juvenile sex offending. In H. E. Barbaree, W. L. Marshall, & S. M. Hudson (Eds.), *The juvenile sex offender* (pp. 164-177). New York: The Guilford Press.

Miner, M. H., Siekert, G. P., & Ackland, M. A. (1997). *Evaluation: Juvenile Sex Offender Treatment Program, Minnesota Correctional Facility—Sauk Centre.* Final report—Biennium 1995-1997. Minneapolis, MN: University of Minnesota, Department of Family Practice and Community Health, Program in Human Sexuality.

National Adolescent Perpetrator Network. (1993). The revised report from the National Task Force on Juvenile Sex Offending. *Juvenile and Family Court Journal, 44*(4), 1-120.

Perry, G. P., & Orchard, J. (1992). *Assessment and treatment of adolescent sex offenders.* Sarasota, FL: Professional Resource Press.

Righthand, S., & Welch, C. (2001). *Juveniles who have sexually offended: A review of the professional literature.* Washington, DC: Office of Juvenile Justice and Delinquency Prevention.

Schram, D. D., Milloy, C. D., & Rowe, W. E. (1991). *Juvenile sex offenders: A follow-up study of reoffense behavior.* Olympia, WA: Washington State Institute for Public Policy, Urban Policy Research and Cambie Group International.

Vizard, E., Monck, E., & Misch, P. (1995). Child and adolescent sex abuse perpetrators: A review of the research literature. *Journal of Child Psychology and Psychiatry, 36,* 731-756.

Yalom, I. D. (1995). *The theory and practice of group psychotherapy* (4th ed.). New York: Basic Books.

24

Crafty Coping:
Coping Tools for College Students

Jennifer Marshall
Trey Fitch

Type of Contribution: Activities

Objectives

These activities have two main objectives:

1. To keep group members' hands busy while they discuss hard issues.
2. To learn effective coping "tools" that can be used out of the group.

Rationale for Use

College students face many issues, including managing academics and negotiating with roommates, dates, friends, and parents. Many of the issues revolve around having a lack of control in a situation, as well as handling the stress involved in daily life issues. Seyle (1974) found that an individual who experiences a stressful event also experiences a physiological reaction, regardless of the type of stressor that was involved. This stress reaction can be destructive to one's health (Seyle, 1956). Among college students, impending exams, fear of failure, and academic ability have been linked to increased stress levels (Hughes, 2005). Further, negative social interactions have also been linked to well-being and health factors (Edwards, Hershberger, Russell, & Markert, 2001).

Effective coping activities, however, can promote personal growth in the wake of stressful events (Park & Fenster, 2004). College students need coping skills to address physical well-being, academic performance anxiety, and negative social interactions. The primary rationale for these activities is to foster coping skills applicable to all college students while addressing current stressors. Specific coping skills that are addressed include positive reframing, catharsis, anger management, and enhancement of communication skills.

Instructions

The group leader begins each session with a topic, such as daily stresses or lack of control. He or she then introduces an activity, such as the Dammit Person or the Tool Box. As the students work on the activity, the group facilitator encourages an open discussion on the topic, concentrating on how this issue has impacted them particularly in recent time and focusing on what has and has not worked. Having members work on the activity while they discuss the issue will help

The Group Therapist's Notebook
© 2007 by The Haworth Press, Inc. All rights reserved.
doi:10.1300/5576_24

link the coping mechanism to the stressful event and, thus, encourage group members to use these coping mechanisms when they are stressed.

Dammit Person

The Dammit Person is an actual doll that the members make in group. It is simply a cotton cloth doll stuffed with batting and sewn/stapled along the edges. This uses the popular Dammit Doll concept (see "How to Make a Dammit Doll at www.warpedworld.org/dammit.html). This activity expands on this concept by having group members make their own Dammit Person that can be individualized. For example, some group members have actually made clothes for their Dammit Person and have given them faces and names. The group leader will need to have needles and thread (or a stapler for those who do not sew), white material, cotton batting (can be found at a sewing store), and markers, cloth, buttons or other materials to decorate and personalize the Dammit Person.

To make the Dammit Person pattern, take the white material and fold it in half. The leader will need to cut the white material into two halves resembling the front and back of a gingerbread man. Each member is given the front and back patterns of the Dammit Person and a needle and thread/stapler. The doll is sewn/stapled around the edges, except for a hole big enough to stuff cotton batting into. The member stuffs the batting into the doll and sews or staples the hole shut. The group member can then personalize his or her person.

After the Dammit Person is complete, the group leader discusses ways to vent anger and frustration using appropriate coping mechanisms. One way they can do this is by kneading, throwing, or hitting the doll. The group leader can also talk about other coping mechanisms, such as deep breathing, guided imagery, and progressive muscle relaxation (see also Hamlin & Kane, 2007).

The Toolbox

The toolbox is a kit, which the member makes, that includes tools which can be used outside of group. Each tool symbolically represents a support which the member can visualize and use in stressful situations. To make the tools for the toolbox, the group leader will need to provide the members with scissors, colored construction paper, and markers and pens.

The leader explains that thoughts and actions can be used as tools to solve problems. The leader asks for one member to specify a current problematic issue, give examples, and identify the emotional and behavioral reactions he or she experienced as a result. The group leader then encourages the members to create a personal toolbox with tools representing coping mechanisms they can use after their presenting problems have been discussed. Each tool in the box has a purpose. Some examples include the following:

- Hammer: Knock off bad thoughts
- Screwdriver: Secure things together and stability
- Level: Make sure a level head is used
- Saw/Scissors: Get rid of destructive thoughts and behaviors
- Flashlight: See things in a brighter perspective
- Lightbulb: Insight

The group leader brings in a sample toolbox that he or she makes outside of the group. For example, one of the authors' toolboxes (J. M.) included individually drawn pictures (light bulb, screwdriver) and printed clip art pictures from a computer (level, hammer, saw, and flashlight). Depending on the group, most students will need a visual example before making their own.

As the group members bring up issues, they should make tools to symbolically represent coping skills. Each member creates his or her own toolbox using the group leader's toolbox as an example. It is emphasized that each tool must represent a coping skill under their control. The member must also be willing to explain how the tool is a metaphor for a specific coping skill. For example, a group member may use a picture of a saw to represent getting rid of unhealthy, destructive, and unrealistic thoughts.

Brief Vignette

Tanya, a nineteen-year-old and a sophomore in college, opened the group by declaring how angry she was with her boyfriend. As she talked about her thoughts and feelings in dealing with her boyfriend, she asked the group for ways to cope with the stress. Ms. Jacobs, the group leader, introduced the toolbox activity. She related how everyone uses different tools to handle different situations. Each member received materials to create their own toolbox. Ms. Jacobs explained how different tools represent different coping mechanisms, such as a light bulb representing insight. Tanya constructed a hammer, nails, and level out of construction paper, using markers and scissors. Tanya expressed that the hammer represented knocking off negative or angry thoughts and the nails symbolized those thoughts. The level represented rational thinking. Tanya was cognizant of her rational and irrational thinking and the level helped her to remember to balance her appraisal of her stressors.

Once complete, the members brainstormed how other tools could be used for Tanya's stressors. Group members suggested that she also use an eraser to help eliminate negative thoughts she had toward herself when she was angry. Tanya had previously related that she would retain thoughts of arguments in her mind long after the arguments were over. She needed to remind herself to more quickly erase her negative thinking. They also suggested glue, which could symbolize keeping close to her support systems. She needed to glue herself to her supportive friends and family when feeling stressed and fight the temptation to isolate herself.

In the following group session, using the instructions outlined previously, the group leader introduced the Dammit Person activity. While talking about her boyfriend Tanya, vented her frustrations using the Dammit Person. Tanya smacked the doll on the table and threw it across the room while releasing her pent-up anger. This helped Tanya express repressed anger toward her boyfriend and herself. Metaphorically, the doll represented her hidden anger and previous failures of expression. Afterward, Tanya appeared calmer, and she and the group were able to joke about the activity now that the tension had depleted. She was encouraged to express herself with the Dammit Person between sessions, along with her newly constructed tools. In future sessions, Tanya reported successfully using her new tools and Dammit Person in a more positive expression of anger.

Suggestions for Follow-Up

Check-in with the participants to make sure the techniques are working. Get a feel for the individual's thoughts and reactions to the activities by asking questions and have them journal their use of the activities out of group. The Dammit Person and Toolbox are meant to be used as supports out of group, as well as in the group. The group leader may want to assign homework which includes using the Dammit Person and the ideas contained in the toolbox outside of the group. It is also helpful to know what the participant put in their toolbox so the group leader can refer back to a member's particular supports when needed.

Contraindications

When personalizing the Dammit Person, the group leader should ensure that members do not name or create the likeness of anyone with whom they have a relationship in order to reduce any transference issues. The Dammit Person is not recommended for use by those who have been accused of battery or domestic violence or who have severe anger management problems. These clients need more intensive treatment than can be provided by this activity.

The group leader needs to stress that while it is appropriate to release anger with or on the Dammit Person, it is never appropriate to physically, emotionally, or sexually abuse, neglect, or exploit another person. The group leader should always inform group members that they are mandated reporters in the case or suspected child or elder abuse, neglect, and exploitation and should be ready to make these reports to the proper authorities if necessary.

In the beginning, members may have trouble using the Dammit Person and the toolbox and may need encouragement and modeling. The students should try out the Dammit Person after construction. Also the group leader may want to rename the Dammit Person a Darn-it Person for individuals who may be offended by the terminology.

Emotional expression can be very difficult for some members and everyone may not choose to participate. Conversely, some members can become emotionally charged through these activities. The group leader must be ready to help process and de-escalate these issues.

Reading and Resources for the Professional

Archer, J., Jr., & Cooper, S. (1998). *Counseling and mental health services on campus.* San Francisco: Jossey-Bass, Inc.

Chickering, A., & Reisser, L. (1993). *Education and identity* (2nd ed). San Francisco: John Wiley & Sons, Inc.

Evans, N. J., Foreny, D. S., & Guido-DiBrito, F. (1998). *Student development in college: Theory, research, & practice.* San Francisco: Jossey-Bass, Inc.

How to make a Dammit Doll. (n.d.). Retrieved April 24, 2005 from http://www.warpedworld .org/dammit.html

Bibliotherapy Sources for the Client

Ellis, A. (1988). *How to stubbornly refuse to make yourself miserable about anything—Yes, anything.* New York: Kensington Publishing Corp.

Kaufmann, Y., & Bernstein, M. (Eds.) (2004). *How to survive your freshman year.* Atlanta, GA: Hundreds of Heads Books, Inc.

Lazarus, A., Lazarus, C., & Fay, A. (1993). *Don't believe it for a minute.* Atascadero, CA: Impact Publishers.

References

Edwards, K. J., Hershberger, P. J., Russell, R. K., & Markert, R. J. (2001). Stress, negative social exchange, and health symptoms in university students. *Journal of American College Health, 50*(2), 75-80.

Hamlin, E. R., & Kane, M. (2007). Learning how to de-stress. In D. R. Viers (Ed.), *The group therapist's notebook: Homework, handouts, and activities for use in psychotherapy* (pp. 33-38). Binghamton, NY: The Haworth Press.

How to make a Dammit Doll. (n.d.). Retrieved April 24, 2005, from http://www.warpedworld .org/dammit.html.

Hughes, B. M. (2005). Study, examinations, and stress: Blood pressure assessments in college students. *Educational Review, 57*(1), 21-37.

Park, C. L., & Fenster, J. R. (2004). Stress-related growth: Predictors of occurrence and correlates with psychological adjustment. *Journal of Social & Clinical Psychology, 23*(2), 195-216.

Seyle, H. (1956). *The stress of life.* New York: McGraw.

Seyle, H. (1974). *Stress without distress.* Philadelphia: Lippincott.

25

A Group Intervention for Athletic Teams

Victoria L. Bacon
Marcia K. Anderson

Type of Contribution: Activity

Objective

The group activity covered in this chapter utilizes critical incident stress debriefing (CISD) with athletic teams in schools and colleges to reduce symptoms of excessive stress and prevent the occurrence of post-traumatic stress disorder symptoms (Mitchell & Everly, 1997). Critical incidents in sport are often related to injury, disability, or death and involve a team member, coach, or individual closely associated with the team.

Rationale for Use

Sport participation brings a risk of injury and disability. Cantu and Mueller (1999) documented 476 fatalities and catastrophic injuries from participation in a sport at the high school and collegiate levels during the years from 1982 to 1996. Examples of other tragic events are accidents while in transit, severe violence, suicide, drug overdose, and sudden death. Lessons learned from the Oklahoma City bombing, the Worcester cold-storage fire, and 9/11 have taught us that we must manage the emotional and psychological needs of all persons involved in a critical incident (Everly & Mitchell, 2000).

A critical incident "refers to an event which is outside the usual range of experience and challenges one's ability to cope. The critical incident has the potential to lead to a crisis condition by overwhelming one's usual psychological defenses and coping mechanisms" (Everly & Mitchell, 2000, p. 212). Given that student athletes are actively engaged in learning as well as performing in sport, involvement in a critical incident could potentially have a negative impact on their ability to perform academically and in their sport, as well as in the social and relational domains.

The various types of critical incidents that occur in sport can be viewed as direct or indirect in nature. Direct incidents are directly related to sport involvement, like the death of an athlete during play. Indirect incidents generally occur off the playing field, such as an automobile or airplane crash involving members of the team, coach, and/or medical staff. When a critical incident occurs, teammates often experience a grief response; first experiencing shock, then preoccupation with the incident and a myriad of acute stress symptoms, including insomnia, fatigue, eating problems, a change in risk-taking behavior, and angry outbursts (Henschen & Heil, 1992; Pedersen, 1986).

Critical incident stress debriefing is a debriefing model designed to provide psychological closure for individuals in a group format in response to a critical incident (Mitchell, 1983).

CISD was developed for the purpose of "mitigation of the impact of a traumatic event, prevention of posttraumatic stress reactions, and acceleration of recovery processes" (Mitchell & Everly, 1997, p. 85). This intervention model was originally designed to help emergency services personnel to process their exposure to extreme stress during traumatic events (Mitchell & Bray, 1990). Since its inception, it has been widely used in a variety of large- and small-scale critical incidents and with a wide spectrum of ages across the lifespan.

Vernacchia, Reardon, and Templin (1997) contend that CISD interventions are a good fit in sport given the similarities that athletic teams have with emergency services personnel; both groups spend the major portion of their time together, share common goals, have a cohesive unit, and experience a sense of immortality, making a catastrophic event even more intense. CISD have been shown to be very effective with emergency services personnel (Robinson & Mitchell, 1993) and, more recently, with athletic teams (Hunt, 2003; Vernacchia et al., 1997).

Instructions

Critical incident stress debriefing is a seven phase debriefing model designed to be employed within fourteen days post incident. CISD takes approximately one to two hours and is facilitated by mental health professionals trained to use this protocol (Mitchell & Everly, 1997). The process involves the following steps:

1. Introduction (5 minutes)
2. Facts (10 minutes)
3. Thoughts (20 minutes)
4. Emotional Reactions (20 minutes)
5. Signs and Symptoms (15 minutes)
6. Teaching (15 minutes)
7. Reentry (15 minutes)

Estimated times are provided based on a two hour intervention. It is recommended that two persons cofacilitate the group intervention.

The job of the cofacilitators is two-fold: (a) to move the members through the stages and (b) to assess group member's psychological reaction and ability to cope. On occasion, it will be necessary to refer a member for individual psychotherapy. It is important to note that athletes respond best to mental health professionals who have a close connection to sport or who were or are currently involved with a sport. Athletes feel a strong sense of connection with professionals who understand the unique stressors of being a competitive athlete and the various aspects of sports participation.

Introduction

It is important to introduce the group facilitators and explain the purpose of the meeting. At this juncture, it is helpful to give the parameters of the meeting, including that this is a one-time, time-limited meeting. Sharing how this meeting will help them process their experience and move forward is helpful, particularly connecting this process to their sport and their role as an athlete. Confidentiality needs to be discussed prior to introducing each of the group members.

Facts

Next, provide facts about the incident, including information about any fatalities or injuries and the status of events and persons directly involved in the critical incident. It is important to differentiate fact from fiction. It is recommended that a rumor-control person be identified and available at this meeting. This person is typically employed by the school or college and is knowledgeable about the facts. Having a rumor-control person available will help reduce fiction and discrepancies regarding facts. The rumor-control person is also used to provide periodic updates (for example, the health status of an athlete).

Thoughts

This phase helps participants transition from information and facts to the affective or emotional aspect of their experience. Begin by asking members to describe where they were at the time of the incident. Encourage participants to include what they saw, heard, and smelled. Explore their thoughts and feelings at the time of the incident and then move to their thoughts and feelings in the present moment. Keep the process moving from member to member, focusing on thoughts and feelings. It is important to curtail efforts at blaming or the desire of members to talk about the future.

Emotional Reactions

In this phase, help participants express their reactions about the event, as well as the meaning of the critical incident on a personal level.

Signs and Symptoms

This phase is intended to move participants from emotionally charged material back to their thoughts and daily activities. It is helpful to use a blackboard to track symptoms. Symptoms are shared and normalized. Ask about sleeping and eating patterns, mood changes, and routines. The most common signs and symptoms include decreased concentration, lowered academic performance, feeling overwhelmed particularly related to feelings of anger, grief, or loss, changes in behavior, and physical signs and symptoms associated with an increase in anxiety.

Teaching

This is an opportunity to provide some education to normalize symptoms, prepare participants for the next few days, and review coping strategies. It is useful to review common reactions to a critical incident and encourage members to identify effective coping strategies during this period.

Reentry

This phase provides closure. Participants are encouraged to ask questions about the material covered in this session and get clarification about the facts. Be certain to keep members focused and do not allow them to move back to an earlier phase of the group process. Depending on the age and particular group, it may be helpful to use an activity such as writing a question on a piece of paper, placing the questions in a hat, and having members pull one out and read it to the group. An activity such as this is less threatening and allows for important questions to surface and be addressed. It is helpful to give age-appropriate handouts that will provide education about common symptoms and referral information. Make certain to end on time.

Upon conclusion of the group intervention, it is important for cofacilitators to debrief with each other. The function of this is two-fold: (a) to review the success of the intervention and (b) to assess for vicarious traumatization. Vicarious traumatization is when a cofacilitator exhibits signs and symptoms of trauma as a result of empathetic engagement with a client's trauma. Cofacilitators need to be aware of the signs and symptoms as well as contributing factors that place facilitators at risk.

CISD is more effective when there is support from key individuals in the system. In sport this would involve the athletic director, athletic trainer, coach, team captain, and other key individuals. Vernacchia et al. (1997) recommend involving athletic staff (athletic trainers and administrators) with other support professionals (counselors, CISD specialists, etc.) trained to respond to sport-related critical incidents. Doing so would allow for maximum support to athletes, athletic staff, and the larger community. A CISD intervention provides an opportunity to process the event and develop a plan to move forward ,as well as reduce the potential negative impact of the critical incident (i.e., psychological symptoms of distress) on the staff and team members.

It is recommended that all athletic programs have a Critical Incident Stress Management protocol as part of their emergency action plan (Hunt, 2003; Vernacchia et al., 1997). All individuals involved in executing the protocol should receive training and meet regularly to assess and evaluate protocols for effectiveness and efficiency.

Suggestions for Follow-Up

It is helpful to identify support service personnel in the school or college prior to conducting the group intervention. Developing a follow-up plan that includes the referral process, monitoring the status of the persons involved in the critical incident, and a discussion of other systems issues and policies will all contribute to the overall success of the intervention. Educating key professionals about stress signs and symptoms that may persist past the debriefing is critical. Mitchell and Everly (1997, p. 23) have identified some of the more common signs and symptoms of excessive stress:

- Cognitive: confusion in thinking, difficulty making decisions, lowered concentration, memory dysfunction, lowering of higher cognitive functions.
- Emotional: emotional shock, anger, grief, depression, feeling overwhelmed.
- Physical: excessive sweating, dizzy spells, increased heart rate, elevated blood pressure, rapid breathing.
- Behavioral: changes in ordinary behavior patterns, changes in eating, decreased personal hygiene, withdrawal from others, prolonged silences.

Contraindications

CISD is a protocol with the intended purpose of mitigating the impact of a traumatic event, helping to prevent posttraumatic stress reactions, and accelerating the recovery process (Mitchell & Everly, 1997). It is important to remember that even the best prepared and delivered group intervention may not be suitable for all individuals or appropriate for all circumstances. Individuals experiencing psychological distress prior to the event will need more assistance and support, which goes beyond what can be provided by CISD. CISD is not a treatment for persons who have a diagnosis of post-traumatic stress disorder or other psychological diagnoses (such as major depression, generalized anxiety disorder, etc.).

Assessment of the level of involvement of each person in the critical incident, the intensity of the incident, and level of exposure is needed prior to agreeing to conduct CISD with a group. Mitchell and Everly (1997) contend that "the more intimately involved in an incident a person is, the more likelihood there is that debriefings alone will not be sufficient to overcome the negative impact of the trauma" (p. 85).

Readings and Resources for the Professional

American School Counselor Association (2003, Nov/Dec). Crisis Response. *School Counselor, 41*(2), 8-44.

Collins, B. G., & Collins, T. M. (2005). *Crisis and trauma.* Boston: Lahaska Press.

Everly, G. S. (1989). *A clinical guide to the treatment of the human stress response.* New York: Plenum Press.

Herman, J. (1997). *Trauma and recovery.* New York: Basic Books.

Hunt, V. (2003, May). Can guidelines ease the aftermath of tragedy? *NATA News,* 10-14.

Lerner, M. D., Volpe, J. S., & Lindell, B. (2003). *Crisis response in our schools* (5th ed.). New York: The Academy of Experts in Traumatic Stress.

Mitchell, J. T., & Everly, G. S. (1997). *Critical incident stress debriefing: An operations manual for CISD, defusing and other group crisis intervention services* (3rd ed.). Ellicott, MD: Chevron Publishing Company.

Pedersen, P. (1986, Winter). The grief response and injury: A special challenge for athletes and athletic trainers. *Athletic Training, 21,* 312-314.

Bibliotherapy Sources for the Client

Lerner, M. (2007). Twenty-one things you can do while you're living through a traumatic experience. Retrieved January 17, 2007 from www.aaets.org/column5.htm.

National Association of School Psychologists (NASP) Resources: www.nasponline.org/resources/crisis_safety/index.aspx#general.

References

Cantu, R. C., & Mueller, F. O. (1999, Aug). Fatalities and catastrophic injuries in high school and college sports, 1982-1997: Lessons for improving safety. *The Physician and Sports Medicine, 2*(8), 35-48.

Everly, G. S., & Mitchell, J. T. (2000). The debriefing "controversy" and crisis intervention: A review of lexical and substantive issues. *International Journal of Emergency Mental Health, 2*(4), 211-225.

Henschen, K. P., & Heil, J. (1992). A retrospective study of the effect of an athlete's sudden death of teammates. *Omega: Journal of Death and Dying, 25,* 217-223.

Hunt, V. (2003, May). Can guidelines ease the aftermath of tragedy? *NATA News,* 10-14.

Mitchell, J. T. (1983). When disaster strikes . . . : The critical incident stress debriefing process. *Journal of Emergency Medical Services, 8*(1), 36-39.

Mitchell, J. T., & Bray, G. P. (1990). *Emergency services stress: Guidelines for preserving the health and careers of emergency services personnel.* Englewood Cliffs, NJ: Prentice Hall.

Mitchell, J. T., & Everly, G. S. (1997). *Critical incident stress debriefing: An operations manual for CISD, defusing and other group crisis intervention services* (3rd ed.). Ellicott, MD: Chevron Publishing Company.

Pedersen, P. (1986, Winter). The grief response and injury: A special challenge for athletes and athletic trainers. *Athletic Training, 21,* 312-314.

Robinson, R. C., & Mitchell, J. T. (1993). Evaluation of psychological debriefings. *Journal of Traumatic Stress, 6*(3), 367-382.

Vernacchia, R. A., Reardon, J. P., & Templin, D. P. (1997). Sudden death in sport: Managing the aftermath. *The Sport Psychologist, 11,* 223-235.

SECTION V:
INTERVENTIONS FOR COUPLE
AND FAMILY GROUPS

26

Make Your Partner Your Friend, Not Your Enemy

Floyd F. Robison

Type of Contribution: Activity/Handout

Objective

This activity is intended to help couples, who are in frequent or seemingly intractable conflict, reframe their attitudes toward one another in ways that will facilitate negotiation rather than quarreling and mutual blaming. The procedure is designed to illustrate to partners that their quarrels are based on their view of each other as enemies and encourages them to revise their thinking about each other as friends.

The purpose of this activity is to help couples successfully work through current and future conflicts by accomplishing the following:

(a) Couples will understand how they have come to construe each other as enemies.
(b) They will decide how they may reinterpret their view of each other as friends who have yet to understand what they need from each other and how to give and receive what they need.
(c) They will identify ways of talking and behaving with each other that are consistent with the ways friends would talk and behave to negotiate solutions to their conflicts.

Rationale for Use

This homework activity is adapted from the cognitive-behavior theory of Aaron Beck (1976), which proposes that persons behave toward others according to their beliefs about others' motives and intentions. In the case of ongoing conflict between partners in a relationship, each partner has developed an attitude that, in effect, construes the other partner as an enemy (that is, one who wants to somehow harm, disenfranchise, or take away something from him or her). These attitudes manifest in "self-talk," or immediate messages and cognitions that people tell themselves about a specific event. When partners experience negative self-talk, they engage in defensive behavior, such as resistance, blaming, undermining, and attempting to justify their respective positions in the conflict.

Instructions

This activity may be introduced in one group meeting and continued over several successive meetings. The following steps are used to introduce and conduct the activity:

Step 1: Setting the stage
Step 2: Identifying "enemy" thinking and behavior

Step 3: Presenting assumptions for change
Step 4: Reinterpreting your partner's behavior and your thoughts about it
Step 5: Negotiating conflict resolution behaviors

Step 1: Setting the Stage

The facilitator should introduce the activity with the following explanation in oral or written form (facilitators may present this explanation in their own words as long as the same ideas are presented):

> When a couple has trouble resolving conflicts that arise between them, they often come to harbor beliefs that enemies believe about one another. These words people think or say to express these beliefs varying from person to person, but beliefs include notions that their partners are intentionally trying to hurt them, take advantage of them, or take something away from them. Think of two people who are sworn enemies of each other. Each has come to decide that the other is, in some way, out to get them, and they must fight back to protect themselves. And fight they do; each will intentionally harm the other in order to prevent what they have decided is an attempt by the other to harm them.
>
> Enemies do not work out conflicts. Instead, each attempts to defeat the other. As long as two parties, whether the parties are individuals or groups of people, deal with one another as enemies, their conflicts can never be worked out. Someone must win and someone must lose, although in many cases, everyone loses because no one has been able to obtain what they wanted or needed from the "war."
>
> How do wars stop? How do people stop being enemies? They do so by first changing how they think about one another then behaving as friends would behave. They decide that those who are their enemies may, in fact, not be trying to harm them but would be willing to negotiate solutions to their disagreements in order to become friends, or at least not enemies. When, and only when, two people decide that they do not have to be enemies, they can negotiate solutions.
>
> Couples who quarrel and cannot let go of their differences have come to evaluate each other as enemies. They have come to believe their partners are trying to hurt them, do not care about them, and are willing to do anything to get their way at their partner's expense. But the vast majority of people do not enter intimate relationships to be enemies. Enemy thinking evolves over time, from the accumulation of little hurts that partners unintentionally inflict on one another.
>
> Perhaps you and your partner can identify ways that the two of you have come to treat each other like enemies in this way. The purpose of this activity is to help you and your partner identify ways that the two of you have come to believe the other is your enemy, evaluate and change your thinking about each other, and negotiate solutions to your conflicts that friends would use.

Step 2: Identifying "Enemy" Thinking and Behavior

The leader distributes a pencil and paper to each participant and continues with the second step:

> For the next three minutes, I would like you and your partner to decide together on a conflict that you've had for a long time—weeks, months, or even years. When the two of you have decided on the conflict you want to use for this activity, write it at the top of the paper I have given you.

The facilitator waits for at about three minutes, then continues with the following:

> For the next three minutes, I would like you to think about that conflict without talking to your partner. When the two of you are caught in this conflict, what are you thinking about your partner? As precisely as you can, write on your paper the thoughts you are having about him or her. Again, don't discuss this with your partner yet.

The facilitator again waits for about three minutes, then continues:

> Now, think about what you do when this conflict arises. How do you behave toward him or her when the conflict arises and you have the thoughts that you've written down? In three minutes, write down what you do when you conflict with your partner over this matter.

After this three minute period has ended, the facilitator asks the participants to share with the group the thoughts they have written. These disclosures should be treated as voluntary, but all participants should be encouraged to share their thoughts at least with their own partners during this discussion period.

At the conclusion of this discussion, the facilitator poses this question: "Reread what you have written about your thoughts about your partner and what you did during the conflict. Now, write on your paper one or two ways that your partner seemed like your enemy during that conflict."

After the leader has allowed about three minutes for participants to write their thoughts, another discussion period follows. During the discussion, the facilitator should link participants' thoughts to the concept of enemy thinking described earlier, helping participants link common elements of their respective enemy thoughts and linking participants' thoughts to their behaviors toward partners that maintain and escalate conflicts. This helps the participants to recognize and stop the negative self-talk they are having about their partner. During this discussion, the leader may want to encourage feedback among participants to help them clarify the relationships between their thinking and behaviors toward their partners during their conflicts.

Step 3: Presenting Assumptions for Change

In this step, the facilitator presents to the group five assumptions that they will asked to accept in order to change their thinking about each other. Some participants may initially resist these assumptions, but in our experience using this activity in groups, we have found that participants are able to reframe their partners' actions and brainstorm new thoughts on managing conflicts more successfully if they will at least "pretend" to accept them. The assumptions are as follows (these assumptions are pulled apart in Handout 26.1 as an optional handout to give to participants):

1. Neither you nor your partner entered your relationship with the intent of being enemies.
2. Neither you nor your partner actually gains anything from being enemies.
3. Most people in relationships are not astute enough to be good enemies, but they are "thick-headed" enough to not know how to be good friends.
4. If given the chance, and if they know how to do it, couples will be friends.
5. Friendship will happen faster if you teach each other how to be your friend.

Step 4: Reinterpreting Your Partner's Behavior and Your Thoughts About It

In this step, the facilitator leads the group in a discussion as to how participants can positively reinterpret their partners' behavior and their own thoughts about this behavior. The group discussion during this step may bring up several side topics as well as some resistance from participants, which can be discussed to the extent necessary to continue with activity. The facilitator introduces this step as follows:

> Let's talk more about your enemy thoughts and your partner's behavior that leads to those thoughts. Considering the five assumptions I have proposed, how might you reinterpret your partner's behavior if you consider the behavior of a friend who just doesn't understand what you need? How would your thoughts about him or her change from what you have written on your sheet? Let's talk about this, and as we talk, you should feel free to write your ideas on your sheets.

The facilitator should encourage the group to discuss these questions and, as appropriate, provide feedback to each participant.

Step 5: Negotiating Conflict Resolution Behaviors

The facilitator leads the group in a discussion of appropriate conflict resolution behaviors between partners who are friends. This step is initiated as follows:

> Now that you've created and written down your positive interpretations of your partner's behaviors that you used to consider as those of an enemy, how would you work through your conflict as friends? Let's discuss this as a group and, as good ideas come to you, write them down in the remaining space on your sheets.

The group's feedback at this step is useful to help each participating couple generate and refine appropriate conflict resolution strategies. Also, the facilitator can use the group discussion at this stage to share information on conflict resolution, negotiation, compromise, assertion, and behavior feedback techniques to further assist couples in planning strategies for working thorough disagreements as friends in the future.

Brief Vignette

Janet, age twenty-four, and Tom, age twenty-seven, were referred to the couples group because they had made little progress in couple's therapy during the past year. They had been together for two years. During this time, their relationship had steadily deteriorated. Janet complained, "Tom doesn't show me that he loves me. He won't do with me the things I like to do, even though I do things with him that he enjoys. When we do go out together, he looks at other women like he wants to be with them instead of me. When I ask him if he'd rather be with them, he just brushes it off and says I'm paranoid. I want us to get married some day, but when I bring it up, he changes the subject. I get so hurt, I start thinking about ending our relationship." Tom stated, "She's always on me about where I go and what I do, even though she knows where I am. If I as much as look at another woman in a restaurant or at a ball game, she accuses me of wanting to go out with the other woman. I've never cheated on Janet, but I hate to go anywhere with her where there might be women. I feel trapped by her jealousy. I love her but don't want to think about marriage with the way things are now. I don't know how much more I can stand."

As Tom and Janet explored their relationship using the Make Your Partner Your Friend, Not Your Enemy activity, they realized that they were telling themselves a number of enemy messages about each other. They were rather surprised at the similarity of their respective self-talk. For example, during their arguments, and often at other times, Janet told herself that Tom actually derived some kind of odd pleasure from avoiding her. Tom often told himself that Janet was "out to make me miserable" and felt that he had to protect himself from her paranoia by refusing to accompany her on some outings. Both partners realized that their construction of each other as enemies had clouded the original issues on which they disagreed. Being at odds with each other had become the central issue in their relationship. The group explained to Tom and Janet that until they could put aside their self-talk of each other as enemies, they could not refocus their energy on negotiating solutions for more straightforward disagreements.

Tom and Janet finally agreed that they were construing each other as enemies, but acknowledged that they had entered their romance as friends and wished to return to that friendship. The group assisted the couple in brainstorming other, more positive, interpretations of each other's behavior, such as Tom's looking at other women in public places (which the group reframed as his way of communicating to Janet that, although there were other attractive women in the place, she was the one with whom he wished to be) and Janet's desire to learn about Tom's work or places where he had been without her (which was reframed as her expression of caring about him). Once the couple had brainstormed more positive interpretations, they were able to explore with each other ways that they, as friends, could negotiate a schedule by which they would alternately have needed time away from each other and spend time in activities that they each enjoyed.

Suggestions for Follow-Up

A follow-up dialogue about the activity should occur in the group from one to three weeks after each couple has started to negotiate conflict-resolution behaviors. The follow-up should address participants' success and problems with conflict resolution and assist participants in summarizing the skills they learned through the activity.

Contraindications

This activity is intended for couples who are in nonviolent, noncoercive, and nonexploitive relationships. If a partner is, in fact, the recipient of physical or psychological abuse or exploitation, then the assumptions presented by the facilitator in Step 3 (Presenting Assumptions for Change) cannot be met, and the activity is inappropriate for the couple until those issues are addressed in the group or in individual therapy.

Reading and Resource for the Professional

Sager, C. J. (1977). *Marriage contracts and couple therapy: Hidden forces in marital relationships.* New York: Brunner-Routledge.

Bibliotherapy Sources for the Client

Beck, A. T. (1988). *Love is never enough.* New York: Harper and Row.
Turndorf, J. (1999). *Till death do us part (unless I kill you first): A step by step guide for resolving marital conflict.* New York: Owl Books.

Reference

Beck, A. T. (1976). *Cognitive therapy and the emotional disorders.* Boston: International Universities Press.

HANDOUT 26.1. ASSUMPTIONS FOR CHANGE

1. Neither you nor your partner entered your relationship with the intent of being enemies.

2. Neither you nor your partner actually gains anything from being enemies.

3. Most people in relationships are not astute enough to be good enemies, but they are "thick-headed" enough to not know how to be good friends.

4. If given the chance, and if they know how to do it, couples will be friends.

5. Friendship will happen faster if you teach each other how to be your friend.

Robison, F. F. (2007). Make your partner your friend, not your enemy. In D. R. Viers (Ed.), *The group therapist's note-book: Homework, handouts, and activities for use in psychotherapy* (pp. 199-204). Binghamton, NY: The Haworth Press.

27

Gender Awareness and Media Messages:
An Activity for Couple Therapy

Toni S. Zimmerman
Jennifer L. Krafchick
Jennifer T. Aberle

Type of Contribution: Activity

Objective

For many couples, conflict is a normal part of life. Some of this conflict may stem from disagreements in housework allocation, parenting issues, how leisure time is spent, occupations, and income. In heterosexual couples, men and women have traditionally stepped into gender "appropriate" roles when it comes to many of these issues. When men and women take on these stereotypical gender roles in their relationships, one person may feel the distribution is unequal or unfair. Therefore, examining how gender-role messages influence people and their beliefs about their relationship is a critical component of therapeutic intervention around role conflict. This activity increases a couple's awareness of the media's influence on constructing gender "norms."

Rationale for Use

Gender is a fundamental organizing principle in society that influences our relationships, families, and communities (Haddock, Zimmerman, & Lyness, 2003). Stereotypes and expectations based on gender can restrict freedom, and individuals can be limited in achieving their full potential. Many of the most serious social problems of our time result from powerful societal forces that prescribe particular expectations for women and men from all racial and socioeconomic backgrounds resulting in serious sexist ideologies. On a societal level, substantial research has been done in the area of limiting and negative stereotyping in the mass media regarding race and gender (Wilson & Gutierrez, 1995; Pipher, 1994; Pollack, 1998).

Socialization pressures on females often lead girls and women to define and value themselves primarily through relationships and physical appearance. As a result, many women suffer from eating disorders, depression, and real and perceived restrictions in life choices (Pipher, 1994). Many scholars argue that societal construction of masculinity—characterized by power, emotional invulnerability, stoicism, and independence—significantly contribute to epidemic rates of male violence, alcoholism and depression, physical and mental health problems, and constricted relationships with partners and children. Researchers have correlated emotional illiteracy in boys, which can result from adherence to traditional male gender norms, to all of these problems

The Group Therapist's Notebook
© 2007 by The Haworth Press, Inc. All rights reserved.
doi:10.1300/5576_27

(Pollack, 1998). These dynamics can set couples up to experience inequality and low marital satisfaction.

We learn about these prescribed gender roles from the world around us. In particular, the media in its many forms continues to reinforce restrictive gender roles. The average American spends a considerable amount of time interfacing with some form of media, especially advertising. These advertisements are displayed on television, in magazines, in movies, and on billboards. Because of the constant exposure to traditional and rigid gender roles portrayed in the media, individuals may begin to think of these roles as normal and desirable. As adults form relationships, they continue to emulate limiting gender expectations learned from the media. Unfortunately, these restrictive roles do not serve couples well in terms of forming a successful relationship. By recognizing and deconstructing traditional gender-restrictive roles, men and women can examine and question the expectations and limitations of these roles.

To overcome the harmful effects of stereotyping, people must learn—ideally in a safe and thoughtful way—to carefully analyze societal messages and develop helpful, practical skills for managing these messages to avoid a negative influence on their relationships. How individuals recognize and interpret messages of gender-appropriate behavior can impact the quality of their relationships in their families, with their partners, and in their careers and communities.

Recognizing the magnitude of gender-restrictive messages displayed in television, magazines, movies, and billboards is an important first step in deconstructing stereotypical gendered behavior and solving gender-perpetuated conflict for many couples. It allows the couple to feel less anger at each other and, instead, have the media as the common enemy. Understanding how the media has influenced their thinking and behaviors can help the couple to resist the media, not each other. They then can decide how they want to relate to each other outside of these restrictive ways.

Instructions

Gender socialization begins at birth, and as a result of this process, members of our society dictate certain expectations for who we are, what we like to do, what we are good at, and how we feel based on if we are a girl/woman or boy/man. Sometimes these gendered expectations or stereotypes can create conflict and discontent in relationships. This activity can provide a foundation for discussing these gendered expectations, whereby setting the contextual stage for couple-related issues. Participation in this activity can assist couples in better understanding how messages from the media, their families, and others can affect their perceptions of critical couple issues (for example, division of labor, parenting, sexual interactions, and employment). It is designed to provide a basic understanding of the influence that gender socialization plays on couples and how couples are taught to "do gender" in our society (West & Zimmerman, 1987). Group members can analyze the affect of gender stereotypes in their relationships and begin to develop the skills to resist these stereotypes. The ability to resist gender stereotypes can result in stronger and more satisfying marriages (Gottman & Silver, 1999).

Groups focusing on premarital couples, couple enrichment, and couples therapy can provide an ideal setting for this activity. It can be difficult to think outside the gender box as most people have spent their lives acting and thinking in ways that are "gender appropriate." It is less threatening for couples to begin group therapy by critically analyzing the media and the impact it has on society than to examine gender in their own relationship. Therefore, this activity is most successful when implemented at the beginning of the group sessions. It can serve as a catalyst to explore gendered expectations and can also be referred back to when issues related to gender stereotyping inevitably emerge within the group. As a result, group members can begin to realize that some of their couple concerns are driven by the gender messages in the media. There are two parts to this activity: the index card sort and the image collage.

Materials

- Index cards
- Enough medium-sized cardboard boxes for each couple
- Glue
- Scissors
- Several magazines for each couple

Index Card Sorting

The index card sorting activity is designed to promote discussion and recognition of gender-restrictive roles portrayed in the media and how these messages manifest in a couples relationship. It is important to recognize that the media sends messages that prescribe gender-appropriate behavior in relationships. Therapists can prepare stereotypical male and female activities written on index cards (or, if time permits, the group members can each take several cards and write down tasks or responsibilities that exist in a relationship or family). For example, activities may include washing the dishes, car repair, cooking, doing the laundry, mowing the lawn, playing golf, working at the office, shopping, taking care of the children, scheduling dates, paying bills, making a significant purchase, keeping in touch with friends or relatives, and other tasks.

Next the group members are asked to categorize whether a male or female would typically or stereotypically perform each task by placing them on a pink (female) or blue (male) sheet of paper. The therapist can hold up each card or distribute them to group members to be sorted. After the tasks (index cards) are sorted, the therapist should help the group members deconstruct the implications of gender expectations. The therapist could begin by asking what the group members notice about the tasks placed on the pink paper (and then the blue paper), keeping in mind that the discussion should emphasize gender on a societal level at this stage. Specifically, group members are asked to discuss the following questions.

- What influences the assignment of some tasks to males, and some to females?
- What do the "female tasks" have in common?
- What do the "male tasks" have in common?
- What do stereotypical female tasks say about the role of women?
- What do stereotypical male tasks say about the role of men?
- What happens if a woman prefers to, or chooses to, consistently perform the stereotypical male tasks?
- What happens if a man prefers to, or chooses to, consistently perform the stereotypical female tasks?
- Are there times when you have felt limited in the tasks or activities you can perform simply because of gender norms?
- Are there times that you limit others in the activities they choose because of stereotypical gender norms?

Discussion may continue and the therapist can be sure to emphasize specific points:

- Stereotypical female tasks are often passive and have to do with being caring, nurturing, and domestic.
- Stereotypical male tasks are often active and outside the home and deal with money and making decisions.

- When men and women, from early ages, are sent messages about what is appropriate and desirable behavior, this is limiting in what they may strive for, or hope to achieve, even in adulthood.
- Men and women should feel free and be encouraged to participate in any activity they choose. They should not feel they are limited to a specific role simply because of their gender.

Image Collage

The therapist provides magazines, a box, scissors, and glue to each couple. Couples are asked to imagine themselves in a confined space, like a box. The space would be confined, restricting, and uncomfortable. Sometimes, gender-restrictive messages make us feel the same way. The therapist will draw two large boxes on a sheet of paper. Each couple is then asked to help the therapist fill in the first box with several characteristics, interests, and behaviors that the media prescribes as valuable characteristics of a man (see Figure 27.1). Next, fill out the second box with characteristics, interests, and behaviors that the media prescribes as valuable characteristics of a woman (see Figure 27.2).

Because we receive such powerful messages about how women and men "should" act, sometimes it is difficult for clients to understand that there are personal attributes, interests, and ways of interacting that do not adhere to the prescribed expectations for individuals. You can describe these characteristics as "out-of-the-box." Ask the couple what types of ways of being might be described as out of the box. You can have them write these characteristics on index cards as well. Spend time brainstorming these qualities with the couple. Ask them to think about ways that they or others they know well embody out-of-the-box characteristics. Examples of out-of-the-box characteristics for men and women are included (see Figure 27.3).

After the couples understand the in/out-of-the-box metaphor, give each couple a flattened cardboard box, glue, scissors, and some magazines. Ask the couples to look through the maga-

FIGURE 27.1. Examples of In-the-Box Characteristics for Men

Strong	Unemotional
Independent	Insensitive
Breadwinner	Leader
Money maker	Initiator
Decison maker	Aggressive

FIGURE 27.2. Examples of In-the-Box Characteristics for Women

Caretaker	Thin
Parent	Nurturing
Passive	Emotional
Follower	Domestic chores
Pretty	Weak

FIGURE 27.3. Examples of Out-of-the-Box Characteristics for Men and Women

Feeling and Thinking		Leading and Following
Earning and Caring		Share in Domestic Labor

zines for pictures of males and females performing in-the-box behaviors or activities. Then have the couple glue the in-the-box pictures to the inside of the cardboard box.

Next, have the couples look for pictures that display males and females participating in activities that are outside of the box. Glue these images to the outside of the box.

After all images are cut and glued to the box, tape or fold the box into form. Image collage discussion questions/points may include:

- Why are these messages damaging to a relationship?
- What activities and feelings are men excluded from when they act in-the-box in regard to their relationship, family, or career?
- What activities and feelings are women excluded from when they act in-the-box in regard to their relationship, family, or career?
- Finding in-the-box images was probably easier to find than that those that were out-of-the-box. This is a clear reminder that it is much more socially acceptable to act in-the-box, and that idea is reflected by the abundance of gender-stereotypic images.
- When males think they have to "act like a man" by being tough, aggressive, muscular, overly independent, unemotional, the breadwinner, and the only decision maker, they are acting inside the box. When females think they have to "act like a lady" be being passive, thin and beautiful, dependent, overly nurturing, and solely responsible for the domestic chores, they are acting inside the box.
- When men and women are only allowed to choose behaviors that are inside the box, they are very limited.
- When men and women live outside the box they are free to be assertive, strong and sensitive, nurturing in relationships, serious about careers, independent, and emotionally expressive if they choose.
- It is okay choose behaviors that are inside the box, as long as each individual does not feel trapped in these roles. The key is to feel you can participate in both in- and out-of-the-box activities, without limits.

The couples are encouraged to take the box home with them as a reminder of ways to behave that are outside of the box and what happens when we behave in-the-box.

Brief Vignette

Sally and Sam planned to get married in six months and thought it would be helpful to participate in a premarital counseling group. At the first session, they met five other couples who were also planning to marry. Some had previously been married, and two group members had children from previous relationships. After introductions and an overview of the group, the therapist explained that they would be doing an experiential activity. The therapist handed out index cards with different chores on them. Sally, Sam, and the other couples were asked to place the card on a pink or blue sheet of paper. Sam had the card "takes care of children" and quickly placed it on the pink sheet. Sally had "financially provide for family" and was having a hard time deciding where to put it. She felt strongly that both women and men could financially support their families, but at Sam's insistence placed it on the blue sheet. When the therapist initiated the discussion about how they decided where to put their cards, Sally explained that Sam told her to put it on the blue sheet. A few other group members supported this choice saying that it was the husband's responsibility to make sure that his family was provided for. Sally shared that she wanted to help support their future family, too; she did not want it to fall on Sam's shoulders alone. Another group member, Katie, said that in her first marriage, her husband was very resistant to her working outside the home and expected her to be the primary care provider for their two children. Katie shared that this disagreement was one of the main reasons her the marriage ended in divorce.

Next, during the image collage, Sam and Sally had no trouble identifying in-the-box images of women and men. However, they were not having any luck finding any out-of-the-box images. Sally kept looking for pictures of nurturing fathers with their children but had a lot of trouble finding them. All she could find was mothers with their babies. The group then discussed their image collages. All of the couples noted that it was easy to find in-the-box images but harder to find the less traditional image. The therapist highlighted how this shortage of nontraditional images fuels our understanding of who does what in our society. Sally said that she did not want to be a stay-at-home mother. Sam looked shocked. It became clear to the therapist that Sam and Sally had never discussed who would be involved in providing for their family. The therapist then facilitated a discussion about financial and child care provider roles in families. This activity provided a catalyst for deeper discussions about expectations for each partner in the relationship and how important it is to negotiate these issues prior to marriage. The group members who had been divorced all echoed how important this was and strongly encouraged Sam and Sally to work on finding a mutually acceptable arrangement.

Suggestions for Follow-Up

The therapist should follow up with further discussions on gender stereotypes and media messages as the need arises in the group. For example, in a later session from the above vignette, the group was discussing financial issues. Bob said that if he was making the money, then he should be able to pick which car he wanted to buy. His partner, Brandy, felt that this was not fair or equitable, and that even if she was not the primary breadwinner, she should still be an equal participant in this important decision. The therapist then reminded the group of the images that we see around us in the media, and how the images fuel expectations for who has the power in relationships. The therapist introduced the couple to research and implications of these ideas from the literature on equal parenting and partnering (such as Haddock, Zimmerman, Current, & Ziemba, 2003). They began to understand their problem as media driven and manifesting from stereotypically limiting expectations and are empowered to make real and lasting changes in their relationship. From this perspective, the therapist cocreated concrete ways to begin debunking the couples' unhelpful perceptions of their roles, power, and how these concepts relate.

Contradictions

Couples who have experienced domestic violence or high volatile couples may do better doing this activity individually, rather than as a couple. This way they are able to look at their own gender roles without their partners present.

Please note: This activity was adapted for couples from the FAIR Curriculum project (a curriculum encouraging Fairness for All Individuals through Respect) designed to increase the awareness of social justice issues. For more information about the FAIR Curriculum Project, or

to download free images for this activity, please visit our Web site at http://mycahs.cahs
.colostate.edu/toni.s.zimmerman/. Other activities are also available on the Web site that could
be adapted for group therapy.

Readings and Resources for the Professional

Haddock, S. A., Zimmerman, T. S., Current, L. R., & Ziemba, S. (2003). Intimate partnership:
The foundation to the successful balance of family and work. *The American Journal of Family Therapy, 31,* 107-124.

Haddock, S. A., Zimmerman, T. S., & Lyness, K. (2003). Changing gender norms: Transitional
dilemmas. In F. Walsh (Ed.), *Normal family processes: Growing diversity and complexity*
(3rd ed.) (pp. 301-336). New York: Guilford Press.

Haddock, S. A., Zimmerman, T. S., & MacPhee, D. (2000). The power equity guide: Attending
to gender in family therapy. *Journal of Marital and Family Therapy, 26,* 153-170.

Rabin, C. (1996). *Equal partners, equal friends.* London: Routledge.

Risman, B. J. (1998). Doing it fairly: A study of postgender marriages. *Journal of Marriage and
the Family, 60,* 23-40.

Risman, B. J. (1998). *Gender vertigo: American families in transition.* New Haven: Yale University.

Steil, J. M. (1997). *Marital equality: Its relationship to well-being of husbands and wives.*
Thousand Oaks, CA: Sage.

Zimmerman, T. S., Haddock, S. A., Ziemba, S., & Rust, A. (2001). Family organizational labor:
Who's calling the plays? In T. S. Zimmerman (Ed.), *Balancing family and work: Special considerations in feminist therapy* (pp. 65-89). Binghamton, NY: The Haworth Press.

Bibliotherapy Sources for the Client

Deutsch, F. M. (1999). *Halving it all: How equally shared parenting works.* Cambridge, MA:
Harvard University Press.

Gottman, J., & Silver, N. (1999). *The seven principles for making marriage work.* New York:
Three Rivers Press.

Hochschild, A., with Machung, A. (1997). *The second shift.* New York: Avon.

Pipher, M. (1994). *Reviving Ophelia: Saving the selves of adolescent girls.* New York:
Ballantine.

Pollack, W. (1998). *Real boys: Rescuing our sons from the myths of boyhood.* New York: Random House.

Schwartz, P. (1994). *Peer Marriage.* New York: The Free Press.

Williams, J. (2000). *Unbending gender: Why family and work conflict and what to do about it.*
New York: Oxford University Press.

References

Gottman, J. M., & Silver, N. (1999). *The seven principles for making marriage work.* New
York: Random House.

Haddock, S. A., Zimmerman, T. S., Current, L. R., & Ziemba, S. (2003). Intimate partnership:
The foundation to the successful balance of family and work. *The American Journal of Family Therapy, 31,* 107-124.

Haddock, S. A., Zimmerman, T. S., & Lyness, K. (2003). Changing gender norms: Transitional
dilemmas. In F. Walsh (Ed.), *Normal family processes: Growing diversity and complexity.*
(3rd ed.) (pp. 301-336). New York: Guilford.

Pipher, M. (1994). *Reviving Ophelia: Saving the selves of adolescent girls*. New York: Ballantine.

Pollack, W. (1998). *Real boys: Rescuing our sons from the myths of boyhood*. New York: Random House.

West, C., & Zimmerman, D. (1987). Doing gender. *Gender and Society, 1,* 125-151.

Wilson, C. & Gutierrez, F. (1995). *Race, multiculturalism, and the media.* London: Sage Publications.

28

Family Mine Field

Dawn Viers

Type of Contribution: Activity

Objectives

This activity has three main goals:

1. To help parents and children learn effective communication skills.
2. To teach families to ignore extraneous information and listen to verbal commands.
3. To help families have fun together.

Rationale for Use

Good parent-child communication is essential to positive family functioning. Yet, many families present in group therapy with communication problems as a top complaint. Parents say their kids ignore their instructions or talk back. Their children say that their parents yell too much or do not listen to them. Most families in group therapy would agree that they want to change their communication patterns but do not know how.

Effective communication with a child generally consists of "being a good listener, working at understanding what your child is trying to tell you, and using words and concepts that he or she can understand" (Christophersen & Mortweet, 2003, p. 45). Open and empathetic communication among families has been associated with a number of positive outcomes for children, including lower rates of early sexual activity, sexually transmitted diseases, and teen pregnancies (Blake, Simkin, Ledsky, Perkins, & Calabrese, 2001; Kirby, 1999; Ramirez-Valles, Zimmerman, & Newcomb, 1998). Further, good family communication has been linked to reduced drug, alcohol, and tobacco use in children (King, Vidourek, & Wagner, 2004). Clearly, there is a need for group therapists working with families to incorporate and teach positive communication skills.

There are a number of parenting education courses which include communication training, such as Systematic Training for Effective Parenting (STEP) (Dinkmeyer, McKay, and Dinkmeyer, 1997) and the Strengthening Families Program (Kumpfer, 2001). This activity is meant to supplement and provide practice for a lesson on effective communication, such as the lessons provided in the parent education courses above. Alternately, a group facilitator can use this activity to begin a dialogue about communication and listening skills between family members.

Instructions

Prior to the group session, the facilitator should gather the materials to set up the mine field. This includes plastic cones or rope to delineate the perimeter of the mine field, plastic toys, balls, crumbled paper, or other materials to act as "land mines." In addition, the facilitator needs to gather enough blindfolds or bandanas so that each person in the group can have his or her own blindfold. This activity should be conducted in room free from obstructions, such as chairs or tables.

It is best to use this activity to punctuate a lesson on positive communication skills. Depending on the developmental level of family members, these skills could include "I-messages," ignoring outside interference, practicing good listening skills, and focusing on one idea at a time. Once the group facilitator has initiated the discussion on family communication, he or she will tell family members that they will now have a chance to put these skills into action with the Family Mine Field activity.

The group facilitator sets up the mine field by laying the rope in a circle or setting up the plastic cones to indicate a beginning and an end. Next, the facilitator spreads the land mines randomly within the perimeter of the circle or cones. It is important to place the mines far enough apart to allow a person to walk through them with guidance, but not so far apart that someone could walk through the field in a straight line. The ages of the children in the group should also guide placement of the mines. Older children and teenagers can handle a greater number of mines or mines placed closer together while younger children may do better with fewer mines to limit frustration. The facilitator should also make sure that the mines are no higher than four to six inches off of the ground as to reduce tripping hazards.

Each parent in the group will pair up with his or her child. If there are more children than parents or vice versa, the unpaired person can either wait for the other members of his or her family to have a turn or can pair up with the group facilitator. The facilitator hands each person a blindfold and explains that one member of each pair will be blindfolded while the other member will act as the blindfolded person's eyes.

The player who is blindfolded will attempt to cross the mine field relying only on the instructions of his or her partner. The facilitator should instruct the player who is not blindfolded that he or she should not touch or physically move the blindfolded player, but should rather help the player cross the field to the opposite side with verbal instructions. The blindfolded player can touch three mines before he or she is out. If the blindfolded person reaches the other side of the mine without touching more than three mines, he or she has successfully crossed the mine field.

Each person will have a chance to cross, with the rest of the group acting as bystanders. After the first member of each team crosses the mine field, the teams will switch positions so that each person has the chance to be blindfolded. As an alternative, each team can surround the mine field and try to cross at the same time. The other players crossing the mine field then act as mines. This variation is more difficult due to the extra mines and the distractions from other players giving commands and is best suited to a smaller group or a group with older members.

After each player has his or her turn to be blindfolded, the facilitator should reconvene the group and lead a discussion on what communication techniques were helpful in getting across the mine field. The facilitator will want to make sure the following points were discussed:

- Need for short, very specific commands
- Importance of giving only one direction or command at a time
- Active listening on the part of the blindfolded person
- How to ignore distractions and focus on the speaker
- Benefits of the listener repeating back directions to the speaker or putting directions in his or her own words

The facilitator should also comment on positive communication skills or patterns he or she witnessed during the activity.

The facilitator should link the lessons learned in the activity back to everyday communication. For example, if a group member stated it was helpful when the speaker slowed down his or her speech and used very specific directions, the facilitator should lead a discussion on how these skills would be helpful in conversations at home. It is also helpful to emphasize that listening is an important aspect of good communication. The facilitator should list specific listening skills that facilitate better communication, including good eye contact and the use of positive nonverbal cues (traits that could not be practiced during the mine field activity). The facilitator should encourage parents and children to use constructive communication skills throughout the week and report back on their progress.

Brief Vignette

Lynette and her preteenage daughter, Chloe, were court-ordered to attend group parenting classes as a result of Lynette's substance abuse history. The group consisted of a parents' group, a separate children's group, and family time where the parents and children interacted and practiced new skills. In the parents' part of the group, Lynette would often complain that her daughter talked back, did not listen, and did not respect her. She would vacillate between blaming her daughter for the family's problems and recognizing her own role in their dysfunctional patterns. Chloe seemed sad and withdrawn, although she would participate in the children's group and thrived on positive attention. Lynette and Chloe initially had little contact with each other during family time, although they began to have more encouraging interactions as the weeks progressed.

After a lesson in both the children's and parents' group about communication skills, the group facilitators introduced the mine field activity. Lynette and Chloe agreed to participate and decided that Chloe would be blindfolded first. Lynette started to give Chloe too many directions at once but was able, with the facilitators' help, to slow down and use specific instructions to help Chloe navigate the field. Lynette began to use encouraging remarks and even praised Chloe when she followed instructions and stepped over a mine. When it was Lynette's turn to be blindfolded, she willingly followed Chloe's instructions and Chloe was able to use positive words when talking with her mother. They even laughed together when they made a mistake and blew up a mine. They were both able to transverse the field without exploding more than three mines, and Lynette gave Chloe a quick hug.

Lynette and Chloe both participated in the discussion part of the group and were able to correctly identify positive communication skills they had used during the activity. At the end of the group, Lynette came up to the parents' group facilitator and stated, "That was fun." Chloe, smiling, nodded her head in agreement.

Suggestions for Follow-Up

At the beginning of the group, the facilitator should check-in with family members to see what new and constructive communication skills they used during the week. The facilitator should highlight and give praise to family members for the use of positive communication strategies. If family members' focus on problems or negative contacts, the facilitator should bring the discussion back to what worked, in order to encourage better communication.

Depending on the needs of the group members, the facilitator may want to extend this activity by incorporating other activities into group time that focus on building and strengthening communication skills. Examples include family meetings, using praise and encouragement, communicating feelings, and setting appropriate limits and consequences.

Contraindications

This activity is best suited to small- to medium-sized groups (six to eighteen participants or three to nine pairs) consisting of upper-elementary to teenage children. It may not work in a larger group of twenty or more participants due to the unavoidable noise level that naturally comes with a large group and from the long wait time for participants. Similarly, participants under age six or seven may not be able to follow or focus on the directives (both when blindfolded and when giving the directives) or may have trouble waiting for their turn. However, as all groups are different, the group facilitator should decide what the group can handle.

This activity should be used with caution with family members who are extremely competitive with one another or with other participants, especially as successful use of this activity depends on cooperation and not competition. Likewise, participants who are "sore losers" may be disruptive if they or their team members are unable to cross the mine field. However, this activity can also provide teachable moments for these participants, especially with extra modeling and encouragement on the part of the facilitator.

Some participants may feel uncomfortable wearing a blindfold or being on the spot in front of other group members. Any individual should not be forced into participating. If one family member wants to participate and another does not, the group facilitator should proceed as part of the team. The family member who does not participate should be encouraged to act as a spectator and to take part in the follow-up discussion.

Readings and Resources for the Professional

McKay, G. D. (2005). *Parent group handbook for calming the family storm.* Atascadero, CA Impact Publishers.

Vangelisti, A. L. (Ed). (2004). *Handbook of family communication.* Mahwah, NJ: Lawrence Erlbaum Associates.

Bibliotherapy Sources for the Client

Christophersen, E. R., & Mortweet, S. L. (2003). *Parenting that works: Building skills that last a lifetime.* Washington, DC: American Psychological Association.

Faber, A., & Brehl, E. M. (Eds.) (1999). *How to talk so kids will listen and listen so kids will talk.* New York: HarperCollins.

Ginott, H. G., Goddard, H. W., & Ginott, A. (2003). *Between parent and child: The bestselling book that revolutionized parent-child communication.* New York: Three Rivers Press.

References

Blake, S. M., Simkin, J., Ledsky, R., Perkins, C., & Calabrese, J. M. (2001). Effects of a parent-adolescent communications intervention on young adolescents' risk of early onset sexual intercourse. *Family Planning Perspectives, 33*(2), 52-61.

Christophersen, E. R., & Mortweet, S. L. (2003). *Parenting that works: Building skills that last a lifetime.* Washington, DC: American Psychological Association.

Dinkmeyer, D. McKay, G. D., & Dinkmeyer, D. (1997). *The parent's handbook: Systematic training for effective parenting (STEP).* Circle Pines, MN: AGS Publishing.

King, K. A., Vidourek, R. A., & Wagner, D. I. (2004). Effect of parent drug use and parent-child time spent together on adolescent involvement in alcohol, tobacco, and other drugs. *Adolescent & Family Health, 3*(4), 171-176.

Kirby, D. (1999). Reflections on two decades of research on teen sexual behavior and intercourse. *Journal of School Health, 70,* 338-344.

Kumpfer, K. L. (2001). *Strengthening Families Program: Parent's manual.* Salt Lake City, UT: Department of Health Promotion, University of Utah.

Ramirez-Valles, J., Zimmerman, A. M., & Newcomb, M. D. (1998). Sexual risk behavior among youth: Modeling the influence of prosocial activities and economic factors. *Journal of Health and Social Behavior, 39,* 237-253.

29

Life's Not Fair

Aaron Oberman

Type of Contribution: Activity

Objectives

1. To discuss positive decision making skills.
2. To teach coping strategies for the healthy management of anger.
3. To demonstrate to family members that they cannot control everything in their life and/or the lives of family members.
4. To teach family members about individual responsibility and how to meet their own needs without hurting other family members.

Rationale for Use

Many people often feel the need to control everything in their lives. When unplanned events happen, they can feel like life is not fair and become angry with themselves or other family members. While anger is a natural emotion, some family members need assistance in improving the skills they use to cope with anger.

The theoretical foundations for this activity are based on William Glasser's (1985) control theory and Alfred Adler's (1924) individual psychology. Control theory is the framework to assist the family in changing their behavior and controlling their actions. The family constellation technique, from Adler's individual psychology theory, will help the therapist develop a better understanding of the family and to gather background information about family behavioral patterns.

Glasser (1985) identified the psychological needs of belonging, power, freedom, and fun, and the physiological need for survival. Control theory illustrates how we function to satisfy our needs. When aspects of our lives fail to fulfill our needs, we are unsatisfied with life. Therefore, family members who make decisions that intrude on the lives of others are acting irresponsibly.

Adlerian (1924) therapy assists the therapist in exploring the client(s) family constellation. Potential assessment questions from this theory that are helpful in learning about the family include (a) what is the father's and/or mother's relationship with the children? (b) what are sibling relationships between each other? and (c) how are these relationships similar/different? These questions will help the family focus on their current situation and aid the therapist in learning about the family's lifestyle.

Instructions

This activity works well with groups of families once the therapist has developed rapport and gained insight into the presenting problem(s). This activity works best when group members are

The Group Therapist's Notebook
© 2007 by The Haworth Press, Inc. All rights reserved.
doi:10.1300/5576_29

over the age of six. It is also best utilized in four or fewer families with no more than three to five members per family. The total number of participants should not exceed sixteen.

Prior to the group, the therapist should gather the materials. Materials should include the following:

1. Small prizes in a grab bag that members of different ages might like (such as candy, pens, pencils, stickers, etc.). Before meeting with the group, collect enough small prizes so that there is a minimum of three per family member. It would be a good idea to have a few extra favors. Place all the prizes in a grab bag large enough so that member's can not see into the bag. A large shopping bag from a department store may work best.
2. One pair of dice per family. It may be a good idea to have an extra pair around in case a pair is lost or misplaced.
3. Timer or stop watch.

When the group members arrive, have them sit together around a table or in a circle. Inform the members that they will be participating in a two-part activity; however, only explain the first phase. Explain the second phase of the activity upon completion of phase one.

Phase one begins with a pair of dice. First, allow all members in each family to roll the dice one time, selecting the person with the lowest number to begin the activity. The person who starts the activity is instructed to roll the dice one time. If he or she rolls doubles, he or she will be able to select a prize from the bag. He or she then passes the dice clockwise to the next player. If doubles are not rolled, the player also passes the dice to the next group member. Each family member continues to roll the dice until the members win all of the prizes in the bag. At the end of phase one, some group members may have more than one prize, while some may have none. Phase one should take ten minutes.

Now it is time to introduce phase two of the activity. The second half of the activity will be timed. Allow five minutes for this part of the activity.

The rules for phase two are similar to phase one; however, when doubles are rolled the group member selects a prize from one of the other members instead of the grab bag. As in phase one, each group member will roll to see who goes first, allowing the lowest number to go first and passing the dice clockwise. Phase two will continue until the allotted amount of time expires. Similar to phase one, some group members may end up with several prizes, while other may end the activity with nothing. Call time to end the activity.

At the end of the activity, ask the members to reconvene as a group. The therapist should ask these questions of the group.

1. How did you feel while playing the game? Angry? Upset?
2. What did you do today to cope with these feelings?
3. What do you do when things in life do not go your way?
4. When do feel like you do not have control over your life?
5. What do you do to cope when life is not fair?
6. What other strategies can you or your family members use when life seems unfair or does not go your way?

Brief Vignette

One family in the group consisted of a mother (Donna), father (Tony), and son (Jared). Donna was a housewife and spent her days cleaning the house, preparing meals, and doing other chores—anything to keep the family happy. She wanted to spend more time with her husband and son as a family. Donna tended to get upset with Tony because of the long hours he worked at the office on the weekdays and weekends. She also complained that Jared spent too much time with his friends from school. All Donna wanted was for the three of them to be able to have some quality time together as a family.

Tony was focused on work and bringing home the money to care for his family. Tony would love a job with fewer hours and that would allow him more time with his family; however, he was laid off from his previous job and needed money to support his family. Most days he came home after nine o'clock at night, had a drink, and went to bed. He left for work by six o'clock and had little interaction with his wife or son. On weekends, if he was not working, he watched football or other sports and just wanted to relax.

Jared was not doing his work at school and tended to fall asleep in class. He almost never did his homework and has stopped doing his chores at home. He was also picking on other students and was hanging out with a different group of friends. Jared's teacher realized that there may be something going on at home and asked him about problems but did not get any answers. Jared also wanted to spend more time with his mom and dad as a family; however, their schedules did not match up. It seemed that a group format, where the family could work together, would be a good fit for this family. The mom, dad, and son all complained in the initial group meeting that "life is not fair."

During one group session, the counselor introduced the Life's Not Fair game. Below is a conversation between family members from the second half of the activity, after members initially selected prizes from the bag.

TONY: (rolls doubles) I want Jared's candy bar.

JARED: That is not fair. Hershey's is my favorite kind of candy.

DONNA: (rolls the dice) Doubles, I want Tony's deck of cards.

JARED: (rolls) I did not get doubles.

TONY: (rolls) I did not get doubles.

JARED: (rolls doubles) I want mom's toy car.

DONNA: (rolls) Darn, no doubles.

COUNSELOR: Time's up.

COUNSELOR: Tony, what did you do today when life was not fair?

TONY: I wanted to take my cards back from Donna. It was not fair; she does not even like to play cards.

COUNSELOR: How did you feel when that happened?

TONY: I got angry.

COUNSELOR: What would make you feel better?

TONY: Taking back my cards.

COUNSELOR: Okay, but what constructive strategy could you use from our previous sessions?

TONY: I could remember that I have a good family, a home, and a job.

COUNSELOR: Good. So, although sometimes things do not happen as you would like, there are things going well in your life. Donna, what are your thoughts about the activity?

DONNA: I was upset when my toy car was taken by Jared. It was just like my first car in high school.

COUNSELOR: How did that relate to other times when life is not fair?

DONNA: Well, it's not fair that Tony has to work long hours and is not able to spend much time with Jared and me.

COUNSELOR: How do you feel when that happens?

DONNA: I get sad and wish our lives could be different.

COUNSELOR: What strategies do you use to cope when feel sad?

DONNA: The other day, I focused on the last fun time we did spend together as a family, when we went to the county fair last month.

COUNSELOR: Great Donna! What did you do differently?

DONNA: I focused on a positive experience rather than dwelling on a negative situation.

The therapist continued with each group of family members so they could understand the purpose of the activity.

Suggestions for Follow-Up

Follow up with the family members by assigning homework to help each of them apply and integrate the concepts from the activity. One task the therapist could give the families for future sessions is to assign each family member to keep track of times he or she felt like life was not fair between sessions. Another example would be to have family members praise one another when they use positive coping strategies when things are not going their way. These homework assignments will help the family to think about strategies they can use when life seems unfair and does not go their way. The therapist should also work with the family to set goals for themselves and to help one another by reinforcing these goals at home. For example, the therapist could have suggested to Tony that he could use the same strategy he used in the activity when his boss needed him to work on the weekends. He could think about how, in general, his job is pretty good, and he has a great family to go home to at the end of the day.

Contraindications

This activity would be contraindicated in abusive families. Further, it may not work in families in which members are sore losers or who cannot let go of losing a game or item. Also, the therapist should instruct families not to argue over the outcome or process of the game outside of session, but rather to bring all arguments to the next group or make an individual appointment with the therapist.

Readings and Resources for the Professional

Horne, A. M. (2000). *Family counseling and therapy* (3rd ed.). Itasca, IL: F. E. Peacock Publishers, Inc.

Jacobs, E. E. (1992). *Creative counseling techniques: An illustrated guide.* Odessa, FL: Psychological Assessment Resources, Inc.

Jones, A. (1998). *104 activities that build: Self-esteem, teamwork, communication, anger management, self-discovery, coping skills.* Richland, WA: Rec Room Publishing.

Wubbolding, R. E. (1988). *Using reality therapy.* New York: Harper & Row.

Bibliotherapy Source for the Client

Bradshaw, J. (1998). *Bradshaw: On the family.* Deerfield, Beach, FL: Health Communications, Inc.

References

Adler, A. (1924). *The practice and theory of individual psychology* (2nd ed. rev.). Oxford, England: Humanities Press.

Glasser, W. (1985). *Control theory: A new explanation of how we control our lives.* New York: Harper & Row.

30

Eight Days in a Week:
Using Calendars in Family Groups

Dawn Viers

Type of Contribution: Handout

Objective

This handout provides group members with a place to record family events and schedules. The calendar can be used to note important events, such as family meetings, visitation schedules, and family-fun time. It can be used with many different group populations, including parenting and divorce support groups.

Rationale for Use

Turecki and Tonner (2000) suggest there are three skills essential to positive family functioning: structure, procedures, and routines. Incorporating the use of a calendar in family activities can help to promote these skills. Structure is encouraged as families can organize and plan their schedules, which will establish predictability and stability. Procedures, defined by Turecki and Tonner (p. 132) as an "established way of doing things," will also be delineated as families will come together to make plans and write down activities or schedules. Finally, having a calendar can help families establish a routine as family members know to expect and will have a reminder of upcoming activities and events.

Instructions

Calendars can be used to supplement a variety of group lessons. Customized calendars can be created using the draw features on a standard word processing program, such as the handout at the end of this chapter (Handout 30.1). Alternately, a calendar template can be found on the Internet through free shareware programs. Date books and calendars can also be found for just a few dollars at many discount stores or the facilitator may want to simply make a copy of a standard calendar. Some suggestions for using calendars in family groups are described here.

Family Meetings

Family meetings, a common activity in many parent education classes, are an effective tool for encouraging positive communication, establishing and maintaining rules and consequences, and creating time for family members to come together and have fun. Family meetings generally follow the following format (Dinkmeyer, McKay, & Dinkmeyer, 1997):

1. Meetings occur once a week, on the same day, and at the same place for a specified time (20-30 minutes).
2. The meetings follow an agenda with topics created with input from each family member (for example, chores to be completed or arguments to be moderated).
3. One family member acts as a secretary or recorder of the items discussed at the meetings and the action plans that come out of the meetings.
4. A fun activity or special snack concludes the family meeting.

The group facilitator should review family meeting guidelines, either verbally or using a handout that outlines the instructions. After the discussion on family meetings, the facilitator should hand out a copy of a calendar for each family. It is advisable, if time allows, for each family to have their first family meeting during the group so that the family can practice this skill and so the group facilitator can help with questions and act as a moderator. Prior to leaving the group, the facilitator should instruct the families to mark the time on the calendar for at least two family meetings to occur within that month. If the calendar includes a notes section, family members can also use this space to write down topics that they want to discuss at the family meeting.

The facilitator should then instruct the family members to post their calendar in a conspicuous place, such as on the refrigerator door, so that all family members will be reminded of the meeting and can have the opportunity to add to the topic list as needed. The facilitator should also send home additional blank copies of the calendar for the families to schedule subsequent family meetings. Encouraging families to schedule family meetings on the calendar helps to proactively address potential barriers to conducting family meetings, including members who say they could not fit it in their schedule or that they did not know when the meeting was to take place.

Divorce Support/Education Groups

Calendars can be used in several ways in groups of parents undergoing or adapting to a divorce or separation. On the calendar, parents can jot down visitation schedules, appointments, extracurricular activities, and court dates. Parents can use a notes section or notes written in the margin as a reminder for upcoming events. Parents can also pass the calendar back and forth during visitation changes to keep everyone on board regarding activities and events and to foster positive communication between parents regarding their children.

The facilitator can use a group session to review the many possible uses of the calendar and pass out a blank calendar. The facilitator will want to use group time to lead a discussion on such topics as how and when to ask for visitation changes and ways to communicate to the other parent important dates and activities that relate to the children. The parents should jot down individual activities and special events, children's schedules and activities, and/or visitation schedules.

The facilitator will want to remind parents that, as the calendar will be posted for all family members to see, parents will want to make sure their entries are positive and constructive. Too often, separated or divorced parents become mired in anger toward the other partner and, thus, may use the calendar as a forum for blame. While it may be important to make a note of certain issues, such as when the noncustodial parent is not following a predetermined visitation schedule, the facilitator will want to remind the group that engaging in blame places the child in the middle of the parents' argument and makes it impossible for either parent to establish structure, routine, and predictability.

Termination

As group therapy is generally limited to a certain number of sessions or within a specific timeframe, the termination of a group is inevitable. In many cases, termination is a happy event, and the group members have achieved at least some resolution to the problem that brought them to the group. However, group members can also experience a flare-up of problems at the end of the group or even after the group has terminated. This can occur as families and couples are fearful of handling problems on their own and may have come to depend on the feedback from the group. Alternately, after the group has terminated, families and couples may not be practicing the skills they learned in the group and thus begin to fall back into dysfunctional patterns and habits. In other cases, the time spent in the group may be the most time that family members or couples spend focused on one another during the week. When the group ends and the group members return to the status quo, family members may unconsciously find new problems and issues to keep members engaged with each other or to restart services. Even very young children often realize that the negative attention they receive for misbehaving is better than no attention at all.

In order to proactively address these problems, the facilitator should encourage family members to mark time on their calendars to focus on their family. As family members have already set aside one night per week to attend the group, they can use this night to continue their own group sessions at home. If family members complete chore charts or token economy charts, families can use this time to celebrate achievements or give rewards. Alternately, the family can plan a family date or family-fun night. Much like family meetings, family members can use this time to talk about issues and problems and have a chance to spend quality time with one another.

Suggestions for Follow-Up

After the calendar is introduced, the group facilitator should ask in the subsequent session how the families used the calendars and inquire about any barriers to implementation. If the families did not write on the calendar between sessions, the facilitator could use group time to have family members note at least one important event on the calendar. If family members forgot an event that was listed on the calendar, the group can process ways to help members remember, including posting the calendar on the refrigerator or having one family member act as a calendar keeper to remind others of events. If families continue to forget activities or to follow through with events on the calendar, the facilitator may want to process this at the group or individual level, as this may be indicative of larger issues.

Contraindications

Keeping a calendar for events may not be suitable for family members or divorcing couples who are extremely antagonistic toward each other as they may use the calendar to post hurtful messages. It is also important to remind family members to include relevant family members when planning and participating in events, so that family members feel like they have ownership in the calendar. Family members should be encouraged to make every effort to follow through with events they write on the calendar, as continually changing or forgetting events will undermine efforts toward establishing structure, routine, and predictability.

Readings and Resources for the Professional

Campbell, D., & Palm, G. F. (2003). *Group parent education: Promoting parent learning and support*. Thousand Oaks, CA: SAGE Publications.

Tillman, D. (2000). *Living values parent groups: A facilitator's guide.* Deerfield Beach, FL: Health Communications, Inc.

Bibliotherapy Sources for the Client

Dinkmeyer, D., & McKay, G. D. (1996). *Raising a responsible child: How to prepare your child for today's complex world.* New York: Fireside Books.
Stahl, P. M. (2000). *Parenting after divorce: A guide to resolving conflicts and meeting your children's needs.* Atascadero, CA: Impact Publishers.

References

Dinkmeyer, D., McKay, G. D., & Dinkmeyer, D. (1997). *The parent's handbook: Systematic training for effective parenting (STEP).* Circle Pines, MN: AGS Publishing.
Turecki, S., & Tonner, L. (2000). *The difficult child: Expanded and revised edition.* New York: Bartam Books.

HANDOUT 30.1.
FAMILY CALENDAR

Month

Notes

Sunday	Monday	Tuesday	Wednesday	Thursday	Friday	Saturday

Viers, D. (2007). Eight days in a week: Using calendars in family groups. In D. R. Viers (Ed.). *The group therapist's notebook: Homework, handouts, and activities for use in psychotherapy* (pp. 223-227). Binghamton. NY: The Haworth Press.

31

Maintaining Stability: Life Cycle Transitions in Families Coping with Childhood Cancer

Jessica A. Russo
Laura Tejada
Randall L. Hilscher
John J. Zarski

Type of Contribution: Activity/Handouts

Objectives

This activity will give caregivers of children with cancer a chance to address their concerns about progressing toward normal family life cycle events. It is designed to be a visual tool for group facilitators to use to validate the ambivalence of caregivers about going on with family life in the midst of illness, while supporting their efforts to regain family equilibrium. The main objectives of the activity are to

1. Identify the developmental stages and needs of the family.
2. Enlarge the network of supportive individuals available to the family (psychological team, medical team, and fellow caregivers).
3. Help caregivers problem solve ways to meet normal, developmental family needs in the midst of caring for a child who has cancer.

The impact of the emotions of grief on the family will be explored as a way to normalize the conflicting emotions the family may be experiencing, while respecting the unique and unfair emotional and life cycle burdens they must bear. While this activity alone will not bring a family back to better functioning, it will augment other interventions to support caregivers struggling to regain some sense of normal family life in the midst of one of the most abnormal situations a family can face—the severe illness and potential death of a child.

Rationale for Use

According to the American Cancer Society (2004), about 1, 368,030 new cancer cases were diagnosed in 2004, and about 563,700 Americans were expected to die from cancer. An esti-

Authors' note: The authors would like to acknowledge posthumously the initial contributions to this project by John J. Zarski, PhD, former director of the Marriage and Family Therapy Program at the University of Akron. The impact of chronic illness on family relationships was a primary research interest of Dr. Zarski, and he shared the opportunity to write this book chapter with the authors. In addition, the authors would like to acknowledge the patience of Dr. Viers, who extended the deadline for this project following the sudden death of Dr. Zarski.

mated 9,200 new cases of cancer were expected to be among children ages birth to fourteen, while approximately 1,500 chilu. ᵃn in this age range were expected to die (American Cancer Society). While childhood cancers aᵣ rare, they still exist.

The impact of a diagnosis of cancer in a child disrupts normal family functioning as the family struggles to cope with acute and overwhelming emotional, physical, and social stressors. These stressors include grief emotions, such as shock, denial, fear, anger, and sorrow; navigating the health care system as the family struggles to define the cancer, including the course of the illness and level of current and/or potential incapacitation; coping skills and barriers; financial burdens; continued disruptions of family functioning; and extended demands on the family's adaptability. Because cancer can become a long-term, "life-threatening illness with an uncertain outcome" (Rando, 1984, p. 368), families often remain in a chaotic state over a long period of time, continually adapting to new courses of treatment, remissions, and relapses. This extended disruption of the family's functioning may derail the normal progression of the family through the family life cycle. Abnormal functioning becomes normal for the family. This disruption can "become more troublesome and incapacitating than the illness itself" (Rando, p. 369).

Fredda Herz (1980) defines four factors that lead to disruption in the family equilibrium during a serious illness:

1. The timing of the serious illness in the life cycle, which identifies at what point in the life cycle the illness occurs (at birth, school-age, adolescent, etc.).
2. The nature of the serious illness. Is the diagnosed cancer an illness with a sudden or gradual onset? Is the prognosis death, recovery with physical impairment, protracted illness and treatments, or uncertain?
3. The openness of the family system to interventions and support from professionals, the community, and each other.
4. The family position of the seriously ill, the individual's significance to the family, and the roles she or he fulfills within the family.

The Family Life Cycle

Each family faces developmental phases and challenges reflecting the needs of its members. These challenges change over time in predictable ways and are determined by the developmental needs of the children and adults within the family. This pattern of developmental stages, tasks, and challenges is termed the *family life cycle* (McGoldrick & Carter, 2003).

Families do not progress through these stages in a lock-step fashion. Instead, the progression of families through the family life cycle is recursive, flowing, and spiraling through the different stages as different members grow and change. Typical stages experienced in the family life cycle are

- joining families,
- raising children,
- families with adolescents,
- launching children/families at midlife, and
- families in later life, often a time where adult children form their own families and initiate the cycle anew.

Families are particularly vulnerable to stressors during transition times between stages of the family life cycle because developmental changes in members mean families must redefine relationships and roles. A diagnosis of pediatric cancer can disrupt the family life cycle, deflecting the energy of caregivers from adapting and responding to developmental needs and changes to coping with the demands of cancer on individuals and the family system.

Resuming the development of the family through the life cycle can be a daunting task. Family resources, such as financial and emotional resources, may be limited and the sense of what is normal or typical is often lost in the midst of the atypical world of coping with childhood cancer. In addition, families may be afraid to resume normal development, because this begins the process of adapting to a new family structure that may not include the ill child. Alternatively, family members and siblings of children with cancer who seek to reestablish a sense of normal functioning are often seen as behaving inappropriately (Rando, 1984).

Families may also avoid or dread resuming normal events and activities because of how grief can impact the already ambivalent feelings these events often arouse (Kübler-Ross, 1969). Families of children with cancer have a double-whammy during nodal events, such as schooling transitions, progressions through adolescence (such as sporting events, proms, and graduations), and progression of the couple's relationship. Each event can be potentially the last for the ill child. Yet, the transitional event celebrates the progression of life; a progression the ill child may not get the chance to experience.

The Role of Therapy

Group leaders can help families of children diagnosed with cancer regain some sense of equilibrium by helping them identify the needs of individual family members, and of the family as a system, and help them find ways to meet these needs within the limitations that cancer places on family resources (Rando, 1984). Families of children with cancer often need "permission for 'time out' periods" (Rando, p. 332) to focus their attention and energy on normal life cycle transitions and meet the ongoing developmental needs of other family members. Helping families regain some sense of equilibrium by resuming normal developmental family life cycle tasks and nodal events can be crucial to helping a family cope with cancer over a long period of time, regardless of the outcome of the cancer process.

A useful model for helping families and clinicians understand the dynamics and challenges faced by families that include children with cancer is the family systems-illness model developed by Rolland (1994). This model highlights the interactions between the psychosocial demands illness makes on families over time and key components of family functioning such as adaptability, cohesion, communication, and family belief systems. The aim of Rolland's model is to help families create a functional family-illness system to meet the challenges illness presents by enabling the family to accomplish four important tasks:

1. Learning the expected pattern of practical and emotional demands the particular type of cancer will create over the course of the illness.
2. Understanding the family as a functional unit in systems terms.
3. Appreciating the various challenges posed by both individual and family life cycles.
4. Considering the ways in which a family's response to illness is affected by family beliefs and values, including the family's multigenerational legacies about how illness, loss, and crisis are to be understood and dealt with by family members.

Integrating these four factors can empower families in dealing with both the demands of illness and the challenges of negotiating life transitions.

Even though there are a small number of children, as compared to adults, diagnosed with cancer every year, it is still imperative that families have the opportunity to be a part of a collaborative approach at the onset and throughout their child's illness. The importance of collaborative care with each and every child with cancer is critical in how families manage the impact of cancer on their lives. For the purpose of this chapter, collaborative care is defined as the combination of the psychological and medical team working jointly with the family at the onset of diagnosis.

Instructions

In order to conduct this activity, a clinician will need a large dry erase chalkboard, dry erase markers, and a magnet for each caregiver that can be personalized with his or her name. Prior to the group meeting, the clinician will need to draw or place an enlarged photocopy of the Family Disequilibrium Handout (Handout 31.1) onto the dry erase board. The handout should be large enough for each caregiver to place his or her magnet on the board. In addition, the clinician will need to make enough copies of the Group Activity Log (Handout 31.2) for each caregiver.

The group leader will introduce the family life cycle, as defined by McGoldrick and Carter (2003). The leader will then present the four factors that lead to family disequilibrium, as adapted from Herz (1980). The group leaders can describe the four factors as:

> Factor 1: *timing of the illness*—the stage where family members display shock, denial, fear, anger and sorrow;
>
> Factor 2: *the nature of the illness*—the stage where the family defines the meaning of cancer, their understanding of prognosis, the level of incapacitation and developmental effects;
>
> Factor 3: *the openness of the family* system—the stage where coping skills are learned and used, support groups are available, and treatment planning and symptom management occur; and
>
> Factor 4: *family position of ill member*—the stage where the family functions through rules, boundaries, flexibility, and roles. This factor is focused on the adaptation of the family to the illness.

The leader will then review the Family Disequilibrium handout. The handout allows the caregiver to disclose where he or she believes his or her family is conceptually and emotionally since the diagnosis of cancer on the child. Once this is identified, the caregiver will place a magnet, with his or her name written on it, on the board at the location that fits for him or her. Each caregiver will receive a magnet and be encouraged to map where he or she is individually in regards to the four factors that can contribute to family disequilibrium.

Group facilitators should keep in mind that caregivers in the same family may not be at the same place emotionally or developmentally, so there may be more than one magnet representing each family. Mapping each caregiver's place will be important, as it will help group leaders and group members gain insight as to the stressors faced by participants. It is important for member to understand that caregivers may be static at times and that that is okay. Members may go back and forth among the factors.

Once the magnet has been placed by all caregivers, the group leaders encourage group discussion by having all members form a circle. Group members can begin by stating where they are in regard to the four factors and what their experiences with childhood cancer have been thus far. The group leader(s) role will be to facilitate discussion between group members. For example, the group leader may ask members to describe what it was like for them at the onset of diagnosis or what coping skills have helped them get through the illness. The key to remember when facilitating the group is to guide the group through discussion. Some suggestions to assist group leaders through this facilitation include the following:

- Feelings and experiences regarding the diagnosis and management of the illness
- Relationships with the medical team (doctors, nurses, etc.)
- Relationships with the psychological team (counselors, social workers, support groups, etc.)
- Barriers to treatment and family coping
- Grief and loss around nodal events
- Past coping skills

Emphasis should be placed on discussions around grief and loss around nodal events. This is encouraged by having members tell their story, with leaders and members helping to process each caregiver's story through support, empathy, circular questioning, and defining new coping mechanisms. Many of these coping mechanisms will come from other group members, but leaders can also assist members with this.

Discussion on the previously mentioned topics will pave the way for other group members to gain insight into new roles and rules for their family. In addition, talking through these problems and getting insight from other group members may help family members overcome some barriers and burdens that have come along the way, thus moving toward better adaptability and flexibility within the family system.

At the start of each subsequent group session, the group leaders will reintroduce the Family Disequilibrium Handout (either on the board or in handout form) and have caregivers change the magnet to another location than they were previously, keep it the same, or even go back to an earlier factor (this may occur if a nodal event arises).

The Group Activity Log is designed for each group member to track weekly where they have placed the magnet and what emotions they have experienced related to their actions toward adapting to their post-diagnosis family structure. This tracking is intended for group members to gain insight into their coping skills and their support around them. The group leaders will facilitate discussion with group members by asking members to share their Family Disequilibrium Handout and Group Activity Log. It is important for group leaders to recognize that not all members will move forward, and that some may stay at the same point for more than one week or even regress. This is effective because the family members can process their position with group leaders and group members. Group leaders should adjourn each group session by focusing on the strengths of the group members.

Brief Vignette

Eight members joined a family group for caregivers of children diagnosed with childhood cancer. Susan, a single mother, introduced herself and said her only child, Emma, was just diagnosed with leukemia. Johnny and Leslie, two other group members, immediately began to console her as she began to cry. Their son was diagnosed with osteogenic sarcoma six months earlier and had the lower half of his left leg removed. Marianne was the grandmother of Jenna, a three-year-old also diagnosed with cancer. Other members of the group introduced themselves and sat quietly or spoke briefly throughout the first session.

Group leaders, Mike and Elaine, presented the handouts to the group members. They explained an overview of the family life cycle and the four factors that can cause family disequilibrium. Once the factors were explained, group members were asked to put a magnet on the board where they were in regard to the factors of family disequilibrium.

During the next group session, group members began to talk about their own family life cycle and their experiences regarding the four factors. Some talked in depth about what things have been like for their family since the diagnosis. Marianne, decided she wanted to tell her story and group members asked questions and offered support. Some began crying and said that they were feeling the same. Trust was beginning to form between members. At the end of the session, the leaders asked the group members to start tracking their weekly progress through the factors using the Group Activity Log.

In the following sessions, group members continued to tell their stories. Members tracked as having different experiences in the factors. Johnny and Leslie reported that their relationship had suffered since their son's diagnosis. In group, they both placed their magnet on different factors. Johnny placed his magnet on Factor 4: *family position of the ill member,* and Leslie placed her magnet on Factor 1: *timing of the illness.* Leslie was angry in group and often became tearful that her son developed cancer. Johnny said that he thought that Leslie should be past that because it had been six months since their son's diagnosis. He said that she enabled their son too much and did not let him do anything on his own. Johnny said that they needed to treat him like a normal kid. Leslie said that her husband had never shed a tear over their son's diagnosis and acted as if the cancer did not exist. The group leaders began to facilitate a discussion about how family members can have different experiences. In a subsequent session, Johnny placed his magnet on Factor 1 and began crying. He stated that he had never grieved regarding the cancer and realized that he had been in denial. Through the feedback from other group members, Johnny was able to gain insight into new coping skills for handling the diagnosis and his child's illness.

Suggestions for Follow-Up

All group members are informed that this in an ongoing group, and they may return at any time for support. Group leaders, at the request a group member, should link the caregiver to continued support within his or her community. In addition to this, ongoing counseling for individuals and families to work through grief and loss issues may be needed. Group members may also find that journaling maybe a useful way to help work through some issues relating to grief and loss.

Contraindications

Families struggling with preexisting issues (such as substance abuse) may find that such issues would be better addressed through individual, family, or couples' counseling. Families struggling with survival needs, such as housing, transportation, or meeting regular household expenses, may be better served by securing assistance for these immediate needs before moving to address the transitional issues posed by the child's illness. Families in a state of acute crisis would be better served by crisis services. Further, family members struggling with difficulties in life cycle transitions that are triggered by family-of-origin issues may benefit from additional individual and/or couples' counseling.

Reading and Resources for the Professional

Brown, F. H. (1988). The impact of death and serious illness on the family life cycle. In B. Carter & M. McGoldrick (Eds.), *The changing family life cycle: A framework for family therapy* (pp. 457-482). New York: Gardner Press.

Herz, F. (1980). The impact of death and serious illness on the family life cycle. In B. Carter & M. McGoldrick, (Eds.), *The family life cycle* (pp. 223-240). New York: Gardner Press.

Rando, T. A. (1984). *Grief, dying & death: Clinical interventions for caregivers.* Champaign, IL: Research Press Company.

Rolland, J. (1994). *Families, illness, and disability: An integrative treatment model.* New York: Basic Books.

Rolland, J. (2003). Mastering family challenges in illness and disability. In F. Walsh (Ed.), *Normal family processes: Growing in diversity and complexity* (pp. 424-489). New York: Guilford Press.

Bibliotherapy Sources for the Client: Publications

Bereavement: A Magazine of Hope and Healing. www.bereavementmag.com.

Brunner, S. H. (1996). *Perfect vision: A mother's experience with childhood cancer.* Fuquay-Varina, NC: Research Triangle Publishing.

Duncan, D. (1994). *When Molly was in the hospital: A book for brothers and sisters of hospitalized children* (MiniMed Series, Vol. 1). Windsor, CA: Rayve Productions.

Fromer, M. J. (1998). *Surviving childhood cancer: A guide for families.* Oakland, CA: New Harbinger Publications.

Hilden, M. (2003). *Shelter from the storm: Caring for a child with a life-threatening condition.* Cambridge, MA: Perseus Books.

O'Toole, D. (1988). *Aarvy Aardvark finds hope.* Burnsville, NC: Mountain Rainbow Publications.

Peterkin, A. (1992). *What about me? When brothers and sisters get sick.* New York: Magination Press.

Schwiebert, P., & DeKlyen, C. (1999). *Tear Soup.* Portland, OR: Grief Watch.

Woznick, L., & Goodheart, (2001). *Living with childhood cancer: A practical guide to help families cope.* Washington, DC: American Psychological Association.

Resources for the Client: Web Sites

CancerHealth Online: www.cancerhealthcentersonline.com

Candlelighters Childhood Cancer Foundation: www.candlelighters.org

KidsHealth for Parents: www.kidshealth.org

Living with Loss Foundation: www.livingwithloss.org

Pediatric Oncology Resources Center: www.acor.org/ped-onc

References

American Cancer Society. *Cancer Facts and Figures 2004.* Retrieved November 16, 2005, from www.cancer.org.

Herz, F. (1980) The impact of death and serious illness on the family life cycle. In B. Carter & M. McGoldrick, (Eds.), *The family life cycle* (pp. 223-240). New York: Gardner Press.

Kubler-Ross, E. (1969). *On death and dying.* New York: McMillan.

McGoldrick, M., & Carter, B. (2003). The family life cycle. In F. Walsh (Ed.), *Normal family processes: Growing in diversity and complexity* (pp. 375-398). New York: Guilford Press.

Rando, T. A. (1984). *Grief, dying & death: Clinical interventions for caregivers.* Champaign, IL: Research Press Company.

Rolland, J. (1994). *Families, illness, and disability: An integrative treatment model.* New York: Basic Books.

HANDOUT 31.1. FAMILY DISEQUILIBRIUM

Family Life Cycle Stage: _____

PSYCHOLOGICAL TEAM

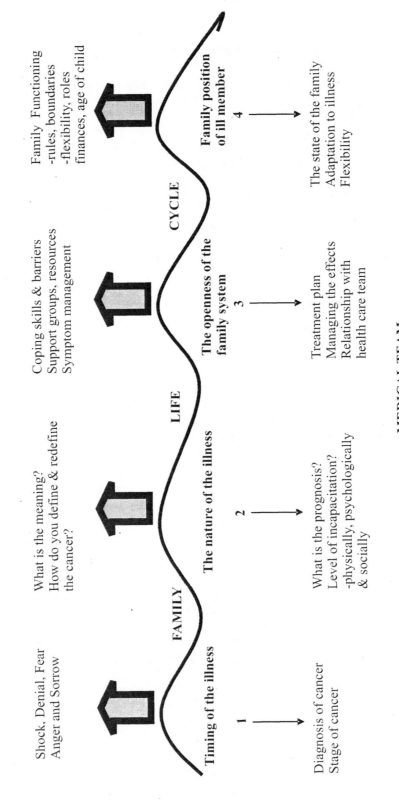

Shock, Denial, Fear Anger and Sorrow

What is the meaning? How do you define & redefine the cancer?

Coping skills & barriers Support groups, resources Symptom management

Family Functioning
-rules, boundaries
-flexibility, roles
finances, age of child

FAMILY **LIFE** **CYCLE**

Timing of the illness

The nature of the illness

The openness of the family system

Family position of ill member

1

2

3

4

Diagnosis of cancer Stage of cancer

What is the prognosis? Level of incapacitation? -physically, psychologically & socially

Treatment plan Managing the effects Relationship with health care team

The state of the family Adaptation to illness Flexibility

MEDICAL TEAM

Factors 1-4 adapted from Freda Herz (1980).

Russo, J. A., Tejada, L., Hilscher, R. L., & Zarski, J. J. (2007). Maintaining stability: Life cycle transitions in families coping with childhood cancer. In D. R. Viers (Ed.). *The group therapist's notebook: Homework, handouts, and activities for use in psychotherapy* (pp. 229-237). Binghamton, NY: The Haworth Press.

HANDOUT 31.2. GROUP ACTIVITY LOG

Directions: Place a check mark under the factor number you feel you are at for each week that you attend group. Add explanatory comments if needed.

	1	2	3	4
WEEK 1				
WEEK 2				
WEEK 3				
WEEK 4				
WEEK 5				
WEEK 6				
WEEK 7				
WEEK 8				
WEEK 9				
WEEK 10				

Russo, J. A., Tejada, L., Hilscher, R. L., & Zarski, J. J. (2007). Maintaining stability: Life cycle transitions in families coping with childhood cancer. In D. R.. Viers (Ed.), *The group therapist's notebook: Homework, handouts, and activities for use in psychotherapy* (pp. 229-237). Binghamton, NY: The Haworth Press.

Index

Page numbers followed by the letter "f" indicate figures.

Parenting
    child with cancer, 229-234
    communication, 213-216
    divorce, 224
    gender roles, 205-211
    programs for, 213
    structure, 223-225, 233
Parents
    alcoholic, 113-118
    death of, 122-123
    transactional analysis, 88, 91, 120, 122
Participants. *See also* Subgroups
    acting out, 10, 41, 42
    advice from, 62, 107, 144, 202
    agreement plan (handout), 161
    attraction between, 72, 161
    in CISD group, 193
    comparisons, 69
    concerns, 7
    confidentiality, 22, 161
    criticism, 12
    dangerous, 22, 26, 53, 116, 190
    dominating personality, 41
    family members, 233-234
    fear and hope exchange, 70-72
    feedback between, 9, 60, 62, 99, 130, 131, 143-144, 144
    fit with group, 15
    group juggle, 142, 158
    interview partners, 157
    membership styles, 16, 19, 41
    orientation, 23
    prior experiences, 2, 5, 8
    problem similarities, 51, 103-111
    relationships outside group, 23
    responsibilities, 26
    roles, 5-7
    sculpting effect, 46
    sex offenders, 182
Participation, encouraging, 29-31, 168, 190
Payment, 22, 25
Pearson, C., 120
Perceptions, 43-47, 59-63
Perfectionism, 50, 88, 91, 114
Performing stage, 16
Personality disorders, 80-81, 175
Photographs, 71
Physical abuse, 109, 116
Physical activity, 157
Physical disabilities, 26
Physical disability, 37
Physical self-care. *See* Self-care
Physical symptoms
    and grief, 130
    and stress, 187, 193, 194
Piaget, J., 96
Pictionary, 157
Planning, 46, 52
    for termination, 68-70

Poems, 156, 158
Post-traumatic stress disorder (PTSD), 34, 191-194
    as contraindication, 53, 80-81, 116
Potter-Efron, P. S., 87-88
Potter-Efron, R. T., 87-88
Premarital group, 205-211
Price, G. E., 4
Privacy. *See* Confidentiality
Privilege, 22, 26
Problems
    clarification, 105-110
    solution focus, 59-66
Procedure, in family, 223
Prochaska, J., 139
Psychoanalytic approach, 16
Psychodrama, 53
Psychoeducation
    for adolescents, 140-145, 171-175
    for children of alcoholics, 115
    and CISD, 193
    and disclosure statement, 22
    in group dynamics, 5-7

Queen, S., 9-10

Racism, 174
Rap songs, 156
Rational Emotive Therapy (RET), 140, 143
Reality
    grasp of, 42
    of loss, 127-129
Reardon, J. P., 192
Reframing, 199-203
Relationships. *See also* Therapeutic relationship
    and adolescents, 143-144, 158
        Latinos, 173, 175
    boundaries, 91, 99, 172
    in couples, 199-204
    within family, 219
    gender roles, 205-211, 220
    and grief, 119, 123, 128
    and group end, 69, 70, 73-74, 144
    with institutions, 106
    interpersonal bridges, 87, 96-97
    mother and daughter, 108-110
    between participants, 23
    pleasing others, 89, 91
    sculpting, 43-47
    and seriously ill child, 231, 233
    and sex offenders, 182, 185
    student and teacher, 143-144
    and substance abuse
        children of alcoholics, 113, 114
        women, 104, 105-106, 109
Relaxation, 33-37